SWAMP WATER
AND WIREGRASS

SWAMP WATER AND WIREGRASS

Historical Sketches
of Coastal Georgia

By
GEORGE A. ROGERS and
R. FRANK SAUNDERS, JR.

MERCER
UNIVERSITY PRESS

ISBN 0-86554-099-3

Swamp Water and Wiregrass
Copyright ©1984 by
Mercer University Press, Macon GA 31207.
All rights reserved.
Printed in the United States of America.

All books published by Mercer University Press
are produced on acid-free paper that exceeds
the minimum standards set by the
National Historical Publications and Records Commission.

Library of Congress Cataloging in Publication Data:

Rogers, George A., 1918–
    Swamp water and wiregrass.

    Bibliography, p. 231.
    Includes index, p. 247.
    1. Georgia—History, Local—Addresses, essays, lectures.   2. Coasts—Georgia—History—Addresses, essays, lectures.   Saunders, R. Frank, 1934–   II. Title.
F286.R64   1984   975.8   84–701
ISBN 0-86554-099-3 (alk. paper)

Table of Contents

Dedication

Dedicated to
"Miss Mollie" L. Saunders and
Betty A. Rogers

*The Ancient ruins will be restored by your own
kindred and you will build once more on
ancestral foundations; you shall be called
Rebuilder of broken walls,
Restorer of houses in ruins.*
—Isaiah 58:12

Introduction:
Of Place and Time

THIS COLLECTION OF ESSAYS is about a place, its people, and selected vignettes of their history. Captivated by the geography, history, and cultural heritage of the Georgia coast south of Savannah to the Altamaha River and the pine barrens of the adjacent hinterlands, we have written about people and events that caught our fancy or appeared neglected. More than a geographic, historical, or rhetorical entity, this region represents paradox and diversity within the wider matrix of Georgia, the South, and the nation. Maybe one has to be born here to understand fully the rhythms and tensions of the society. Even this premise is shaky, however, because it assumes that a native can transcend his regional pride, twisted apologetics, and vengeful past. Undoubtedly, the modernizing influences and rapidly changing values common to late twentieth-century life have heightened this regional consciousness. Our experience has convinced us that "the Southerner" still exists—at least in Georgia, in company with the region's rich cultural legacy and splendid countryside.

By whatever other standard one may choose to judge the region, it does possess an abundance of natural beauty. Protected from the battering assault of the Atlantic by Ossabaw, St. Catherines, Sapelo, St. Simons, Jekyll, and Cumberland Islands, the Georgia coast south of Ossabaw Sound is a delicate ecological system. Sluggish tidal creeks and serpentine rivers such as the Jerico, Medway, North and South Newport, Altamaha, Turtle, Satilla, Crooked, and St. Marys flow from higher, inland elevations through

Elbow, Bull Town, Big Mortar, Buffalo, and Turkey Swamps down to marsh-lands where they form a network of intracoastal waterways.

The humid subtropical climate and black alluvial soil support a dense vegetation pattern of marsh grass, cypress, gums, pine, undergrowth, and vines. Live oaks that appear to drip with Spanish moss, myrtle, and pal-mettos prevail on the hammocks and sand knolls. In springtime, the woods are fragrant with magnolia and yellow jasmine. Aquatic life, water birds, and reptiles (including deadly moccasins and menacing alligators) dwell in the dark water and bogs; stealthy deer, fox, opossum, and bobcat inhabit the wilds. During summer, this natural beauty is more comfortably beheld from the window of an air-conditioned car since the hot, humid environment is a paradise for noxious mosquitoes, flies, gnats, chiggers, and ticks. Settled by Englishmen, Scots, transplanted South Carolinians, and slaves from "Gola," this region was the setting of rice and sea-island cotton plantations during the nineteenth century. It has been trampled and shaped by settlers who arrived with James Edward Oglethorpe in 1733, the Creek Indians, Spaniards, British regulars, Gullah slaves, planters, Yankee invaders, Northern millionaires, developers, tourists, and assorted newcomers.

Some twenty miles inland, the coastal lowlands rise slightly to become the pine barrens that sprawl across the southern half of the state. Char-acterized by sandy soil, lighter rainfall, and greater extremes in tempera-ture, the pine barrens is a region of small farms and woodlands. Farming is profitable here only when the soil is fertilized and irrigated. Upland cotton, once king, has given way to other crops like soybeans, peanuts, corn, and tobacco. Slash and loblolly pines still cover thousands of acres while hard-woods such as gum, poplar, and maple grow along the streams and their branches. Scrub oaks dominate the sand ridges.

The pine barrens is the natural habitat for *Aristida stricta*, better known as wiregrass. This hardy plant thrives in the partial shade of the pine forest and is amazingly resistant to drought, fire, man, and beast. For decades landowners observed open-range grazing, allowing small farmers and share-croppers to turn their stock loose on the open lands. Piney-wood rooters and raw-bone cattle foraged on pine mast, acorns, and wiregrass. In an ef-fort to support their livestock, farmers destroyed or stunted many a stand of turpentine and saw timber by the spring ritual of burning off the woods so that the wiregrass would come out, green and tender, providing grazing for their cattle.

The woods and fields of the region are the habitat of game animals such as deer, dove, quail, and the like. Diamond-backed rattlers, fire ants, pesky gnats, and flies are unfriendly natives. Fishing for bass, bream, and catfish in the rivers, lakes, and farm ponds has always been a popular pastime for country folks. Skillet-fried fish and hush puppies rank close to barbecue as the regional delicacy. Writing about the piney woods as late as the 1940s, a former director of the Southern Regional Council observed that, except for its rich port cities of Savannah and Brunswick, and an occasional patch of land planted in some specialty crop, there were only four things to be found in the whole of that remote piece of country—sand, swamps, pine trees, and poor folks.

In retrospect, how very personal the study of this region has become for us. Unlike historians, novelists seem to know better than to try to make sense out of this Southern preoccupation with place. Yet, where else can one find clearer perceptions of what it means to be Southern than in the fiction of Flannery O'Connor, Lillian Smith, and Alice Walker? In a quest to know this region and its people, we have not only plundered libraries, archives, courthouses, newspaper files, family Bibles, albums, attics, and trunks, but we have also traveled miles and miles of country roads, paused at country stores, met the "little old ladies in tennis shoes" (bless their generosity), and visited many graveyards. Sure enough, South Georgia folks live up to their reputations as good story tellers. We discovered the genre is still alive and well wherever friends and neighbors congregate.

Along the way we have collected images: a mule grazing near a deserted tenant house now overgrown with kudzu; abandoned cotton gins, turpentine stills, and sawmills; country towns that seem to have dried up; billowing smoke stacks at Rayonier; the bulldozer revolution—condos, shopping malls, and four-lanes; a family reunion at Magnolia Springs State Park; homecoming at Elam Missionary Baptist Church at Four Points (Jenkins County) on the second Sunday in June; a baptism in Bay Gall Creek; Confederate Memorial Day at the historic Midway Congregational Church; a political rally on the courthouse square in Statesboro; black and white youth on the athletic field and marching abreast in the high school band; a community meeting in Springfield to save the Savannah River from pollution; the "Onion Festival" in Vidalia; a raft race on the Canoochee; restoration of an old Victorian farm house; grafitti that read "Down with Niggers—Join the KKK"; cheese-and-butter lines at the local welfare office;

an all-night gospel sing in the stadium at Waycross; and the unspoiled natural beauty of Cumberland Island.

For those who expect us to mention the freaks and grotesques, we have encountered our share of snuff-dippers, Holy-Rollers, and rednecks. They have always thrived here, as in other places, alongside the pillars, movers, and the "better sort" of good small-town and country people. There was I. C. who was saving his money—except to buy a jug of moonshine—so he could send off to a lonely-hearts club for a mail-order bride; Pug's wife, Dang, who sat on the hard road eating clay with a rusty spoon; and Rosa who lived "between Nervine and God" to ward off conjure. How often we have pondered: where else but here did past and present conspire to produce so much beauty, nobility, and civility, as well as so much ugliness, evil, and what is pitiable in the human condition?

To paraphrase Irving Babbitt's observation about the Spanish, there seems to be something southern about Southerners, indeed about South Georgians, that causes them to behave in a southern manner. This singular character has been the subject of satire, ridicule, apology, and eulogy; it has been ascribed to defeat and occupation, poverty and deficiency in all of the major economic social indices, agrarianism, slavery, racism, religious fundamentalism, political conservatism, a hierarchical society, romanticism, laziness, violence, diet and disease, weather and climate, and the mythos of a "Lost Cause." Endowed with neither more nor less virtue, Southerners share many of the traditional qualities of rural Americans. "To be Southern today," according to Louis Rubin, "is still to be heir to a complex set of attitudes and affinities, assumptions and instincts that are the product of history acting upon geography, even though much of the history is now forgotten and geography modified." Kinship ties, attachment to community, hospitality, special foods and drinks, the traditional rituals of daily life—being born, growing up, marrying, and dying—and a unique sense of time are separate components of this cultural mosaic. William Faulkner, perceiving how the past haunted the lives of Southerners, aptly noted, "The past is not dead; it isn't even past." For South Georgians, history is the depth dimension of their present, a venture in self-understanding. In a rather strange way Southerners do seem to belong to the region and the region to them. Flannery O'Connor captured this mystique of the Southern character by dispelling the romantic myths; she acknowledged that it wasn't really "connected with mocking birds and beaten biscuits and white columns any more than it is with hookworm and barefeet and muddy clay roads. . . . It is not made from what passes, but from those qualities that endure . . . because they are related to truth. . . . Of those who look for it, none get so close as the artist."

Since Southerners are afflicted with this character, whatever one chooses to call it, should they try to get rid of it, cherish it, or share it? Is it a handicap or an advantage? If their countrymen have become alienated and cut off from larger social units, Southerners have remained attached to family, church, community, and place. This sense of belonging fosters self-definition as well as a shared identity. Undaunted by epitaphs and farewells, the South seems timeless. Even though survival has become a regional habit, it will be interesting to observe how Southern cultural resources and institutions can withstand and assimilate the onslaught of industrial and urban changes in the rush "to develop" a region that appears to be the frontier of the 1980s. Are they destined to repeat the same mistakes of other regions? A strong religious fabric, the closely knit family structure, the enduring power of community heritage, and the ability to individualize and humanize experience remain the South's most viable resources for survival.

The rediscovery of the Sun Belt in recent years is attracting newcomers as well as descendants of émigrés who fled poverty, peonage, and second-class citizenship in the early decades of the twentieth century. How strange that black people whose ancestors were enslaved for two centuries could feel any sense of belonging to the region or it to them. Nostalgia, memories of parents and grandparents, a search for their roots—none of these really explains why blacks return south. This mystery was really brought home to us some years ago when we received a request from a former resident of Liberty County who had learned from some mysterious source that we were gathering materials for a book about coastal Georgia. Written in a shaky, laborious hand and postmarked Philadelphia, Pennsylvania, it read: "Will you send me some free history on Dorchester Academy in Midway Ga please. Thank you answer soon." Enclosed was a post card. Needless to say, we honored the request.

For the past decade our interest has been state and local history. While we would never argue that national history should be just the sum of state and local history writ large, we have discovered that by exploring the records of families, towns, and communities, we are thus able to ask new questions and test familiar generalizations about the past. These essays were written for presentation at various professional meetings and several have already appeared in scholarly journals. The decision to publish them as a collection came *de facto* when Professor Rogers decided to retire at the end of the summer in 1983. A representative sample of our efforts over the past decade, these essays are the fruits of what we consider to have been a rewarding and productive collaboration.

As the reader will discover, except for the centrality of place, this disparate collection of essays is not unified by time, character, or plot. Perhaps more subtle, but nonetheless poignant, are the recurring themes of dreams fulfilled, dreams compromised, and dreams frustrated. But the dreams never dominate; the good ones are tempered with a realization of limits, and the bad ones are saved by a restoration of reason and sanity. This remote and isolated landscape in South Georgia is the stage of high drama reproduced on a manageable scale; in many ways it is a microcosm of sectional and national life. The key players are all, to some extent, spiritual or semimystical personalities who tried to transform their dreams into reality. Results were sometimes constructive, often ambivalent, and occasionally even detrimental.

The founders of the Midway settlement, lineal descendants of the New England Puritans, envisioned a society based on order and morality. Their efforts were compromised by population growth, expansionism, and adaptation to the exigencies of rice culture in South Carolina and Georgia. Theirs was a chronicle of pride shattered by the Civil War. The life of Stephen Elliott was more nearly an example of a dream fulfilled. Yet his publication of the first major botanical study of South Carolina and Georgia was not without costs; it excited strong personal and professional rivalries and brought him to the brink of financial ruin. Charles Colcock Jones, a leading advocate of Christian paternalism and the religious instruction of slaves, failed to realize his dreams of a model biracial community because he could not resolve the paradox of slavery and Christianity. By contrast, the efforts of Bishop Stephen Elliott, Jr., to evangelize slaves succeeded in part, not because of the appeal of Episcopal doctrine, but due to the personal dedication of individual missionaries. More pragmatic than Jones, Elliott was able to accept emancipation and the defeat of his beloved South.

Reconstruction brought an opportunity for abolitionists and reformers to regenerate the fallen South. Eliza Ann Ward and others sent forth by the American Missionary Association came south to bring light and love to the freedmen. The desire to impart traditional New England values and morality, as noble as they were, also reflected their doubts that blacks were ready for freedom and citizenship. Based on fallacious assumptions, their efforts were doomed because they failed to comprehend the cultural differences that separated them from the newly emancipated blacks.

Henry Ford's Richmond Hill experiment was inspired by the desire to make his winter home in Georgia a national showplace, to dabble in what he called "scientific farming," and to rehabilitate the land and people around him. During the years 1925-1947, Ford invested millions to improve the educational opportunities and health of a generation of local residents. It is difficult to determine whether Ford's efforts made a permanent impact on a region that had been deprived for generations.

Some dreams became nightmares. Sherman's men brought war to the home front in Liberty County during December 1864. A hapless countryside was plundered, plantations burned, and livestock slaughtered by Kilpatrick's calvarymen who left destruction and a demoralized people in their wake. Many natives took refuge in southwest Georgia. With the end of slavery and the emergence of new systems of labor management and land tenure, the antebellum rice and sea-island cotton plantations never recovered. War, callous and inhumane, claimed victims in the prison pens, North and South. Camp Lawton near Millen, never as crowded and unsanitary as Andersonville, was nonetheless a living hell for Northern prisoners. Private Benjamin Darsey of Liberty County survived the deprivations of Camp Chase, the Union prison near Columbus, Ohio, and later recorded his prison experiences for posterity. These essays afford some basis for comparing how the antagonists dealt with prisoners of war.

The Liberty County Christ craze of 1889 was a pre-political response by blacks to the frustration and deprivation of the post-Reconstruction years. Isolated, illiterate, economically depressed, and politically powerless, the credulous followers of Dupont Bell, a self-proclaimed messiah, sought to escape their plight through millennialism. Before order was restored, the craze excited wild passions and violence that seemed to confirm already widely held racial stereotypes.

The enduring struggle to wrest a livelihood from the land, the use and abuse of the natural environment, and the uneasy relationship between white and black residents whose lives are so inextricably bound together by history and mutual interdependence are maincurrents in these essays that speak a telling relevance. However hard it has been for South Georgians to escape the past, the scars and inferiorities born of defeat, of being poor and out of the mainstream for too long, their willingness to embrace change has not yet been destroyed. Perhaps the noblest expression of this indomitable spirit is revealed in the heroic struggle of coastal blacks to acquire land and learning in the post-Civil War decades. The record of their dedication and sacrifice is nothing short of inspirational.

If we attempted to acknowledge everyone who has assisted with this book, we could easily fill several pages. Consequently, at the embarrassing risk of omitting someone, we express our sincere thanks to all those who have shared their memories, knowledge, research materials, expertise, and support. We owe special gratitude, however, to Josephine Bacon Martin of Flemington, and Bessie Lewis of Pine Harbor, both now deceased, who were not only respected local historians but exemplars of the genteel tradition associated with Southern ladies. Eliza Bacon Martin of Flemington helped us locate invaluable materials that remain in private hands and arranged numerous introductions. Others to whom we owe special thanks are Barry and Bill Rosier, Midway; Richard Cohan, Hinesville; H. G. Ukkleburg, Richmond Hill; Bill Haynes, Darien; Norman B. Turner, Springfield; Gordon B. Smith and Clermont Lee, Savannah; Lanie P. Clemmons, Tequesta, Florida; and Edward H. Hahn, Pittsburgh, Pennsylvania.

We are also indebted to the Faculty Research Committee of Georgia Southern College that awarded us grants over the past decade to purchase microfilm and to visit archives not only around the state, but also in Boston, New York, Philadelphia, Washington, New Orleans, and Chapel Hill. Dr. Leslie M. Thompson, Dean of the Graduate School of Georgia Southern College, supported our efforts from the beginning and secured funding for preparing the manuscript for publication. We appreciate his commitment to research. Harriet Agnew, our fast and efficient typist, helped us to meet the deadlines—which usually came before the final draft was ready; Edd Rowell and India Fuller of Mercer University Press patiently and expertly directed us and our manuscript through publication. These people share whatever credit this book merits. We assume full responsibility for flaws and errors. Paraphrasing the conclusion that Richard Steel wrote for the final issue of the *Tatler* in January 1710: "We have published our names to our writings and given ourselves to words up to the mercy of the town and with all our imperfections on our heads."

Statesboro, Georgia
September 1983

R. Frank Saunders, Jr.
George A. Rogers

ONE

The Dorchester Connection:
The Genesis
of the Midway Settlement*

ABOUT THIRTY MILES SOUTH of Savannah on the old coastal highway in Liberty County stands the venerable Midway Congregational
Church. Reminiscent of a New England meeting house, this historic edifice was the nucleus of what Dr. James Stacy, historian of the Midway community and of Presbyterianism in Georgia, considered the sixth and last
major settlement in coastal Georgia.

The adjacent cemetery, shaded by magnificent moss-draped oaks, is the
hallowed resting place for many Georgians who attained prominence in the
state and nation. Robert Manson Myers observed in his prologue to *Children
of Pride* that the record of the Midway district was both astonishing and
unique for a small rural community that never had a population of more
than a few hundred people and that was dispersed a little more than a century after its founding.[1]

According to historical tradition, the original settlers of the Midway
district were lineal and cultural descendants of the English Puritans. Their
ancestors had left their homes in Dorchester, England, aboard the *Mary and
John* in 1630, at the beginning of the Great Migration, to embark upon an
"errand into the wilderness." Arriving before the *Arbella* that brought John

---

*This paper was presented at a symposium in Savannah, 9-11 February 1983, celebrating
the 250th anniversary of the founding of Georgia.

[1]Robert Manson Myers, ed., *The Children of Pride* (New Haven: Yale University Press,
1972) 8.

Winthrop and his associates to Salem, the covenanted band founded Dorchester, Massachusetts. In 1635 a large contingent of these settlers joined Thomas Hooker in an exodus to the fertile Connecticut River valley where they founded old Windsor.

In 1695 a small congregation of the church in Dorchester, Massachusetts, banded together and followed the Reverend Joseph Lord to South Carolina. There they founded a planned community on the Ashley River about 18 miles from Charles Town which they also named Dorchester. In the 1750s practically the entire community migrated to coastal Georgia. Although their departure sealed the fate of the once prosperous South Carolina village, this influx of new settlers and their slaves expanded the South Carolina rice frontier into the swamps of coastal Georgia.

What can be discovered about these wandering Puritans through a study of their previous Dorchester connections? What motives prompted them to leave New England for the southern colonies? How did the geographic and socio-cultural conditions in South Carolina and Georgia change the character of Congregationalism, and conversely, what effects did their ideology have on the new region?

The founding of Dorchester in New England was inspired by the Reverend John White, rector of Trinity Parish, Dorchester, England, who was a Nonconformist though not a Separatist.[2] Along with a group of west-country investors, White was interested in establishing fishing settlements along the New England coast. A man of vision, reputedly able to control both his passions and his parishioners' purses, White also perceived these

---

[2]Within the context of English Protestantism, a Nonconformist was a member of the Anglican Church who did not adhere to certain prescribed beliefs and rituals, whereas a Separatist was a Nonconformist who was disassociated from the Anglican Church. Both of these dissenting groups were generally labeled "Puritans." American scholars have depicted Puritans as being the heirs of Augustine, Calvin, Ramus, Cartwright, and Perkins, whose watchwords were predestination, original sin, congregationalism and the authority of the scriptures. See Richard Schlatter, "The Puritan Strain," in *The Reconstruction of American History*, ed. John Higham (New York: Harper and Bros., 1962) 25-45. Also see M. M. Knappen, *Tudor Puritanism, A Chapter in the History of Idealism* (Chicago: University of Chicago Press, 1939) 339-480.

Perry Miller described Puritanism as that point of view and code of values carried to New England by English Protestants who were in fundamental agreement with John Calvin's adherents in Geneva. He contended that the isolation of the New England colonies, the homogeneous culture of the people, and the special geographic environment transformed these English Protestants into a "peculiar people." See Perry Miller, *The American Puritans* (New York: Doubleday Anchor Books, 1956) ix.

settlements as a refuge for persecuted Puritans. After the failure of the initial venture at Cape Anne, White enlisted the support of a number of influential London investors. They secured from the Council of New England a land grant that lay between the Merrimac and Charles Rivers. White, seeking confirmation of the company's territorial rights, received a royal charter for the Massachusetts Bay Company in 1626. The first emigrants sent forth by the new company, many of them from Weymouth and Dorchester, settled in Salem. [3]

White, who came to be known as the "Patriarch of Dorchester," then began to assemble another company in the western counties. Writing to Governor John Endecott of Salem in the summer of 1629, White requested that habitation be designated for 60 families from Devonshire, Dorsetshire, and Somerset who were to arrive in the Bay colony in the spring of 1630. The Reverend John Maverick, an elderly minister of the Established Church from Devon who was described as a "man of exceedingly humble spirit," and the Reverend John Warham, a minister of the Church of England in Exeter, were recruited to serve as spiritual leaders of the new plantation. Both had been ordained as Anglicans but were now "thorough non-conformists." Edward Rossiter, a man of estate from Somerset, and Roger Ludlow, said to come from Wiltshire, were named as assistants. Several middle-aged gentlemen with adult families also joined the association; however, a majority of the company were adventuresome young men of good rank. Three experienced military men added an element of safety to the enterprise.

Of those who came, apparently only Rossiter, Ludlow, and John Glover were stockholders in the venture. A company of 140 members, both families and single males, assembled at Plymouth where the *Mary and John* awaited embarkation. The 400-ton vessel, reportedly owned by John Os-

---

[3]Charles M. Andrews, *The Colonial Period of American History* (London: Oxford University Press, 1934) 1:344-99; Herbert L. Osgood, *The American Colonies in the Seventeenth Century* (Gloucester: Peter Smith, 1957) 1:128-66; Frances Rose-Troup, *John White, the Patriarch of Dorchester and the Founder of Massachusetts, 1575-1648* (New York: G. P. Putnam's Sons, 1930), and *The Massachusetts Bay Company and Its Predecessors* (New York: The Grafton Press, 1930) are good background works on White and the early Dorchester Company. See also Francis J. Bremer, *The Puritan Experiment* (New York: St. Martin's Press, 1976); Perry Miller, *Errand into the Wilderness* (Cambridge: Harvard University Press, 1956); Darrett B. Rutman, *American Puritanism: Faith and Practice* (Philadelphia: Lippincott, 1970); and Larzer Ziff, *Puritanism in America: New Culture in a New World* (New York: Viking Press, 1973); *The Dictionary of National Biography* (London: Oxford University Press, 1937-1938) 21:59-61.

good, was commanded by Captain Squeb. The original passenger list has not survived, but reconstructed lists that include children under two years of age indicate that perhaps as many at 160 persons made the voyage. After a solemn day of fasting, praying, and a sermon by Reverend White, the company sailed on 20 March 1630 for their new home on the Charles River. During the ten-week passage, the gospel was preached and expounded daily. On May 30, they reached Nantasket where Captain Squeb landed the passengers on the southside of Dorchester Neck in Old Harbor. Eager to reach the intended place of settlement, Captain Richard Southcote led a party up the Charles River as far as Watertown only to be recalled when the company decided to settle at Matapan in order to save their starving cattle. They rechristened their settlement Dorchester in honor of their homeland in Old England.[4]

There is no record of any special grant of lands to the west-country settlers, but they doubtless had the sanction of the Court of Assistants since they were authorized the use of their corporate name by September 1630. Although the court prescribed that settlements in Massachusetts had to be compact to insure defense and social order, rapid population growth and the end of Indian threats made these regulations meaningless. The loss of the early pages of the town's records renders it impossible to document the first land grants awarded in Dorchester. A £50 share in the company, however, entitled the holder to 200 acres, a town-house lot, and 50 acres for each member of his family. An additional 50 acres were allotted for each servant transported by a shareholder. Non-stockholders received 50 acres for the head of the family and such quantity of land "according to their charge and quality" as the governor and council saw fit to award.[5] Although the Dorchester settlers suffered hardships during the spring and summer of 1630, they soon began to trade with the Indians, erect houses, gather fod-

---

[4]Maude P. Kuhns, The "Mary and John": A Story of the Founding of Dorchester, Massachusetts, 1630 (Rutland VT: The Tuttle Publishing Company, Inc., 1943); pages 5-6 contain a passenger list compiled from various sources; Ebenezer Clapp, History of the Town of Dorchester, Massachusetts (Boston: Ebenezer Clapp, Jr., 1859) 3-33; James Stacy, History of the Midway Congregational Church (Newnan GA: S. W. Murray, 1951) 7-18. "Introduction," Records of the First Church at Dorchester in New England, 1636-1734 (Boston: George H. Ellis, 1891) iii-xxiii. See also James Blake, Annals of the Town of Dorchester (Boston: David Clapp, Jr., 1846); "Puritan Pilgrams and Their Four Dorchesters," in The Blue Banner (West Columbia SC, 1953) 1-27.

[5]Clapp, History of Dorchester, 23.

der to winter their cattle, and engage in fishing, an occupation familiar to inhabitants from the channel ports in England. According to tradition, the Dorchester settlers were the first to "set upon fishing in the Bay."

The congregation erected its first meeting house the next year, using it for religious services and as a depot for military stores. Because the Dorchester congregation had organized as a church fellowship and settled the salaries of its ministers independent of government, and prior to leaving England, the congregation was given precedence in all civil assemblies and military musters in the colony.[6] The affairs of the plantation were controlled by the clergymen and Magistrates Ludlow and Rossiter during the early months, since the majority of the settlers had no political rights. The General Court, however, extended freemanship to 24 persons in October 1630; the principal qualification was apparently church membership. Besides the right of suffrage, freemen also enjoyed advantages in the division of land and membership in the General Court, at least before adoption of the representative system. In October 1633, the first town government in Massachusetts, indeed in the English colonies in North America, was organized in Dorchester.[7]

Although some of the original settlers such as Captain Richard Southcote returned to England, the population of Dorchester was multiplied by a steady stream of new arrivals. A contemporary described Dorchester in 1638 as a frontier town of 200 houses surrounded by orchards and gardens. Residents owned abundant corn land and cattle. Dorchester was, for a time, the largest town in New England until Boston surpassed it. A second wave of emigrants began to arrive in 1635 when at least five vessels reached Boston with more west-country settlers on board. To accommodate this growth, in 1636-1637 the General Court awarded expanded grants to Dorchester that encompassed several adjacent towns. New names continued to appear in church and town records until 1640 when political changes in England arrested and even reversed the tide of emigration.[8] Many of these new arrivals purchased the property of older settlers who joined the migration to the Connecticut River valley. In addition to problems associated

[6]Ibid., 24.

[7]Ibid., 31-32. For a different interpretation of the founding of the congregation, see Rose-Troup, *White*, 199-203.

[8]Clapp, *History of Dorchester*, 29, 100-102.

with population pressure and the lure of fertile land, many had become weary of domination by Governor John Winthrop and an authoritarian clergy. John Warham, one of the original ministers who accompanied the west-country company on the *Mary and John* in 1630, led a large delegation that included Roger Ludlow and Bray Rosseter to found a new settlement in Connecticut on the Farmington River in the vicinity of Palisado Green. After a prolonged controversy with the settlers of Plymouth and the "Lords and Gentlemen," the Dorchester people laid the foundations of Old Windsor in 1636.⁹

Although two attempts failed to establish Puritan colonies on the Cape Fear River in the Carolinas in the 1660s, the founding of Charles Town in 1670 provided new opportunities. Since the lords proprietor were committed to religious toleration, they welcomed not only Congregationalists but other Nonconformists including Quakers, Huguenots, Presbyterians, and Anabaptists. Dissenters from the northern colonies, the West Indies, and Europe were thus attracted to South Carolina. Among the influential families of dissenters who came from England were the Blakes, Axtells, and Mortons. In 1680 a Congregational church was organized in Charles Town and in 1691 the Reverend Benjamin Pierpont became its first pastor.¹⁰

With the development of outlying plantations along the Ashley River, William Norman journeyed to Dorchester, Massachusetts, to seek a new minister to serve the South Carolina frontier. Norman, a Congregationalist and perhaps a former New Englander, was the owner of a 320-acre tract along the Ashley River. The records of the First Church at Dorchester, Massachusetts, indicate that on 20 October 1695, Joseph Lord, Increase Sumner, and William Pratt were "dismissed" from the church for "Ye gathering of A church for ye South Carolina." Two days later, Joseph Lord was ordained "to be pastuer to a church gathered that day for to goe to South Carolina to settell the gospell there. . . ." Eight brethren then entered into a solemn covenant to establish the ordinances of Jesus Christ in South Carolina, but only three actually accompanied Norman back to South Carolina. Joseph Lord, a native of Charlestowne, Massachusetts, and a graduate of Harvard College, like many aspiring clergymen, had served as a school-

⁹Ibid., 148; *Records of the First Church of Dorchester*, vi-xxiii; Daniel Howard, *A New History of Old Windsor, Connecticutt* (Windsor: The Journal Press, 1935) 13-14.

¹⁰Francis J. Bremer, "'A New Errand': Massachusetts Puritans and the Founding of Dorchester, South Carolina," *Bulletin* of the Congregational Library 28 (Winter 1977): 4-5.

master in Dorchester from 1692-1695. For Lord and his followers, South Carolina offered rich lands, a congenial climate, and an opportunity to spread the gospel in a distant colony that guaranteed religious freedom.[11] This evangelical impulse was forcefully stated in 1696 by the Reverend John Danforth, pastor of the Dorchester church, in a sermon preached to a group departing for South Carolina. He denounced those who had become too provincial and had lost their concern for the rest of Christendom. The labors of New England's sons in the wilderness, supported by the prayers of those who remained behind, Danforth exhorted, would restore the colonies to their proper relationship with God in preparation for the Second Coming.[12]

According to Elder Pratt's diary, the single most important source for the study of the South Carolina migration, the covenanted band sailed from Boston on 14 December 1695 and landed in Charles Town on 20 December where they lingered for the next three months prior to selecting a site for their settlement. They were apparently housed by local inhabitants who desired them as neighbors. Both William Norman and Lady Rebecca Axtell, a widow of Landgrave Daniel Axtell, offered lands on the Ashley River. Governor Joseph Blake and Landgrave Joseph Morton urged them to settle at New London, south of Charles Town. After Elder Pratt and Increase Sumner reported the results of their inspections to Lord, they decided to accept land adjacent to William Norman's holdings. Already Lord had preached at Norman's residence and at the Ashley River where he administered communion to those who gathered. In February 1696, Elder Pratt returned to Massachusetts to remove his and three other families to South Carolina.[13]

During Pratt's absence, two tracts of land known as "Boo-shoo" and "Rose's Land," 4,058 acres in all, were secured by John Stevens for the in-

---

[11]Clapp, *History of Dorchester*, 261-62; *Records of the First Church at Dorchester*, 13, 109. William Pratt, "Journal of the Elder William Pratt," in *Narratives of Early Carolina*, ed. Alexander S. Salley (New York: Charles Scribner's Sons, 1911) 194-200; Stacy, *History of Midway Church*, 6-10; Henry A. M. Smith, "The Town of Dorchester in South Carolina—A Sketch of Its History," *South Carolina Historical and Genealogical Magazine* 6 (April 1905): 65-66.

[12]The Reverend John Danforth, "Kneeling to God at Parting with Friends," based on Acts 21:4-6 and cited in Stacy, *History of Midway Church*, 5.

[13]Pratt, "Journal," 194-98; Smith, "Town of Dorchester," 68-69. Babette M. Levy, "Early Puritanism in the Southern and Island Colonies," American Antiquarian Society *Proceedings* 70 (1960): 265-66.

tended settlers of the new community. The congregation and "others that were concerned" gathered on 23 March 1697 to draw lots that were marked off the following day. Preliminary to dividing the private holdings into 26 parts, the settlers designated 115 half-acre lots for the place of trade, the village of Dorchester. A public square and 20 acres between the town and Dorchester Creek were reserved for common use. A 50-acre meadow was laid out adjacent to the town on the west and 123 acres were set aside for mill land. The remaining divisions were surveyed into two ranges for private use. The first range consisted of 26 lots of 50 acres each that became productive rice fields along the Ashley, while the second range north of the highway was divided into 26 lots of 45 acres each. Although the original map showing the division of the whole 4,058 acres and the list of grantees no longer survives, old wills and conveyances identify the names of John Stevens, Joseph Lord, Increase and Samuel Sumner, William Pratt, William Norman, Michael Bacon, and several Ways.[14] In 1698 the Reverend Lord returned to New England to marry Elizabeth Hinckley, the daughter of a former governor of Plymouth. When they returned to South Carolina, the couple was accompanied by new settlers and were joined by other New Englanders in later years. Likewise the congregation welcomed neighbors from surrounding plantations into communion.

Pending construction of the "Old White" meeting house, a brick church completed in 1700, the Dorchester congregation met in a temporary wooden structure. Besides allowing the Reverend Lord to share in the original drawing for lots, they had set aside one-twenty-sixth of the entire survey for the permanent support of the church and ministry.[15] Lord, true to his Puritan training, was the missionary of a culture as well as a theology. Attempting to model this new Dorchester after its New England prototype,

---

[14]Smith, "The Town of Dorchester," 70-75; Bremer, "A New Errand," 7; Henry A. M. Smith, "The Upper Ashley, And The Mutations of Families," *The South Carolina Historical and Genealogical Magazine* 20 (July 1919): 153-59. For a plan of the village of Dorchester in 1742 that also names some holders of lots, see Stacy, *History of Midway Church*, 18-19. Richard F. Carrillo, *Archeological Investigation at Fort Dorchester: An Archeological Assessment* (Columbia: University of South Carolina, 1976) 7-8.

[15]For an etching of "Old White" Puritan meeting house at Dorchester, South Carolina, as it looked before the Charleston earthquake of 1886, see cover of the *Bulletin* of the Congregational Library; also note the letter which won for the builder the contract to construct the church, ibid., 3. Smith, "The Town of Dorchester," 77; Bremer, "A New Errand," 7-8. Letters of Joseph Lord to James Petiver of the Royal Society printed in *South Carolina Historical and Genealogical Magazine*, vol. 21.

he founded a school in the settlement. Fascinated by his new environment, he also found time to make extensive notes on Southern flora and fauna which he communicated to the British Royal Society. As a devoted pastor, he ministered to his flock, taught the youth of the community, and attempted to preserve the orthodoxy of his faith and ward off the advances of the Anabaptists. Lord won few converts but was moderately successful in dispelling the unfavorable opinion of New Englanders held by many South Carolinians.

As the surrounding countryside became more densely settled, Dorchester became a place of trade, and by 1708 the town had a population of 350 inhabitants. The Dorchester congregation, like dissenting churches in other colonies, engaged in a continual struggle to preserve its rights against an intolerant establishment. Following the appointment of Sir Nathaniel Johnson as governor in 1703, the colonial assembly excluded dissenters from political participation and established the Anglican Church in South Carolina. Dissenters were successful in getting this unpopular act disallowed, but a new law in 1706 divided the colony into six parishes. In 1717 Dorchester and the surrounding territory were organized into St. Georges Parish and plans were laid to erect an Anglican church in the center of Dorchester village.

Joseph Lord remained in South Carolina long enough to witness the loss of dissenter influence and in 1717 he returned to Massachusetts where he served as pastor of the church in Chatham until 1748.[16] The Reverend Hugh Fisher, a Presbyterian, succeeded Lord and ministered to the congregation until 1734. The Reverend John Osgood, a native of Dorchester, South Carolina, and a graduate of Harvard College, was called to lead the congregation in 1735. Osgood moved to Georgia in 1754 as pastor of the Midway Church where he served until his death in 1773.[17]

In the year that Lord returned to Massachusetts, the parish reportedly contained 115 English families or 500 free persons, and 1,300 slaves. Roads were extended into the interior and a fair and market were established at South Carolina's Dorchester. In 1734, acts were passed to build a free school in the village and to clear the Ashley River for navigation to Slann's Bridge. These changes caused the congregation, like their fathers before

---

[16]Smith, "The Town of Dorchester," 79-91; Bremer, "A New Errand," 7-9.

[17]Stacy, *History of Midway Church,* 15.

them in Massachusetts, to feel the impact of population growth. The desire for more and better land threatened the future of their compact settlement. In creating the township, the founders had adopted a system of land tenure alien to the region. If 50 acres had been sufficient for the production of cereal crops in New England, such small holdings were hardly adequate for a plantation-slave economy devoted to production of rice, the major cash crop. By 1737, so many planters had spread out into the Beech Hill section, higher up and across the Ashley River, that another meeting house was constructed. The congregations, however, remained so small that one minister served both churches.[18]

During their time in South Carolina, the transplanted New Englanders had retained many traditional values and institutions, but they had also acclimated to the economic and socio-cultural environment of low-country South Carolina. Like the earliest settlers in the region they too had learned to cultivate rice in the swamplands along the Ashley River and Dorchester Creek. As rice production increased, the demand for slaves rose proportionately. A census of Dorchester in 1725 revealed that 40 out of 52 families were slaveholders. Although Lord's friend and correspondent, Judge Samuel Sewall of Massachusetts, had convinced him to oppose the intrusion of heretical Anabaptists, Sewall's condemnations of slavery went unheeded.[19]

Leaders of the Dorchester community realized that their holdings were inadequate for commercial rice culture and too small to be subdivided among their children. New lands had to be found in South Carolina or elsewhere if they were to arrest dispersal and preserve the identity of their settlement. Now surrounded by established settlements, they searched unsuccessfully for suitable rice lands in South Carolina. Apparently upon the suggestion of William G. DeBrahm, the Dorchestrians then turned their attention to Georgia. Two scouting parties visited the Midway district in the spring and summer of 1752. Their favorable reports resulted in petitions to the Georgia authorities who awarded them two grants totaling

[18]Smith, "The Town of Dorchester," 80-81; Bremer, "A New Errand," 9; see also a signed article by E. Lawrence Lee, *Charleston News and Courier*, 22 February 1959.

[19]David R. Chesnutt, "South Carolina's Expansion Into Colonial Georgia, 1720-1765" (Ph.D. dissertation, University of Georgia, 1973) 84. Lord's letters to Samuel Sewall referred to in *The Letter Book of Samuel Sewall*, Massachusetts Historical Society *Collections*, 6th series, vols. 1 and 2.

31,450 acres. On 11 July 1752, a grant of 22,500 acres was awarded to 44 petitioners. Of these, 41 persons received 500 acres, and one other received 300 acres. A second grant of 9,650 acres was issued on 6 August 1752 to 28 persons of whom 12 received 500 acres, one 400 acres, three 300 acres, three 250 acres, eight 200 acres, and one 100 acres. Grantees were expected to bring ten able-bodied servants to settle their land.[20]

Despite the protests of a minority who opposed moving to Georgia, practically the entire Dorchester congregation resettled in the Midway district. Benjamin Baker and Samuel Bacon arrived with their families in early December 1752; only the family of Parmenas Way arrived the next year. Way owned 10 or 12 slaves and was typical of the churchmen who migrated. He settled on the Medway River and became one of the congregation's first rice planters. The decisive move, however, came in 1754 when the Reverend John Osgood and 16 other families transferred the church to Midway. After holding services temporarily in private homes, Osgood preached the first sermon in the newly constructed log church on 7 June 1754. On 28 August, the settlers drew up articles of incorporation to establish a "Society Settled Upon Medway and Newport in Georgia." The society consisted of all adult male members of the church and others who agreed to subscribe. Mindful of the need for "good order and social agreement," the dissenting congregation formed the corporation to establish peace and harmony among themselves and inoffensiveness to their neighbors. They agreed to meet annually during March at the Midway Church for the management of their public affairs and to elect three or more selectmen. There is little in-

---

[20]Stacy, *History of Midway Church*, 20-25; Louis DeVorsey, Jr., ed., *DeBrahm's Report of the General Survey in the Southern District of North America* (Columbia: University of South Carolina Press, 1971) 141, also 288, n. 20. George G. Smith, *The Story of Georgia and the Georgia People* (Baltimore: Genealogical Publishing Co., 1968) 44; George White, *Historical Collections of Georgia* (Baltimore: Genealogical Publishing Co., 1969) 34-36. Allen D. Candler, comp., *The Colonial Records of the State of Georgia* (Atlanta: Franklin Printing and Publishing Co., 1906) 26:416. For accounts of the early history of the Midway community, also see Myers, *Children of Pride*, 7-31; J. Edward Kirbye, *Puritanism in the South* (Boston: The Pilgrim Press, 1908) 95-125; C. C. Jones, Jr., *The History of Georgia* (Boston: Houghton, Mifflin Co., 1883) 1:481-501; Paul McIlvaine, *The Dead Towns of Sunbury, Ga. and Dorchester, S.C.* (Asheville NC: Groves Printing Co., 1975); Orville A. Park, *The Puritan in Georgia* (Savannah: Georgia Historical Society, 1929); Allen P. Tankersley, "Midway District: A Study of Puritanism in Colonial Georgia," *Georgia Historical Quarterly* 32 (September 1948): 149-57; Josephine B. Martin, *Midway, Georgia in History and Legend* (Savannah: Southern Publishers, 1936); Neyle Colquitt, *An Historette of Midway* (1915).

20 / *Swamp Water and Wiregrass*

dication from their transactions, however, that the society was ever concerned exclusively with secular matters.[21]

Between 1755-1758, 13 more families, two single men, and a widow
joined the settlement. Others trickled in during succeeding years with
three families arriving as late as 1771, at which point the immigration practically ceased. Stacy listed 43 early settlers, most of whom had families, and
71 who received grants of land. To explain this discrepancy, he speculated
that some grantees failed to move to Georgia or that the church and society
records were possibly incomplete. He also estimated that there were 350
whites and 1,500 blacks associated with the Midway settlement by the eve
of the Revolution. A more recent compilation counted approximately 224
whites and 438 blacks in the district in 1760. The records of the Midway
Society indicated that one family came from Charles Town, four more from
the Pon-Pon district, and the others from Dorchester and Beech Hill.
These settlers were middle-class South Carolinians; no wealthy merchants
or planters migrated to Georgia, but neither did the movement include the
destitute or poorer classes.[22]

Already experienced in rice culture, the transplanted South Carolinians settled on grants of 200 to 500 acres in the chain of swamps about ten
miles inland between the Medway and Newport Rivers. Even though the
ban on slavery had been removed in 1749, according to DeBrahm there were
scarcely more than three dozen slaves in Georgia in 1751. In the next two
years, the Midway settlers brought in several hundred slaves who cleared the
land, dug canals, built dams, and cultivated rice and subsistence crops. In
a short time, they transformed wild swamps into productive rice plantations. John Stevens, the largest planter in the congregation, had accumu-
lated 2,000 acres and 35 slaves by 1758. William Graves, an original
petitioner who was the second largest planter, moved in a carefully planned
sequence. He sold part of his estate at Beech Hill in South Carolina and
planted rice on the remainder. Simultaneously he began to clear land in the
Midway district. The next spring he moved his family and slaves to Georgia

---

[21]Stacy, *History of Midway Church*, 25-27, 36-44; for transactions of the Midway Society,
see pages 1-102. Josephine Martin, "The Society of the Midway," *Georgia Historical Quarterly*
11 (December 1927): 321-29. Pat Bryant, comp., *Entry of Claims for Georgia Landholders,
1733-1755* (Atlanta: State Printing Office, 1975).

[22]Stacy, *History of the Midway Church*, 23-25, 113-14; Jones, *History of Georgia*, 1:493;
Chesnutt, *South Carolina Expansion*, 99, 102.

and began full-scale planting. Within ten years he owned 1,700 acres and 47 slaves. John Elliott, within a year of his arrival in 1754, had 1,400 acres and 22 slaves. John Mitchell and Samuel Burnley were representative of the middling planters. Mitchell owned 1,050 acres and 20 slaves by 1765; Burnley, who received a 500-acre grant and arrived with 11 slaves, held 900 acres and 20 slaves by his death in 1768.[23]

Among the Carolinians who settled in the Midway district were Parmenas Way, Moses Way, Samuel Way, Edward Way, Nathaniel Way, and Andrew Way. Henry Way (the Puritan), a native of Bristol, England, came over on the *Mary and John* in 1630. He settled in Dorchester, Massachusetts, where he died in 1667. The Ways who came to South Carolina were the descendants of Richard and Aaron Way, sons of Henry the Puritan. According to family tradition, his grandsons, Aaron and William Way, migrated to Dorchester, South Carolina, to escape the witchcraft hysteria. The grandchildren of these emigrants moved to Midway in the 1750s.[24] Dr. Stacy remarked that the Midway Church records literally teemed with Ways. During the depression of 1843, a Liberty County wit, Dr. W. P. McConnell, wrote that "We have Hams and Dun-hams, Bacons and Greens, Manns and Quartermans, Plenty of Ways but no Means."

Although only the Ways can be traced back to the original passengers on the *Mary and John* in 1630, other families such as the Osgoods, Sumners, and Bacons were part of the 21,000 who came to Massachusetts during the Great Migration of 1630-1640. Of the 26 family names listed by Stacy among the original Midway settlers, nine appeared in the church and town records of Dorchester, Massachusetts, before 1700. Elizabeth Anne Poyas, a South Carolina historian, added two more, and Stacy's list of church members and subscribers to the Midway Society included additional family names of Massachusetts origin. Conservatively, more than a third of the original Midway settlers have surnames that connect them with Dorchester, Massachusetts.

---

[23]Ibid., 103-109. For quotation by DeBrahm, see Spencer B. King, Jr., *Georgia Voices, A Documentary History to 1872* (Athens: University of Georgia Press, 1966) 30.

[24]Stacy, *History of Midway Church*, 356-57; Kuhns, *The "Mary and John,"* 83-84; Charles G. Way, *George Way and His Descendants* (Boston: E. P. Whitcomb, 1887); Mary E. Way, *The Way Family* (Martinez CA, 1969); Arthur M. Martin, *The Flemington Martins* (Columbia: The State Printing Co., 1970) 29-30; Mabel L. Webber, "Dorchester Families," handwritten manuscript, South Carolina Historical Society, Charleston.

Before the arrival of the Congregationalists from South Carolina, the Midway district was already sparsely settled. In 1751, Audley Maxwell represented the district in the colonial assembly. Families that joined the settlement included the Dunhams, Elliotts, Flemings, and Joneses from Charleston, South Carolina; Highlanders like the Martins and McIntoshes from Darien and the Frasers from Georgetown, South Carolina. The Girardeaus from Goose Creek, South Carolina, and the LeContes from New Jersey were of Huguenot descent; the Laws were supposedly from the West Indies.[25]

The founding of the seaport town of Sunbury in 1758 was an indication of the district's prosperity. Mark Carr conveyed 300 acres of his 500-acre grant, including the portion that fronted on the Medway River, to James Maxwell, Kenneth Baillie, John Elliott, Grey Elliott, and John Stevens for the town site. As trustees, they planned and laid out 496 lots around King's, Church, and Meeting Squares; by 1775, 117 of the lots were sold. Governor Henry Ellis recommended to the Board of Trade that Sunbury should be made a port of entry in October 1757. Again recommended by Governor James Wright in 1762, Sunbury was officially declared Georgia's second port of entry the next year. A lucrative trade in lumber, tar, rice, corn, indigo, and hides, largely with the West Indies, led Sunbury to rival Savannah by 1769. Writing to Lord Halifax in 1763, Wright reported that Sunbury had 80 dwellings and three considerable mercantile firms. He observed that the area for about 15 miles around the seaport was one of the most densely settled parts of the colony. In his report on the province in 1773, Wright stated that 56 vessels of various sorts cleared customs at Sunbury the previous year. At the oubreak of the Revolution, Sunbury had an estimated population of 1,000.[26]

---

[25]Kuhns, The "Mary and John," 5-6, 88-89; Clapp, History of Dorchester, Massachusetts, 38-39, 101-102, 143-48, 199-200; Records of the Church of Dorchester, v, xii-xvi; Webber, "Dorchester Families"; Elizabeth Ann Poyas, Our Forefathers: The Homes and Their Churches (Charleston: Walker, Evans and Co., 1860) 94-96. Smith, "The Town of Dorchester," 73-75; Stacy, History of Midway Church, 25-26, 113-14; Martin, Flemington Martins, 2, 33, 38-40; Richard L. Anderson, Le Conte History and Genealogy (Macon: R. L. Anderson, 1981) 2:732-824. John B. Mallard, "Historical Sketch of Liberty County, Ga.," (handwritten manuscript, C. C. Jones Papers, Tulane University), stated that the Midway people made up about a half of the lower part of the county where they settled.

[26]C. C. Jones, Jr., Dead Towns of Georgia (Savannah: Georgia Historical Society, 1878); Virginia F. Evans, comp., Liberty County, Georgia: A Pictorial History (Statesville: Brady Printing Co., 1979) 23-30; John M. Sheftall, Sunbury on the Medway (Georgia Department of Natural Resources, 1977); Chesnutt, South Carolina Expansion, 120-24; Colonial Records

The Puritan attempt to create a Christian commonwealth in colonial America was not long confined to New England. By the end of the colonial era Puritans had penetrated as far south as Dorchester, South Carolina, and Midway in coastal Georgia, as well as to the West Indies. Puritan expansionism, long the subject of debate, was inspired by religious and economic motives. Although first institutionalized in New England in the 1630s, Puritanism was never a monolithic movement. The history of the Midway settlement and its antecedents in Dorchester, South Carolina, and Dorchester, Massachusetts, demonstrated that American Puritanism was a tough and vibrant ideology.

As Calvinists who believed in the doctrine of the elect, Puritans were elitists who selectively recruited new members for their church and society. Their theology offered psychological certitude and undoubtedly helped many to cope with changing circumstances. From the advent of their errand into the wilderness, the covenant was the basis of the congregation and local government. In both Massachusetts and South Carolina, the township bore the hallmark of a civil covenant, but in the Midway district where families were widely dispersed, the Midway Society insured a cohesive social order. Communities were based upon closely knit families, early marriages, numerous offspring, and an obvious aversion to bachelors and widowhood. Neither prudish nor profligate, they participated conscientiously in their secular roles and diligently performed their religious duties. Whether attempting to farm the rocky top soil of New England, or clearing and cultivating rice lands in South Carolina and Georgia, their success might be ascribed to their belief in thrift and the moral dignity of hard work, private property, social and racial inequality, and profit-making.

The Midway settlers wrought an agricultural revolution in the struggling province by expanding commercial rice production and introducing extensive use of slave labor. For the first time, Georgia had a profitable staple crop and a dependable source of labor. The district reputedly contained at least one-third of the wealth in colonial Georgia at the eve of the Revolution. This prosperity supported an indigenous planter aristocracy that produced many of the political and intellectual leaders of colonial and antebellum Georgia. True to the example of their New England forebears who believed that education gave direction to piety, the Midway settlers were the

---

of Georgia (Athens: University of Georgia Press, 1976) 28, Part 1:73, 382-83, 463-65. For the plan of Sunbury, see McIlvaine, *The Dead Towns*, 12.

first to establish a school of any prominence in Georgia. The academy established at Sunbury in 1788 by the famous schoolmaster, Dr. William McWhir, attracted pupils from throughout the state. The Newport and Midway Library Society, the successor of the Beech Hill Alphabet Society, held approximately 500 volumes and continued for more than a century.[27] For higher education, the more affluent families sent their sons to Harvard, Yale, and Princeton. Without repeating all of Stacy's enumerations, a partial list of the noteworthy people who came from the Midway district included 82 ministers, among whom were Daniel Baker and Charles C. Jones; a host of educators; Governors Nathan Brownson, Richard Howley, John Martin, and Lyman Hall; United States Senators John Elliott, Alfred Iverson, and Augustus O. Bacon; Continental Congress member Benjamin Andrew; two members of the House of Representatives, John A. Cuthbert and William B. Fleming; and the first U. S. Minister to China, John E. Ward. Dr. Louis LeConte, who owned a famous botanical garden at "Woodmanston," was the father of two famous scientists, John and Joseph LeConte. Generals James Screven and Daniel Stewart were heroes of the American Revolution. Dr. Francis Goulding, author of *The Young Marooners* and inventor of the lock-stitch sewing machine, and many others merit recognition.[28]

The Midway settlement, unique in the history of colonial Georgia, rested on the pillars of the Puritan faith: the covenanted church, the corporate community, the education of youth, the work ethic, and an economic system based on rice and slavery. This legacy was transplanted to Georgia by the Reverend John Osgood and his band whose ancestors could be traced back to Dorchester, South Carolina, Dorchester, Massachusetts, and ultimately to Dorchester, England. Their encounter with the Southern wilderness not only transformed their mission, but shaped the course of the fledgling colony.

---

[27]William Harden, "William McWhir, An Irish Friend of Washington," *Georgia Historical Quarterly* 1 (September 1917): 197-219; Stacy, *History of Midway Church*, 99.

[28]Jones, *The History of Georgia*, 2:167; White, *Historical Collections*, 532; Stacy, *History of Midway Church*, 112-91.

TWO

Stephen Elliott:
Early Botanist
of Coastal Georgia

It was drawing on towards the close of day, the skies
serene and calm, the air temperately cool, and gently zephyrs
breathing through the fragrant pines; the prospect around
enchantingly varied and beautiful; endless green savannas,
checquered with coppices of fragrant shrubs, filled the
air with the richest perfume. The gaily attired plants
which enamelled the green had begun to imbibe the pearly
dew of evening.

—William Bartram,
Travels, 20

DURING THE FIRST CENTURY of botanical exploration in Georgia, collectors and natural scientists were fascinated by the new flora of the region. These early visitors came with the hope of finding plants with economic or medicinal values; they were enthralled by the lure of the rare or exotic; or they were merely curious and adventurous. Supported by a variety of patrons ranging from royalty to private persons, such expeditions in the eighteenth century had as their primary activity the collection and shipment of seeds, roots, and dried specimens, supplemented by drawings, paintings, and descriptions of the plants and their habitats. Investigation began in 1722 soon after the arrival of Mark Catesby and reached a preliminary synthesis in the work of Stephen Elliott early in the nineteenth century.

In that first century a mere handful of men and a few women confronted hundreds of new species in a nearly virgin wilderness. These early botanists engaged vigorously in the discovery, naming, and classification of hitherto unknown plants. Adoption of the sexual system of classification developed by Linnaeus stimulated scientific communications with European botanists and patrons. The hardships of travel and collecting in a frontier district were ever present, and there were few material rewards. These early naturalists were driven to persevere by the thrill of discovery, the sheer delight of being in the presence of unspoiled nature, and the prospect of enduring fame from the publication of their findings. Competition for priority in publication sometimes led to rivalry, disputes, and what appeared as petty squabbles. The rival scientists, however, viewed publication as a matter of prime importance; their public reputation, a limited financial remuneration, and their private sense of accomplishment and personal worth were at stake. Such a rivalry was illustrated in the relationship between Stephen Elliott and William Baldwin.

Although Georgia had not yet been named when Mark Catesby explored, collected, and painted scores of its plant species, he contributed much to Georgia botany. Using Charleston, South Carolina, as his base, he spent three years (1722-1725) "in Carolina and the adjacent parts (which the Spaniards call Florida, particularly that province lately honoured with the name of Georgia). . . ."[1] During those years he was often at or near Fort Moore on the Carolina side of the Savannah River, not far from the future site of Augusta, Georgia. His exact travels in Georgia are unknown but his drawings and commentary were to serve as fundamental sources for many who followed him.

Brief notice must be taken of Johann Martin Bolzius, pastor at Ebenezer, and Philip Georg Friedrich von Reck, a young man who conducted groups of Salzburgers to Georgia in 1734 and again in 1736. Bolzius wrote detailed reports containing occasional items of botanical interest and revealed an accumulating knowledge at Ebenezer about the Georgia flora.[2] Von Reck kept a careful journal of his 1735-1736 trip and also preserved his drawings of plants, birds, animals, and Indians. Unfortunately von Reck's works re-

---

[1]See reprint of The Natural History of Carolina, Florida and the Bahama Islands Containing two hundred and twenty figures of Birds, Beasts, Fishes, Serpents, Insects and Plants by the late Mark Catesby, F.R.S., with an introduction by George Frick and notes by Joseph Ewan (Savannah: The Beehive Press, 1974) iii-v; George Frederick Frick and Raymond Phineas Stearns, Mark Catesby the Colonial Audubon (Urbana: University of Illinois Press, 1961) 22-32.

[2]For examples, see George Fenwick Jones and Renate Wilson, Detailed Reports on the Salzburgers Emigrants Who Settled in America. . . . , ed. by Samuel Urlsperger (Athens: University of Georgia Press, 1981) 6:27, 40, 76, 111.

mained unpublished and unknown to researchers until 1976, consequently they played no role in the early botanical history of Georgia.[3]

About 30 years later, in 1765-1766, John Bartram (1699-1777) and his son, William (1739-1823), visited Georgia together.[4] Their mission was to fulfill John's obligations as King's Botanist and to send seeds, roots, and specimens to Peter Collinson, British friend and patron of John Bartram. William acted as assistant to his father, drawing and painting many of their discoveries. The two crossed the Savannah River from Purysburgh, South Carolina, in a bateau 3 September 1765, landing about ten miles downriver near Abercorn on the Georgia bank. They lodged nearby and reached Savannah the next morning.[5]

After meeting the governor and other prominent Georgians, they set out for Augusta. Their route took them along the west bank of the Savannah River through the Salzburger settlement of Ebenezer and past Sisters Ferry. They crossed Brier Creek near its mouth, at the place where the battle of Brier Creek would be fought several years in the future. They continued northward to Shell Bluff in Burke County where Bartram described the giant oyster shells which can still be found there. They crossed into South Carolina, continued past George Galphin's trading post, and recrossed the river to Augusta. Retracing their route to Shell Bluff, they rode southwestward to cross Brier Creek where Thompson's Bridge is today. In his diary, John Bartram referred to the many large sturgeons jumping in the Savannah River and at Blue Springs took note of the "evergreen casseena," source of the black drink of the Indians, and commented that "it is very wholsom."

---

[3]Kristian Hvidt, ed., *Von Reck's Voyage: Drawings and Journal of Philip Georg Friedrich von Reck* (Savannah: The Beehive Press, 1980). Plates on pages 65, 91, 93, 97, 99, 101, 103, 105, 109; discussion on preceding pages.

[4]For general treatments, see Ernest Earnest, *John and William Bartram, Botanists and Explorers (1699-1777) (1739-1823)* (Philadelphia: University of Pennsylvania Press, 1940); N. B. Fagin, *William Bartram, Interpreter of the American Landscape* (Baltimore: The Johns Hopkins Press, 1933); Edmund Berkeley and Dorothy Smith Berkeley, *The Life and Travels of John Bartram: from Lake Ontario to the River St. John* (Tallahassee: University Presses of Florida, 1982); see also Betsy C. Corner and Christopher C. Booth, *Chain of Friendship: Selected Letters of Dr. John Fothergill of London, 1735-1780* (Cambridge: Harvard University Press, 1971).

[5]John Bartram, "Diary of a Journey through the Carolinas, Georgia, and Florida from July 1, 1765 to April 10, 1766," annotated by Frances Harper, *Transactions of the American Philosophical Society*, n.s., vol. 33, part 1 (Philadelphia: American Philosophical Society, 1942): 23.

Soon they rejoined the road through Ebenezer and reached Savannah on 23 September, soaked through from incessant rains.[6]

After numbering and packing their specimens and writing some letters, the Bartrams left Savannah for St. Augustine. They crossed the Ogeechee River, passed Midway, and traveled the obscure road toward Fort Barrington on the Altamaha River. As they approached the fort, they lost their way and camped four miles downriver. During this interval they found the beautiful small tree, *Franklinia alatamaha*, which Bartram named for his good friend Benjamin Franklin. Among other plants observed near the fort, he described the overcup oak (*Quercus lyrata*) and the Ogeechee lime (*Nyssa ogeche*), the latter "with large red acid fruite . . . which is used for punch." A half-century later Stephen Elliott remarked that "the pleasant acid of its fruit induced some of the early inhabitants of Georgia to use it as a substitute for the lime . . . but its last flavour is austere." Both trees are still abundant in the area. After crossing the Altamaha, they rode southward toward St. Augustine. Just beyond the Little Satilla River they found a "very odd Catalpa" with pods round as an acorn, a description that is still puzzling. On 10 October, they crossed the Cowford, the site of modern Jacksonville, and spent the winter in Florida. When William Bartram determined to seek his fortune as a planter of indigo in Florida, his father sailed to Philadelphia from St. Augustine in March 1766.[7]

William's adventure as an indigo planter brought quick disillusionment and termination; he had probably returned home by early 1768. After another failure in business in Philadelphia in 1770, William moved to North Carolina. In 1772 he sent some of his drawings of natural objects to Dr. John Fothergill in London and apparently expressed his interest in undertaking another southern trip. After Dr. Fothergill agreed to underwrite his expenses, William returned to Philadelphia to make his preparations and sailed for Savannah on 20 March 1773.[8]

---

[6]Ibid., 24-29; on the black drink, see Charles M. Hudson, ed., *Black Drink: A Native American Tea* (Athens: University of Georgia Press, 1979).

[7]Bartram, "Diary," 31-32, 49; William Bartram, *Travels through North and South Carolina, Georgia, East and West Florida* (Philadelphia: James and Johnson, 1791) 16, 467-68; Stephen Elliott, *A Sketch of the Botany of South Carolina and Georgia* (Charleston: J. R. Schenck, 1824) 2:685.

[8]William Bartram, "Travels in Georgia and Florida, 1773-74: A Report to Dr. John Fothergill," annotated by Francis Harper in *Transactions of the American Philosophical Society*, n.s.,vol. 33, part 2 (Philadelphia: American Philosophical Society, 1943): 125-26.

From Savannah he rode south to Sunbury and on nearby Colonel's Island he found the soap tree (*Sapindus marginatus*), *Magnolia pyramidata*, and *Fothergilla gardeni*. His route took him to Darien, Fort Barrington, Brunswick, and back to Savannah. He then rode north toward Augusta and revisited Blue Springs near Beaverdam Creek in Screven County. From Augusta he accompanied the surveying party marking the boundaries of the 1773 cession of Indian lands to Georgia. Not far from the intersection of the survey line with the Savannah River, he found "a very beautiful Shrub, bearing long loose spikes of sweet white flowers. . . ." From the specimen and colored drawing William sent to Dr. Fothergill, it was later identified as the rare *Elliottia racemosa*. The site must have been in present-day Hart County or in eastern Franklin or Madison Counties.[9]

After hearing disquieting news of Indian disturbances in the back country from Augusta, he turned southward toward Florida by way of Savannah, Darien, and St. Simons Island. Here he found *Lycium carolinianum*, commonly called Christmas berry. Elliott later wrote that it was "found by Mr. William Bartram, in the saline rushy marshes of Carolina" and puzzled future botanists by recording its common name as "Johnny Bartram." William sailed from Florida in November 1774, stopping at Sunbury, Georgia. From there he shipped his specimens and a written report to his patron, Dr. Fothergill. Late in March of 1775, he arrived in Charleston to confer with Dr. Lionel Chalmers, Fothergill's agent for William's explorations, so as to plan future trips.[10]

Late that April, he crossed into Georgia at Sisters Ferry (near Clyo in Effingham County) and found *Dirca palustris*. He rode through Augusta toward Fort James Dartmouth on the Broad River. En route he spent the night near the ford across Little River and found a second colony of *Elliottia racemosa*. The site is now submerged under the dammed-up waters of the Savannah River. Bartram then visited the Cherokee country before heading west across central Georgia where he found *Hypericum aureum* (now *Hypericum frondosum* Michx) just west of the Flint River. He went on into Alabama to Mobile and thence to the Mississippi River in Louisiana; he

---

[9]Ibid., 134-43; Bartram, *Travels*, 6, 28-46; Joseph Ewan, ed., *William Bartram: Botanical and Zoological Drawings, 1756-1788* (Philadelphia: American Philosophical Society, 1968) Plate 39, pp. 71, 161.

[10]Bartram, *Report to Dr. Fothergill*, 144-45, 163, 192-93; Bartram, *Travels*, 48-59, 305-307; Elliott, *Sketch*, 1:200.

arrived back in Augusta in mid-January 1776. Taking the familiar route to Savannah, he made a brief stop at Blue Springs in Screven County. On a visit to Fort Barrington he found the *Franklinia alatamaha* in bloom and nearby a "new, singular and beautiful shrub," the *Pinckneya pubens* or Georgia bark. In late October or early November of 1776, William Bartram turned homeward; riding north from Savannah, he crossed into South Carolina at Zubly's Ferry. He reached Philadelphia in early January, in ample time for many conversations with his father before the latter's death later that year.[11]

A few years later another father and son, Andre Michaux (1746-1802) and Francois Andre Michaux (1770-1855), arrived in the United States from France. Michaux had gained a reputation as an enthusiastic plant collector and had received a commission from his government to search for trees that might be useful in France. The French government was interested in species with shipbuilding potential, but Michaux seems to have been searching for horticultural plants as well. Their first holding garden was established in New Jersey, but they moved to Charleston in 1787 and launched a new one.[12]

On their first collecting trip, they crossed into Georgia at Sisters Ferry on 26 April 1787. They found many species still to be seen there, such as *Dirca palustris*, *Kalmia latifolia*, and an *Azalea* the color of the orange day lily. They also found an *Asclepias* (perhaps *Matelea*) and a new *Magnolia*, probably *pyramidata*. Their explorations carried them southward through Ebenezer to Savannah.[13] In early May they were at the Ogeechee River and collected the Ogeechee lime (*Nyssa ogeche*) of Bartram. They went on to Sunbury where Andre remained to collect plants while his son and two others made a separate expedition to the banks of the Altamaha. On 10 May, they turned north and collected *Halesia diptera* four miles from Ebenezer. In Screven County they collected the buckwheat tree (*Cliftonia monophyllum*)

[11]Elliott, *Sketch*, 1:448; Ewan, *Drawings*, frontispiece and plates 23, 46, pp. 13, 76-77; Bartram, *Travels*, 308-470, 481.

[12]Dumas Malone, ed., *Dictionary of American Biography* (New York: Charles Scribner's Sons, 1933) 12:591-93.

[13]C. S. Sargent, "Portions of the Journal of Andre Michaux, Botanist, written during his Travels in the United States and Canada, 1785 to 1796, with an Introduction and Explanatory Notes," *Proceedings of the American Philosophical Society* 26 (January to July 1889): 9-10.

and a *Rumex* that has been identified as *Brunnichia cirrhosa*. By 27 May, they were in Augusta heading north.[14]

In late May of the following year, Michaux entered Georgia from Florida, with collecting stops at St. Marys, and on Cumberland, St. Simons, Sapelo, and St. Catherines Islands. After a brief visit to Savannah, he reached Charleston 6 June 1788.[15] He was again in Georgia in Augusta in mid-November and nearby he found a new buckeye and what may have been *Ceratiola ericoides*, commonly called rosemary. He then swung southward into Screven County, found the buckwheat tree again, returned to Augusta only to head west into Wilkes County and then northward.[16] He spent one more month (19 April-18 May 1791) in Georgia, collecting from St. Marys northward to Savannah and finding *Nyssa ogeche*, *Lyonia ferruginea*, *Kalmia hirsuta*, and the beautiful *Befaria racemosa*. He was back in Charleston 22 May 1791.[17]

In addition to the collections, the Michaux contributions included three major publications. In 1801 in Paris, Andre Michaux published the *Histoire des Chenes de l'Amerique, ou descriptions et figures de toutes les especes et varietes de Chenes de l'Amerique Septentrionale*. His *Flora Boreali-Americana, sistens caracteres Plantarum quas in America Septentrionali collegit et detexit Andreas Michaux* appeared posthumously in 1803, edited by Claude Richard. Francois Andre Michaux published his *Histoire des Arbres forestiers de l'Amerique Septentrionale* in three volumes, 1810-1813; it was reissued as *The North American Sylva . . .* in 1818-1819. Along with *Bartram's Travels Through North and South Carolina, Georgia, East and West Florida . . .* , these quickly became standard reference works for Stephen Elliott and his contemporaries.[18]

Stephen Elliott (1771-1830) was born at Beaufort, South Carolina. He graduated from Yale College in 1791 after being elected to Phi Beta Kappa. During his senior year, he delivered an oration entitled "On the Supposed Degeneracy of Animated Nature in America," probably based upon Thomas

[14]Ibid., 11-14.

[15]Ibid., 39.

[16]Ibid., 43.

[17]Ibid, 65-67.

[18]Malone, *Dictionary of American Biography*, 12:592-93.

Jefferson's *Notes on the State of Virginia*. In it the youthful Elliott refuted the theory advanced by the French scholar, Georges de Buffon, and revealed his growing interest in natural history.[19]

After graduation he returned home to manage his several plantations in South Carolina and Georgia. The latter included properties in Chatham, Bryan, Liberty, and Camden Counties. In the ensuing years, he married Esther Wylly Habersham of Savannah, served in the South Carolina legislature, and dabbled in natural history as a collector of plants, minerals, seashells, and insects. He bought books in the areas of history, literature, and natural history and began to assemble a magnificent private library that finally numbered 2,500 volumes.[20]

In the summer and fall of 1808 Elliott traveled northward to Pennsylvania with his wife and daughter and followed a route along the eastern flank of the mountains, probably to escape the coastal heat, enjoy the scenery, and collect rocks and mineral specimens.[21] He carried with him a flowering specimen of a shrub found near Waynesboro (Burke County), Georgia, which he gave to the Reverend Henry Muhlenberg of Lancaster, Pennsylvania. Muhlenberg, the outstanding botanist in America, promptly named it *Elliottia racemosa*. From this visit and the long correspondence that followed, Elliott was persuaded to concentrate on botany. He freely acknowledged Muhlenberg's influence and admitted that he might have turned toward mineralogy and geology had circumstances been different.[22]

-----

[19]Stephen B. Barnwell, *The Story of an American Family* (Marquette MI: n.p.) 30, 50; Thomas Jefferson, *Notes on the State of Virginia*, edited with an introduction and notes by William Peden (Chapel Hill: University of North Carolina Press, 1955) 53-58; Franklin Bowditch Dexter, *Biographical Sketches of the Graduates of Yale College with annals of the College History* (New York: H. Holt and Company, 1885-1912) 4:704-707.

[20]*Georgia Gazette*, 4 February 1796, p. 3, c.3; Joan Schriner Reynolds Faunt, Robert E. Rector, David K. Dowden, *Biographical Directory of the South Carolina House of Representatives* (Columbia: University of South Carolina Press, 1974) 1:242; Emily Bellinger and Joan Reynolds Faunt, comps., *Biographical Directory of the Senate of the State of South Carolina* (Columbia: South Carolina Archives Department, 1964); South Carolina Archives, "Inventory of Estate of Stephen Elliott," *Inventories*, Book G, 387-88.

[21]Joseph and Nesta Ewan, "John Lyon, Nurseryman and Plant Hunter, and His Journal, 1799-1814," *Transactions of the American Philosophical Society*, n.s., 53, part 2 (1963): 37. Letter, C. W. Peale to Stephen Elliott, 14 February 1809, Peale Papers, American Philosophical Society.

[22]Henry Muhlenberg to Stephen Elliott, 9 November 1808. The correspondence is preserved in 30 letters from Muhlenberg to Elliott at the Arnold Arboretum Library, Harvard University (hereafter referred to as AAL), and 16 letters from Elliott to Muhlenberg at the Historical Society of Pennsylvania; Elliott, *Sketch*, 1:448.

When he died in 1830, Stephen Elliott was widely recognized as "The Southern Botanist." Between 1816 and 1824 he had published what he modestly called *A Sketch of the Botany of South Carolina and Georgia*. Originally issued in 13 separate fascicles, the *Sketch* was bound in two volumes and comprised more than 1,300 pages of plant descriptions in Latin and English.[23] In preparing this work, Elliott studied with minute care the publications of European botanists and those of his American predecessors such as Mark Catesby, Thomas Walter, William Bartram, and Frederick Pursh, comparing their descriptions with specimens in his herbarium.[24] He drew upon his contemporaries for specimens, commentary, and inspiration, and readily admitted his indebtedness to them. He delighted in going afield with James Macbride, John Brickell, or Alexander Wilson, and found much pleasure in the collections and conversation of John Lyon, Correa da Serra, and Thomas Nuttall.[25] Many collectors like John Abbot, Augustus Oemler, and James Jackson contributed hitherto unknown species and, despite a certain rivalry, Elliott managed to incorporate some achievements of Louis and John Eatton LeConte.[26]

---

[23]John Hendley Barnhart, "Dates of Elliott's Sketch," *Bulletin of the Torrey Botanical Club* 27 (1901): 680-88; Joseph Ewan, ed., "Introduction" to a facsimile reprint of Elliott, *Sketch* (New York: Hafner Publishing Company, 1971) xix-xxiv.

[24]Thomas Walter (1740-1789) published his *Flora Caroliniana* in London in 1788. Walter's plants were in South Carolina, but many occur also in Georgia. Frederick Pursh (1774-1820) published *Flora Americae Septentrionalis; or, A Systematic Arrangement and Description of the Plants of North America* in London in 1814. Pursh collected Southern plants in 1806.

[25]James Macbride (1784-1817) was a South Carolina medical doctor and a close friend of Elliott. The second volume of the *Sketch* was inscribed to his memory. The Elliott-Macbride correspondence is at the Charleston Museum. John Brickell (1749-1809) was a Savannah doctor who regarded Elliott as his friend and who sent specimens and letters to Muhlenberg. Elliott named *Brickellia cordifolia* in his memory. Alexander Wilson (1766-1813) published *American Ornithology; or, the Natural History of the Birds of the United States* in Philadelphia between 1808-1814. George Ord completed volume eight and wrote volume nine because of Wilson's death. Elliott was a subscriber and insisted that Wilson use his home in Chatham County as a base. Elliott furnished Wilson with specimens and some acute observations on the fish crow and towhee. John Lyon (?-1814) was an English gardener and plant collector who was Elliott's house guest and botanizing companion on several occasions. Jose Francisco Correa da Serra (1751-1823) was a house guest of Elliott for about two weeks. As Minister of Portugal, he knew Thomas Jefferson well and told Jefferson that Elliott was the best Southern botanist. Thomas Nutall (1786-1859) was an English botanist who published *The Genera of North American Plants* in 1818. He and Elliott were together for a considerable period in Charleston during late 1816 and early 1817.

[26]John Abbott (1751-ca.1840) spent most of his life in Georgia. He painted birds, insects, and spiders. One set of his paintings was published in London in 1797 by James Edward

Louis LeConte (1782-1838) published nothing, but the reputation of his botanical garden at Woodmanston Plantation in Liberty County and the testimony of his relatives and friends point to a truly scientific mind. John Eatton LeConte (1784-1860), his younger brother, published 35 papers of which 12 were on botanical subjects, including the genera *Paspalum*, *Utricularia*, *Gratiola*, *Tillandsia*, and *Viola*. Both had sons who achieved a reputation for scientific eminence.[27] But it was Stephen Elliott who combined his own extensive original research with all other available sources and produced a synthesis that is still fundamental to the science. During the critical years when the concept and the specific form of the *Sketch* were taking shape, Muhlenberg encouraged him to publish and, by correspondence, introduced him to Dr. William Baldwin.[28] Between Elliott and Baldwin there developed a very special friendship interlaced with competition. Their strained collaboration produced a partial coauthorship that profoundly affected the *Sketch* and through it the future of southeastern botany.

William Baldwin was born 29 March 1779 in Chester County, Pennsylvania. In his late teens his acquaintance with Dr. Moses Marshall provided the opportunity to study the plants in the Marshallton Botanic Garden, prompting his interest in botany. He became a pupil and assistant of Dr. William A. Todd, a local physician, and attended medical lectures at the University of Pennsylvania in 1802-1803. There he formed a lifelong friendship with William Darlington, who later published a collection of

---

Smith as the *Natural History of the Rarer Lepidopterous Insects of Georgia*. Elliott possessed a set of his paintings. He provided specimens of *Sabatia gentianoides* for Elliott who reciprocated with insects. Augustus G. Oemler was a Savannah druggist who collected specimens for Elliott, among them *Coreopsis oemleri*. James Jackson (1787-1857) was a professor at the University of Georgia who sent Elliott specimens that included *Elliottia racemosa* and *Penstemon dissectum*.

[27]John Hendly Barnhart, "John Eatton LeConte," *The American Midland Naturalist* 5 (1917-1918): 135-38; Clark A. Elliott, ed., *Biographical Dictionary of American Science, The Seventeenth through the Nineteenth Centuries* (Westport: Greenwood Press, 1979) 153; Richard LeConte Anderson, *LeConte History and Genealogy* (Macon: privately printed, 1981) 2:776-836.

[28]Henry Muhlenberg to Stephen Elliott, 5 January 1812, AAL. Henry Muhlenberg to William Baldwin, 4 November 1811, in William Darlington, comp., *Reliquiae Baldwinianae* (Philadelphia: Kimber and Sharpless, 1843) 51-53.

Baldwin's papers. He worked again as a medical assistant to Dr. Todd until 1805 when he embarked as ship's surgeon aboard a merchant vessel in the China trade. Upon his return he resumed his study of medicine at the University of Pennsylvania under Professor Benjamin Smith Barton, who further stimulated his zeal for botany. He was awarded his M.D. in 1807 and moved to Wilmington, Delaware, to begin a medical practice. He soon married Miss Hannah W. Webster of Wilmington and ever afterwards, despite his travels, regarded that city as home.[29]

Apparently he found time to continue his botanical studies and somehow came to the attention of Henry Muhlenberg. Muhlenberg initiated correspondence in January of 1811; Baldwin replied within a week with genuine pleasure and delight.[30] Six months later Muhlenberg wrote Elliott that Baldwin was an excellent botanist and desired to introduce him.[31] Baldwin was already suffering from tuberculosis and was traveling south for the winter of 1811-1812; he arrived in Savannah in December and met Elliott that January. Baldwin spent several months at the Indian agency on the Flint River and was commissioned as a surgeon in the U.S. Navy in the spring of 1812. He was stationed mostly in St. Marys and Savannah. In 1816 he sent his family home to Wilmington while he explored the botany of East Florida. In 1817 the Navy sent him on a mission to South America aboard the U.S.S. *Congress*, and upon his return in 1818 he spent nearly a year with his family in Wilmington. In 1819 he was appointed surgeon and botanist on Major Long's expedition up the Missouri River. He died 1 September 1819 and was buried along the Missouri.[32]

What can be reconstructed about the nature of the Elliott-Baldwin relationship? What was it like in 1812? How did Elliott regard it? What did Baldwin see as his role? By 1816-1817, how had their relationship evolved?

If Elliott followed his usual procedure during their first meeting in January 1812, he asked Baldwin to send him specimens with appropriate comments on habitat, date and site of collection, and other interesting details about the plants. Correspondence between them reveals Baldwin's eager-

---

[29]Darlington, *Reliquiae Baldwinianae*, 7-14.

[30]Ibid., 15-19.

[31]Henry Muhlenberg to Stephen Elliott, 29 July 1811, AAL.

[32]Wayne Rasmussen, "Diplomats and Plant Collectors: The South American Commission, 1817-1818," *Agricultural History* 29 (January 1955): 22-31.

ness to provide both data and specimens, and Elliott's delight in finding a new botanical friend who was a new source for botanical treasures and information as well.[33] The subsequent attributions to Baldwin in the *Sketch* number only 94 specimens, 15 of which were described as Baldwin's new plants, out of a total of 3,089. Almost certainly Baldwin sent more than 94 specimens and for reasons of his own, Elliott did not include Baldwin's name. Commonly Elliott limited specimen credit to only three or four of the earliest authorities for each species.[34]

Elliott was already planning publication of a work on southeastern flora and perceived in Baldwin another collector-correspondent who would send notes and specimens as contributions. In all, nearly 60 different persons collected specimens for Elliott. Some contributed only an occasional plant, while some like James Macbride sent a great many. Most of them were interested in botany as a hobby, although physicians were seeking plants as a source of prescriptions for many ailments.[35] Some were farmers or outdoorsmen who had a keen eye for the new or unusual. Most had no ambitions for publication on their own and apparently took substantial pleasure in forwarding flora to Elliott. In 1812, Baldwin was also an amateur botanist who was just beginning to study the southeastern flora. Quite likely, Baldwin perceived his role as being one of contributor; maybe he had not yet thought through what he wanted to do in botany. Certainly, some of his specimens went to Muhlenberg and not to Elliott.[36] For example, neither *Collinsonia verticillata* nor *Erianthus strictus* was published in the initial printing of the *Sketch*'s first fascicle although Muhlenberg received the former and possibly the latter from Baldwin some years earlier. Both appeared in the revised version of the first number as Baldwin's plants. Obviously, Elliott did not have them at first although Baldwin and Muhlenberg did.[37]

---

[33]William Baldwin, Correspondence, Stephen Elliott, 1815-1819, New York Botanical Garden Library (hereafter referred to as NYBG).

[34]Elliott, *Sketch*, tabulation by author.

[35]James Macbride to Stephen Elliott, 24 December 1811, 10 February, 7 March, August, and 18 December 1812, AAL. Thomas J(arram) Wray to Stephen Elliott, 17 February 1819, AAL. There are numerous references to the medicinal properties of plants in the *Sketch*.

[36]William Baldwin to Thomas M. Forman, 11 March, 6 May 1813, Forman-Bryan-Screven Papers, Georgia Historical Society, Savannah.

[37]See initial version of the first number of the *Sketch*, De Renne Collection, University of Georgia, Athens; compare with later version. Darlington, *Reliquiae Baldwinianae*, 207. It should be noted that von Reck painted *Erianthus strictus* in 1736.

Baldwin was different in another way. He was an enthusiastic amateur with a sound foundation through his training under Benjamin Smith Barton; and with each letter from Muhlenberg, he received encouragement to continue to determine the identity of his plants with precision. Such training in taxonomic exactness, coupled with the example of Muhlenberg, Barton, and Elliott, prompted him to publish his own work. By early 1814, he was planning to issue a botanical guide for ladies in collaboration with Miss Louisa Greene.[38] In addition, he met Louis and John Eatton LeConte early in 1812 and both of them were inclined toward publication. The role of author rather than that of mere contributor to the work of others began to take definite shape in Baldwin's mind.

His letters to Elliott show that he was frequently with the LeContes—they told him the names of several plants; they claimed a new species of *Ludwigia*; their garden had a new *Thalia* shooting up; they believed the range of the *Canna flaccida* terminated at the Ogeechee River. Baldwin was irked in June of 1816 when LeConte requested specimens from him and afterwards let it be known that he would send them to European botanists for identification.[39] Nevertheless, Baldwin wrote William Darlington in February 1817 of his disagreement with some identifications made by Elliott and his agreement with "my truly scientific friends, the LeContes."[40]

When Elliott forwarded impressions of the first illustrations for the *Sketch*, Baldwin, the LeContes, and Augustus Oemler of Savannah criticized both the design and the execution of the plates.[41] Since the original drawings for the plates had been done by Elliott, such criticisms were probably not easy to accept, especially since the drawings were well done. There were other evidences of rivalry, if not hostility, between Elliott and the LeContes. For example, John Eatton LeConte instructed that specimens intended for him that came through Charleston might be sent there to anyone "except Stephen Elliott" and in his published articles he expressed with acerbity his particular disagreements with Elliott. Although Elliott used John Eatton LeConte's notes in his treatment of the genus *Utricularia* and

[38]William Baldwin to General Forman (date missing, but the reply was dated 7 April 1814), Forman-Bryan-Screven Papers.

[39]Baldwin to Elliott, 7 June, 25 June, 11 November 1816, William Baldwin Correspondence, Stephen Elliott, 1815-1819, NYBG.

[40]Darlington, *Reliquiae Baldwinianae*, 207.

[41]Baldwin to Elliott, 25 June 1816, NYBG.

Louis LeConte's specimen of *Tillandsia bartramii* with appropriate acknowledgments, he omitted the LeContes from notices in his preface. Baldwin was undoubtedly influenced by these competitive attitudes.[42]

The crisis in the Baldwin-Elliott relationship came in early October 1816 when Baldwin received the first number of the *Sketch*. Six weeks earlier Baldwin had expressed his disappointment in his inability to give Elliott all the assistance that he had intended and the day before he received his copy, Baldwin had written that since Elliott had led him "into the labyrinth of the panicums," he would probably need Elliott's help to get out. He felt proud to claim scientific kinship with Elliott. A few days later after examining the first number, Baldwin first praised it and then launched into a vigorous criticism of details. He did not approve of the specific names given the *Kyllingias* (sedges) or the *Collinsonia tuberosa* and he denied collecting *Stipulicida setacea* near St. Marys. He was irked because Elliott had attached Baldwin's name to *Xyris setifolia* and was certain that he (Baldwin) had not given it that specific name. Elliott used the common name, Linear-leaved Xyris, and described the leaves as "filiform." Baldwin feared that his name attached to the plant would injure his botanical reputation since he questioned how leaves could be both linear and filiform. Twice among a good many attributions of specimens Elliott had used the passage "From specimens sent me (without leaves) by Dr. Baldwin"; Baldwin was distinctly not flattered. But the crucial matter was Baldwin's determination to secure publication credit for those plants that were his own discoveries. Baldwin announced that he would gladly have his name removed from the first number.[43]

Elliott replied four days later (11 October 1816) in a letter no longer extant; however, one can infer much of its contents. Elliott hoped there would be no "loss of friendship," assured Baldwin of no intent to injure him, and reminded him that he had presented a manuscript portion for his approval on the use of Baldwin's name. Baldwin disclaimed any problem about intent to injure or damage to their friendship, nor could he recall any issue concerning his name in the sample manuscript in which only one plant and its description was ascribed to him (*Sabbatia corymbosa*). Baldwin's

---

[42]Elliott, *Sketch*, preface and plates; John LeConte to James Macbride, 24 December 1814, James Macbride Papers, Library of Congress.

[43]Baldwin to Elliott, 7 October 1816, NYBG; see initial version of *Sketch*, De Renne Collection, and Darlington, *Reliquiae Baldwinianae*, 334.

wounded vanity and injured self-esteem then poured forth. He would sustain hurt to his botanical character to be termed a mere collector, and he was still offended about the "leafless specimens." He alluded obliquely to Elliott's preface as an indication of how his assistance was regarded; Baldwin had not been mentioned. He would not permit Elliott to name, describe, and publish his plants. He blamed himself for failing to make clear that he wished to name and write the descriptions under which his plant discoveries were published. He had expected Elliott to ask for descriptions, "if he were to be considered in "any *Character* higher than that of a *Collector*." Baldwin boasted that "in less than five years . . . I have discovered nearly as many new plants" as Elliott had in his life. He queried "is it any wonder that I should begin to think of dissolving partnership and setting up for myself? You have taught me to feel my own importance. . . ." Baldwin then reiterated his desire to continue to supply Elliott with specimens, names, and descriptions to be published in Elliott's work, but as Baldwin submitted them. He offered specific criticisms of the first number involving the changing of names in a species of *Xyris* and of *Dichromena* and then ventured (as Baldwin put it) "upon *privaledged ground*" when he disagreed with the medical comments of Dr. James Macbride concerning *Monarda punctata*. In closing, he asserted vigorously how important his correspondence with Elliott was.[44]

Elliott obviously agreed to these conditions since Baldwin requested on 24 October that Elliott "inform the public of our *new arrangement*, in your *second number*, as an apology for my not having described my own plants in the *first*." Despite the extra financial costs, Elliott's solution was to recall all copies of the first number and have it reprinted in accord with their agreement; Baldwin responded on 11 November that he was very satisfied. On 30 November Baldwin wanted to see publication delayed until others could collaborate. He wrote Elliott that the LeContes would have contributed if they had been permitted. Later letters contained specific corrections and the admonition to refer to Baldwin's letters for detail and not to quote from memory.[45]

Baldwin's feisty temperament showed in other ways. Once James Jackson, professor of natural history at Athens, sent a packet of specimens for

[44]Baldwin to Elliott, 13 October 1816, NYBG.

[45]Baldwin to Elliott, 24 October, 11 November, 30 November 1816, and 18 February, 16 April 1817, NYBG.

Elliott via Oemler with some material in the packet destined for Baldwin. He happened to be out of town so Oemler sent the entire packet to Elliott. Baldwin was annoyed and complained; Elliott in due time sent the specimens back to him. When Thomas Nuttall collected plants in the Southeast, he chose to honor Baldwin by naming a genus of the Aster family *Balduina*. Twice Baldwin wrote Elliott that he especially (and strenuously) objected to the "u" instead of the "w."[46]

What can be said then about these two botanists? Baldwin had a fiery, impetuous, forthright personality whereas Elliott seemed quieter, steadier, and more willing to adjust to Baldwin's changing requirements. Both were good botanists, but Baldwin was a perfectionist who did not wish to publish until he knew every detail was correct. Elliott was more of a realist and accepted the fact that he would inevitably make errors for future botanists to correct. Elliott accepted the possibility of mistakes; Baldwin abhorred the very idea. Baldwin accepted Elliott's invitation to contribute plants, came to desire collaboration, and would have been thrilled to have been named as coauthor. Elliott started with the assumption that Baldwin was a collector and came to accept the idea that the *Sketch* had become the vehicle for the publication of Baldwin's plant names and descriptions. The overwhelming fact was that Baldwin did decide to provide Elliott with plants and descriptions and Elliott did provide an opportunity to publish them. As a consequence Baldwin's work on southeastern flora was not lost and Elliott's *Sketch* was significantly enriched.

Catesby, Bolzius, von Reck, John and William Bartram, Andre and Francois Andre Michaux, and other predecessors of Elliott had explored, collected, and published. Elliott made careful use of the published works based on their efforts. Nearly 60 persons of his own generation contributed specimens, notes, paintings, and encouragement to the writing and publication of the *Sketch*. When Elliott first began assembling his herbarium in 1810, he was still an amateur collector. By 1824, when the second volume of the *Sketch* was completed and bound, he had become a taxonomic scientist. His most important influences were his early teacher, Henry Muhlenberg, and his erstwhile collaborator and critic, William Baldwin. Nevertheless, the *Sketch* remained preeminently the work of one man, Stephen Elliott. He took the work of others, meshed them with his own col-

---

[46]Baldwin to Elliott, 12 March, 16 September 1817; 4 December 1818; 26 February 1819, NYBG.

lections and observations, and produced the first major synthesis of Georgia botany. It was Elliott who wrote 1,305 pages of text in parallel columns of Latin and English and prepared the glossary, index, and illustrations. It was he who saw the book through the tedious process of printing despite a very serious illness in 1819-1820. It was Elliott who paid for publication and took the risk of never recovering his investment (his costs probably contributed to a severe personal financial stringency in the mid-1820s). Without his synthesis, southeastern botany remained in separate pieces; with the *Sketch*, we have the culmination of a century of work and the foundation on which succeeding botanists might build.

Most of these "succeeding botanists" would have concurred most fervently with Stephen Elliott when he said, "The study of natural history has been, for many years, the occupation of my leisure moments; it is a merited tribute to say, that it has lightened for me many a heavy and smoothed many a rugged hour, that beguiled by its charms, I have found no road rough or difficult, no journey tedious, no country desolate or barren. In solitude never solitary, in a desert never without employment. I have found it a relief from the languor of idleness, the pressure of business, or from the unavoidable calamities of life."[47]

[47]Stephen Elliott, *An Address to the Literary and Philosophical Society of South Carolina* (Charleston: Printed by W. P. Young, 1814) 10.

THREE

The Reverend Charles C. Jones and Bishop Stephen Elliott: Southern Evangelicals and the Burden of Slavery*

SPIRITUAL REDEMPTION OF BLACKS was an earnest concern of the major Protestant denominations in the antebellum era. The Reverend Charles Colcock Jones and Bishop Stephen Elliott of Georgia, like other Southern clergymen, struggled with the paradox of Christianity and slavery. How could they be loyal to their faith and fail to evangelize the slaves? Conversely, how could they evangelize slaves effectively without endangering the central institution of Southern society? As liberal leaders of the Presbyterian and Protestant Episcopal Churches, both desired to reform their society from within by advocating the religious and moral instruction of slaves. They regarded slavery not as a positive good, but as a permissible institution sanctioned by the scriptures. God had ordained the apparent evil of slavery so that a "primitive" race might be Christianized and civilized. Impelled by missionary zeal and a sincere desire to meliorate the system and uplift the slaves, they were aware that white Southerners were suspicious of their intentions. Religious teachings and organizations might subvert slavery and encourage rebellion. Ironically, conversion and control thus became the major goal and constraint of their mission.[1]

---

*This paper was prepared for presentation at the Third Citadel Conference on the South, 23-25 April 1981, in Charleston, South Carolina.

[1]See Anne C. Loveland, *Southern Evangelicals and the Social Order, 1800-1860* (Baton Rouge: Louisiana State University Press, 1980); chapters seven and eight are devoted to slavery and religious instruction of the blacks. For study of Southern religious thought, see Donald G. Mathews, *Religion in the Old South* (Chicago: University of Chicago Press, 1977); H.

Although many slaveowners shared the motivations of the clergy, their concerns tended to be more pragmatic. They wanted to cultivate docility and efficiency in their slaves and to combat the attacks of abolitionists by demonstrating the stability of their conservative, yet humane, social order. If slaves could be taught to believe that obedience to their masters was a religious duty, then the authority of the planters would be established upon a solid foundation. Slaves, however, were not just passive recipients of the teachings of Christian missionaries. Even within the restraints of bondage, slaves clung tenaciously to their African heritage and found ways to protest within their seemingly helpless status. They dared to walk out on young C. C. Jones and refused to assemble for William C. Williams, Episcopal minister to the Ogeechee mission. While many slaves were genuinely interested in salvation, they were also mindful of the rewards and punishments inherent in the slave system. When given a choice, they preferred freer forms of worship conducted by black ministers in separate churches.[2]

Georgians apparently attempted no systematic efforts to Christianize slaves in the colonial period. Instructed by individual planters, slaves were received into white churches where they worshiped with white members, were extended the privileges of the sabbath, and were occasionally taught to read. After the Revolution, Baptists led all other denominations in missionary work among the slaves. The First African Baptist Church was established in Savannah by George Liele in 1792. The Second African Baptist and the Ogeechee Colored Baptist Churches were formed out of the First Church in 1802–1803. The anomalous Sunbury Association that embraced Baptist churches in the coastal area between the Savannah and St. Marys Rivers was founded in 1818 with two all-black congregations out of a total of 13. According to C. C. Jones, Baptists licensed more black preachers than all other denominations combined. The Methodist Church in 1796 reported only 148 black members in Georgia. Strongly influenced by the great Kentucky revival that began in 1799, however, they began to con-

---

Shelton Smith, *In His Image, But. . . Racism in Southern Religion, 1780-1910* (Durham: Duke University Press, 1972); Russell B. Nye, *The Cultural Life of the New Nation, 1776-1830* (New York: Harper & Row, 1960) 216-34; William W. Sweet, *Religion in the Development of American Culture, 1765-1840* (New York: Charles Scribner's Sons, 1952).

[2]For studies of slave religion, see Eugene D. Genovese, *Roll, Jordan, Roll* (New York: Pantheon Books, 1974); Albert J. Raboteau, *Slave Religion: The "Invisible Institution" in the Antebellum South* (New York: Oxford University Press, 1978); Lawrence Levine, *Black Culture and Black Consciousness* (New York: Oxford University Press, 1977) 136-89.

duct camp meetings that gave a new impetus to their ministry. Across the South local preachers, circuit riders, missionaries, and black ministers had won more than 170,000 black church members to the fold by 1861.[3]

The Midway Church, only nominally Congregationalist, was the center of Presbyterian evangelism among slaves in coastal Georgia. As early as 1770 the Midway Society ordered the erection of a shelter for blacks at the meeting house. After the Revolution, individual planters like John Lambert and Robert Quarterman laid the foundation for the later ministry of C. C. Jones. Unlike the other Protestant denominations, the Episcopal mission to the slaves was conditioned by its conservative social character. Its highly elaborate doctrines and litany undoubtedly proved an obstacle in winning converts from the slave population. Prior to 1841, the wives and daughters of wealthy planters, such as Misses Anne Clay and Esther Elliott, the bishop's older sister, attempted to impart Christian knowledge to their slaves. When Bishop Elliott assumed office in 1841, his records showed regular churches in Savannah, Augusta, Macon, and St. Simons with a total of 323 white communicants; there was no mention of black members.[4]

In the 1830s as Jones and Bishop Elliott were beginning their missions to the slaves, the South was moving toward an evangelical, neo-Calvinist orthodoxy. Liberal theology, exemplified in unitarian-transcendental Christianity, posed embarrassing questions about the peculiar institution. A renewed Calvinism, supported by the evangelical impulse of the "second awakening," furnished Southerners their best justification for slavery. The quickening interest in the evangelization of the slaves was a peculiarly Southern manifestation of the nationwide humanitarian movement asso-

---

[3]For convincing arguments that Southern churches were not so clearly aligned with the racial mores of their region, see Kenneth K. Bailey, "Protestantism and Afro-Americans in the Old South: Another Look," *The Journal of Southern History* 41 (November 1975): 451-72. Charles C. Jones, *The Religious Instruction of the Negroes in the United States* (Savannah: Thomas Purse, 1842) 92-97; *Proceedings of the Meeting in Charleston, S.C., May 13-15, 1845, on the Religious Instruction of the Negroes, Together with the Report of the Committee and the Address to the Public* (Charleston: B. Jenkins, 1845) 68-70. Jones and Elliott attended this meeting; Jones wrote the *Report*.

[4]Jones, *Religious Instruction of the Negroes*, 92-93, 95-96; Erskine Clarke, *Wrestlin' Jacob* (Atlanta: John Knox Press, 1979) 32-34; Bailey, "Protestantism and Afro-Americans," 458; Stiles B. Lines, "Slaves and Churchmen: The Work of the Episcopal Church Among Southern Negroes, 1830-1860" (Ph.D. dissertation, Columbia University, 1960) 268.

ciated with Jacksonian democracy, the South's conscientious alternative to the antislavery crusade.[5]

Charles Colcock Jones was the chief advocate of the movement to develop an adequate system of religious instruction for slaves. His book, *Religious Instruction of the Negroes in the United States*, was the movement's standard history; his reports and catechisms, its theory and guidebook; his native Liberty County, its laboratory. Yet, his life is a study of the incongruent themes that disturbed the consciences of Southern clergymen who believed they could be paternalistic and humane without destroying slavery.[6]

Jones was born near Sunbury in 1804 into a prosperous planter-slaveholding family. Orphaned at age six, he was reared by relatives who were staunch members of the old Midway Congregational Church and religious society. His forebears had migrated from Charleston to settle among the descendants of the Puritans in the Midway district. Young Jones attended the Reverend William McWhir's academy at Sunbury, and at age fourteen he was apprenticed to a merchant in Savannah. A close encounter with death in 1822 led to his religious conversion and soon thereafter he joined the Midway Church. While in Savannah he began to teach Sunday school, joined the Brotherly Society, and attempted serious study of the theology of Jonathan Edwards and Timothy Dwight. During this period he decided to enter the ministry, and in 1825 he went north to Phillips Andover Academy, and after two years, he enrolled in Andover Theological Seminary, a stronghold of Congregational orthodoxy.

---

[5]For a good summary of the South's response to growth of heterodoxy and liberalism in Northern religion, see Robert F. Durden, "The Establishment of Calvary Protestant Episcopal Church for Negroes in Charleston," *The South Carolina Historical Magazine* 45 (April 1964): 63-64.

[6]While there is no biography of C. C. Jones, his papers are voluminous and are located at Tulane University, the University of Georgia, and Duke University. See Robert M. Myers, *Children of Pride* (New Haven: Yale University Press, 1972); James Stacy, *History of the Midway Congregational Church* (Newnan GA: S. W. Murray, 1951); Clarke, *Wrestlin' Jacob*, 3-81; Edward N. Loring, "Charles C. Jones: Missionary to Plantation Slaves" (Ph.D. dissertation, Vanderbilt University, 1976); Donald G. Mathews, "Charles Colcock Jones and the Southern Evangelical Crusade to Form a Biracial Community," *The Journal of Southern History* 41 (August 1975): 299-320; and Wayne C. Tyner, "Charles Colcock Jones: Mission to Slaves," *Journal of Presbyterian History* 55 (Winter 1977): 363-80; T. Erskine Clarke, "An Experiment in Paternalism: Presbyterians and Slaves in Charleston, South Carolina," *Journal of Presbyterian History* 53 (Fall 1975): 223-38.

Jones was introduced to reform thought and the American Colonization Society while at Andover, which apparently had a disturbing effect on his attitudes toward slavery. After visiting home, he seriously reflected whether he was becoming a Southern-Northerner or a Northern-Southerner. By the end of 1828 he was advocating the American Colonization Society to his friends and relatives in Liberty County. For a time he believed and promoted the society's watchword that it would be benefical to free slaves and return them to Africa. In a letter to Mary Jones, his first cousin and future bride, Jones confided that he had always held views hostile to slavery.[7] Although he was probably homesick, he was disturbed by the contrast between Southern and Northern society. "There is a calmness, an order, a morality, a general sentiment of right and wrong, a justice, an equality, in this society which is not looked for in ours." In New England, but not in the South, he observed that man could freely discuss great social issues such as slavery. He conceded that his generation was not responsible for the evil that had been entailed upon them, but since he was obligated to slaves for his "conveniences of life" he felt a strong sense of personal guilt for the sinful institution.[8] For Jones, slavery had become "A violation of all the Laws of God and man at once. A complete annihilation of justice, an inhuman abuse of power, an assumption of the responsibility of fixing the life and destiny of immortal beings, fearful in the extreme." In his despondency, he told Mary that he wished to postpone their marriage until he could find a livelihood that was not dependent upon slavery. "What would I not freely give if our family were freed from this sort of property and removed beyond its influence?"[9] So earnestly did Jones fast, pray, and agonize over the perfection of his own life and the resolution of this moral dilemma, that his friends and relatives hoped for some relief, humor, or other sign of human frailty.

Jones, sensing that he was out of place in the North, left Andover in October 1829, and entered Princeton Seminary, a citadel of "Old School" Presbyterian orthodoxy. Within a few months he organized the "Society of Enquiry Concerning Africans" to collect information concerning the ac-

---

[7]Charles C. Jones to Mary Jones, 8 September 1829, C. C. Jones Papers, Tulane University.

[8]Ibid.; Charles C. Jones to Mary Jones, 15 October 1829, Jones Papers.

[9]Charles C. Jones to Mary Jones, 8 September 1829, Jones Papers.

tivities of benevolent societies among slave and free Africans at home and abroad. In the fall of 1830, he traveled to New York, Philadelphia, and Washington to discover his "path of duty." He considered the foreign mission field, work among the Indians, and service with the American Colonization Society.[10] Finally settling upon a plan for missions among the slaves, he still pondered whether he should emancipate his own servants. "As to the principle of slavery it is wrong," he wrote. "It is unjust, contrary to nature and religion to hold men enslaved."[11] But could he do more for his slaves by holding or freeing them? In September 1830, he divulged his "General Plan" to Mary. He was going to return to Liberty County to introduce a system of religious instruction by word-of-mouth for the slaves. If the plan succeeded, he would devote his life to the mission.[12] After completing his studies at Princeton, he returned to Liberty County in November 1830.

During the winter of 1831-1832, Jones began discussions with planters and church members that led to the organization of "The Liberty County Association for Religious Instruction of the Negroes." Twenty-nine planters who represented the wealth and leadership of the community, including James S. Bulloch, Odingsell Hart, John Dunwoody, Barrington King, and William Maxwell, assembled at the little courthouse in Riceboro on 10 March 1831. The meeting was sponsored by the Midway Congregational Church and the Sunbury Baptist Church under their respective pastors Robert Quarterman and Samuel Spry Law.[13] In his sermon before the gathering, Jones emphasized that the primary duty of religious life was evangelism. "We are bound to give the Negroes the Gospel," he exhorted. "Should we continue to neglect them, our neglect might not only shut their souls out of heaven, but our own." Believing slaves to be an ignorant, degraded,

---

[10]Charles C. Jones to Mary Jones, 3 February, 8 May, 5 June, 24 June, 25 August 1830, Jones Papers.

[11]Charles C. Jones to Mary Jones, 18 May 1830, Jones Papers.

[12]Charles C. Jones to Mary Jones, 18 September 1830, Jones Papers.

[13]Jones published 13 reports of the association; the *Eighth Annual Report of the Association for Religious Instruction of the Negroes in Liberty County, Georgia* (Savannah: Thomas Purse, 1843) gives a history of the association; the *Thirteenth Annual Report of the Association for the Religious Instruction of the Negroes in Liberty County Georgia* (Savannah: Edward J. Purse, 1848) reviews Jones's mission to the slaves; also, Erskine, *Wrestlin' Jacob*, 21.

destitute, neglected, and perishing people, he believed that religious instruction was the duty of masters, ministers, and churches.[14]

Without attacking the institution of slavery, Jones condemned planters
for the low moral condition of slaves. He advocated that the planters should
form a voluntary association and personally assume responsibility for religious instruction. The executive committee of the association should ap-
point teachers and establish stations for instruction during the week and on
the sabbath. Oral instruction should embrace the principles of the Christian religion, yet carefully avoid points of doctrine that separated denominations. Teachers would not be allowed to visit any plantation without the
consent of its owner and would confine their duties exclusively to religious
instruction. Jones recommended that a missionary should be appointed to
supervise the sabbath stations, preach during the week on plantations, and
assist in developing courses of instruction.[15] Anticipating criticisms, Jones
explained that the mutual relationships between master and servant would
be better understood through religious instruction.[16] He assured the planters that "Our plan carries our security in it."[17] The gospel would enlighten
the slaves, restrain their passions, reform their habits and manners, correct
their superstitions, promote self-respect, cleanliness, honesty, industry,
family affection, chastity, and obedience to superiors. Jones reminded the
planters that faithful servants gave more and better work and, thus, were
more profitable than unfaithful ones.[18] Lest his mission be misunderstood,
Jones reaffirmed that "The great object for which we would communicate
religious instruction to them [slaves] is that their souls may be saved. To this
all other objects should be subordinate."[19]

The 29 planters who came to Riceboro that March signed the constitution of the new association and paid their dues.[20] Jones accepted the call

[14]Charles C. Jones, *The Religious Instruction of the Negroes. A Sermon Delivered before As-
sociations of Planters in Liberty and McIntosh Counties, Georgia* (Princeton: O'Hart & Con-
nolly, 1832) 6-17. Jones, *Thirteenth Annual Report*, 59.

[15]Jones, *Sermon*, 18-26.

[16]Ibid., 25-32.

[17]Ibid., 20.

[18]Jones, *Thirteenth Annual Report*, 59.

[19]Jones, *Sermon*, 30.

[20]For the constitution of the association, see Charles C. Jones, *Seventh Annual Report of
the Association for the Religious Instruction of the Negroes in Liberty County, Georgia* (Savan-

from the Midway Church Missionary Society to become the associational missionary which entailed preaching two Sundays each month to the whites in the destitute parts of the county, two Sundays to the blacks, and to the slaves during the week.[21] The Reverend Samuel S. Law became vice-president of the association. Hardly had Jones begun his mission, however, when he realized that he was unprepared for the work. Disappointed when both planters and slaves questioned his plan, he decided to accept the pulpit of the First Presbyterian Church in Savannah. He remained committed to his mission while in Savannah, however, and succeeded in bringing the issue of religious instruction of slaves before the Synod of South Carolina and Georgia.[22]

After 18 months in Savannah, Jones returned to Liberty County to renew his missionary work among the slaves.[23] Except for the years he served as professor of history and church polity at Columbia Theological Seminary, 1837-1838, and again in 1848-1850, and for the three years he was corresponding secretary of the Board of Domestic Missions of the Presbyterian Church in Philadelphia, Jones resided in Liberty County. He supervised his three plantations—Arcadia, Montevideo, and Maybank, which consisted of 3,748 acres on which 107 slaves labored—and continued his evangelization of the blacks.[24]

In an attempt to reach the 4,577 slaves of the 15th Georgia Militia District, an area approximately 25 miles long and 15 miles wide that included 100 to 125 plantations, Jones established six stations—Sunbury, Pleasant Grove, Newport, Midway, Fraser's Plantation, and Sand Hills.[25] His sabbaths were spent laboring among his flock from sunrise to sunset. The day began with an early prayer meeting, followed by the morning worship serv-

---

nah: Thomas Purse, 1842) 22. Jones, *Tenth Annual Report* (Savannah: Office of P. G. Thomas, 1845) 14-15, 18.

[21]Jones, *Tenth Annual Report*, 15-16.

[22]Charles C. Jones to Mary Jones, 3 December, 6 December 1831, Jones Papers.

[23]Jones, *Tenth Annual Report*, 16.

[24]Myers, *Children of Pride*, 1567; U. S. Census return 1850, C. C. Jones, Liberty County, Georgia, 1 June 1850, Jones Papers; Erskine, *Wrestlin' Jacob*, 10.

[25]For discussion of "stations," see Loring, *Charles C. Jones*, 158-74.

ice and sabbath school.[26] Initially, Jones preached sermons that emphasized duties and fidelity, about biblical slaves like Eliezer, Gehazi, and Onesimus.[27] When half of his congregation left a meeting and those who remained challenged his interpretation of the scriptures, Jones tempered his emphasis on duties and obedience and thereafter preached on Christian ethics as generally applied.[28] In the afternoon, he presided over the inquiry meeting and occasionally met with the black watchmen who were charged with watchcare over the morals and conduct of slaves who were church members. Watchmen meetings tried those cases of immorality that were not serious enough to warrant excommunication. They also collected and prepared evidence for cases to be brought before the congregations.[29] By 1845, Jones estimated that 800 to 900 slaves, one-sixth of the slave population in the district, attended worship services regularly.[30] According to his account, more than 1,000 slaves were brought into church membership between 1833 and 1847.[31]

From the beginning, Jones recognized that moral reformation of young slaves was the main hope for the success of his missions. Between 1834 and 1835, he organized seven sabbath schools in the district.[32] "Confinement to oral instruction," Jones lamented, "was among the peculiar and great difficulties to be overcome."[33] Even though Georgia law prescribed that slaves should be kept illiterate, Jones declared that those "who would keep the Bi-

[26]"Activities of the Sabbath Day," ibid., 175-81.

[27]Erskine, *Wrestlin' Jacob*, 40.

[28]Jones, *Tenth Annual Report*, 24; *Third Annual Report*, 14; Erskine, *Wrestlin' Jacob*, 40-41.

[29]Jones, *Tenth Annual Report*, 9-10, 27-28; Charles C. Jones, *Minutes of Watchmen's Meeting for Midway Church, Instituted March 8, 1840, By the Consent and Order of the Church*, Jones Papers; Erskine, *Wrestlin' Jacob*, 52-55.

[30]Charles C. Jones, *Eleventh Annual Report of the Association for the Religious Instruction of the Negroes in Liberty County, Georgia* (Savannah: Office of P. G. Thomas, 1846) 15-16.

[31]Charles C. Jones, *Twelfth Annual Report of the Association for the Religious Instruction of the Negroes in Liberty County, Georgia* (Savannah: Edward C. Councell, 1847) 13.

[32]Information on the separate sabbath schools scattered through various *Reports*. See Jones, *Tenth Annual Report*, 25; *Fifth Annual Report* (Charleston: Observer Press, 1840) 9; *Twelfth Annual Report*, 4; *Eleventh Annual Report*, 9, and others.

[33]Jones, *Religious Instruction of the Negroes*, 183.

ble from their fellow creatures are the enemies of God and man. The Bible belongs of right to every man. It is the property of the world."[34] After deciding that none of the existing catechisms met his needs, Jones wrote and published the most widely used catechism ever written for slaves.[35] In 1833 his 108-page *Catechism for Colored Persons* was issued; it was revised in 1837 and 1845, and reprinted again in 1852.[36]

Read by the free and memorized by the bound, Jones's catechism became the Bible in his sabbath schools. An excellent Bible student, Jones selected passages from the Old and New Testaments that emphasized obedience to God and master. His obvious intent was to produce good masters, Christian though submissive slaves, and peaceful plantations. The catechism taught the omnipotence and omniscience of God, the certainty of punishment for sin and the promise of a heavenly paradise for the godly, keeping of the sabbath, and the principles of morality. Since God had arranged a static hierarchy in human society, slaves were morally bound to be humble, diligent workers. Even when abused, they should return good for evil, for God in his sublime righteousness would judge ungodly masters. The catechism denounced lying, stealing, infidelity, running away, and defined the Christian obligations of husbands, wives, parents, and children.[37]

Jones not only was a missionary to the slaves, he was their chief advocate to the white masters. At first, some planters opposed slave evangelism because they feared large assemblages of slaves, night meetings, and the special attention given to their servants. Gradually Jones convinced them of the practicality of his prudential plan. "We believe," Jones explained, "that the authority of masters can be strengthened and supported in this way only; for the duty of obedience will never be felt or performed to the extent that we desire it, unless we can bottom it on religious principle."[38] Unfortunately, Jones's critics would misconstrue these pronouncements to dis-

---

[34]Jones, *Tenth Annual Report*, 42.

[35]Smith, *In His Image*, 153-54; Jones, *Tenth Annual Report*, 21-22; Charles C. Jones, *A Catechism for Colored Persons* (Charleston: *Charleston Observer* Office Press, 1834) iii.

[36]Charles C. Jones, *A Catechism of Scripture, Doctrine and Practice: For Families and Sabbath Schools. Designed also, for the Oral Instruction of Colored Persons* (Savannah: T. Purse and Co., 1837).

[37]Ibid, passim.

[38]Jones, *Sermon*, 26.

credit his mission as another ploy to increase the control and profits of the planter class.[39]

After winning their confidence, Jones admonished masters to assume pastoral care over their slaves, to allow them to observe the sabbath, to recognize the sanctity of slave marriages, to preserve the slave family, and to provide just and equal treatment. He taught that they should improve the standard of living of their servants by providing adequate food, clothing, shelter, and medical care for them.[40] In return, masters would reap profits, obedience, tranquility, and be relieved of their "great responsibility."[41]

Jones, "Apostle to the Negro Slaves," was an exemplar to his people—a kind master and a dedicated Christian who ministered to the slaves and planters of Liberty County. He actually served without pay for the first seven years of his ministry. In spite of frail health, he traveled to plantations and preaching stations from 1833 to 1847. When Frederick Law Olmstead visited coastal Georgia, he acknowledged that "in no other district has there been displayed a general and long continued interest in the spiritual well-being of the Negroes."[42] Jones lived long enough to witness the collapse of the stable biracial community he had labored to build in Liberty County.

A contemporary of Jones, Stephen Elliott, Jr., was a Southern aristocrat in the truest sense. He was born in 1806 in Beaufort, South Carolina, the son of botanist Stephen Elliott, and his wife, Esther Habersham Elliott. He attended Harvard College, but received his degree from South Carolina College in 1825. After reading law under James L. Petigru, he was admitted to the bar in 1827. While practicing law in Charleston, Elliott assisted his father with *The Southern Review*, and in the 1830s returned to Beaufort as a law partner of C. C. Pinckney.[43] Here he had a vivid conversion experi-

---

[39]Erskine, *Wrestlin' Jacob*, 26-27.

[40]Jones, *Tenth Annual Report*, 16-18; Jones, *Fifth Annual Report*, 21-23; Jones, *Religious Instruction of the Negroes*, 115-17, 138-39, 207-209, 242; Jones, *Twelfth Annual Report*, 21; Jones, *Thirteenth Annual Report*, 16.

[41]Jones, *Sermon*, 31-32.

[42]Frederick Law Olmstead, *The Cotton Kingdom* (New York: Mason Bros., 1862) 2:215.

[43]Likewise there is no major published biography of Bishop Stephen Elliott. Papers and other records are located at the University of the South, the University of North Carolina, the University of Georgia, and others. The published *Journals of the Protestant Episcopal Diocese of Georgia* are in the Georgia Historical Society, Savannah. See Stephen B. Barnwell, *The Story of an American Family* (Chicago: Marquette, 1969); Thomas M. Hanckel, *Sermons of the Right Reverend Stephen Elliott, D.D., Late Bishop of Georgia with a Memoir* (New York:

ence during a revival conducted by the Reverend Daniel Baker, a Presbyterian missionary from Liberty County. In addition to Elliott, five other
young men from the same law firm decided to enter the ministry. The Cal-
vinistic fervor of the Beaufort revival had a lasting influence upon young
Elliott.[44]

Soon after his ordination in 1835, he was elected chaplain and professor
at South Carolina College. During his summer vacations Elliott supervised
sabbath schools for slaves at Beaufort. He was elected first bishop of the new
Diocese of Georgia in May 1840. As bishop he was confronted with the
challenge of building and expanding the church over the vast area of a
largely frontier state, a task that entailed establishing outposts in strategic
places. His ministry became a striking example of the influence that could
be wielded by a dynamic bishop.[45]

Elliott's interest in the welfare of slaves had deep and pervasive roots.
His father was a church vestryman who was paternalistic toward his own
slaves. Elliott was familiar with the sabbath school for black children at his
family's church, St. Paul's Radcliffeborough, in Charleston. His religious
mentor in Beaufort, Dr. Joseph R. Walker, had urged that blacks should be
associated with whites in "pastoral and sacramental privileges." Elliott's sister, Esther, presided over her Georgia plantation on the Ogeechee River and
faithfully provided religious instruction to her slaves.[46]

Pott and Amery, 1867); Stiles B. Lines, "Slaves and Churchmen: The Work of the Episcopal
Church Among Southern Negroes, 1830-1860" (Ph.D. dissertation, Columbia University,
1960); Virgil S. Davis, "Stephen Elliott: A Southern Bishop in Peace and War" (Ph.D. dissertation, University of Georgia, 1964); Doris K. Collins, "The Episcopal Church in Georgia From the Revolutionary War to 1860" (M.A. thesis, Emory University, 1957); Edgar L.
Pennington, "Stephen Elliott, First Bishop of Georgia," Historical Magazine of the Protestant
Episcopal Church 7 (September 1938): 203-63.

[44]William M. Baker, The Life and Labours of the Rev. Daniel Baker, D.D., Pastor and Evangelist (Philadelphia: Presbyterian Board of Publications, 1859) 146-48; Lines, "Slaves and
Churchmen," 256-57.

[45]Henry T. Malone, The Episcopal Church in Georgia 1733-1957 (Atlanta: The Protestant
Episcopal Church in the Diocese of Atlanta, 1960) 68-107; Daniel Walker Hollis, University
of South Carolina: South Carolina College (Columbia: University of South Carolina Press,
1951) 1:125-26, 128; Maximilian Laborde, History of Carolina College (Charleston: Walker,
Evans and Cogswell, Printers, 1874) 35-40; Bishop Elliott's activities on behalf of the church
can be traced in the Journals of the annual conventions.

[46]Stephen B. Barnwell, "The Confederate Episcopacy, Slavery and Stephen Elliott," The
Michigan Academician 1 (Spring 1969): 58-59. Jones and Elliott were obviously acquainted;
see Charles C. Jones to Mary Jones, 5 November 1835, Jones Papers. Jones and Elliott met

In his first address to the convention of the diocese, Elliott urged each clergyman to establish a sabbath school for slaves since they direly needed "sound religious instruction." He deplored their access only to "a religion of excitement, occupied entirely with feeling." The Episcopal arrangement of worship, he was certain, best met the needs of the blacks.[47] So convinced was he that he attempted to demonstrate that the Episcopal Church could satisfy even the preference of blacks for baptism by immersion. In January 1843 at St. Simons, he led a group of 21 candidates to the river bank, read aloud the canon that permitted immersion, waded into the wintry waters, and proceeded to baptize five of them in the river. The remaining candidates promptly announced they would prefer to be sprinkled indoors from the baptismal font.[48]

Bishop Elliott decried the failure of his church to serve the needs of blacks and worked to awaken its ministers and communicants to their Christian responsibility. Admonishing his subordinates in 1843, he reminded them that at least one-half of the large slaveholders on the Savannah, Ogeechee, Altamaha, and Satilla Rivers, as well as those on the coastal islands, were Episcopalians. "But it is useless to arouse the Planters to their duty," he proclaimed, "so long as the ministers of the Church and her candidates for Orders shut their eyes to the vast work which is here spread out before them. From this city [Savannah]," he continued, "we can look out upon at least ten thousand slaves whose masters are willing that they should be religiously instructed—willing to pay and yet among all that vast multitude there is not heard the voice of a single Episcopal Pastor." Only St. David's Church, Glynn County, existed to spread the gospel. Why were there no pastors from their master's church? He encouraged young men who were willing to dedicate themselves to this work to enter the field.[49]

---

at the plantation home of Miss Anne Clay, Bryan County, March 1842, to discuss religious instruction of slaves. Barnwell, *An American Family,* 157; C. C. Jones, *Sketch of the Life and Character of Miss Anne Clay* (Boston: Crocker and Brewster, 1844) 18. A copy is preserved in Jones Papers.

[47]*Journal,* Diocese of Georgia (1841) 7.

[48]Charles L. Hoskins, *Black Episcopalians in Georgia: Strife, Struggle and Salvation* (Savannah: Hoskins, 1980) 32; *Journal,* Diocese of Georgia (1843) 11-12.

[49]Ibid., 11; Pennington, "Stephen Elliott, First Bishop of Georgia," 213-14.

Elliott realized that sabbath schools and church services as extensions of existing white congregations were not reaching the slaves. Aware of Jones's personal ministry, he decided that the most effective approach required a resident white missionary to labor among the slaves of several contiguous plantations. This concept was tested when mistresses of two Ogeechee plantations requested that an Episcopal missionary be appointed to serve their slaves. Elliott also owned a plantation on the neck between the Great Ogeechee and the Little Ogeechee Rivers, an area approximately six miles long and three miles wide. Here local planters employed more than 1,500 slaves in profitable and intensive rice culture. Bishop Elliott chose the Reverend William C. Williams for the assignment. Williams, the son of a prominent Virginia lawyer and graduate of the College of William and Mary, had come to Georgia to regain his health. While recovering he had studied theology under the direction of Bishop Elliott. As a member of the Bishop's household, he became interested in the need for converting slaves. Although many of the neighboring planters were communicants of the Episcopal Church, no systematic effort had been made to introduce the Episcopal form of worship. Methodist and Baptist missionaries had long visited the neck and were already entrenched.[50] Bishop Elliott conceived both the grand design and the strategy of the mission, but the Reverend Williams deserves full credit for its success. After his ordination in November 1845, Williams began a 19-year ministry that would surely have been abandoned by one of weaker convictions.

Several years of rejection and discouragement elapsed before Williams was able to prove to the slaves that he was not an agent of the planters.[51] Since there was no chapel, Williams conducted services initially in barns, slave cabins, or outdoors under trees. By the end of the first year, he had organized schools for catechizing the children on four plantations and built a new chapel, but only six adults had been baptized and eight confirmed.[52] Four years later, the mission had only 14 communicants. The cholera epidemic of 1852 and the devasting flood of 1854 that destroyed the chapel en-

[50]Hoskins, Black Episcopalians, 35-40; "A Sketch of the Ogeechee Mission," Southern Episcopalian 1 (February 1855): 494-97. For best treatment of Ogeechee Mission see Lines, "Slaves and Churchmen," 201-14.

[51]For resistance by slaves to Williams, see Lines, "Slaves and Churchmen," 204-205.

[52]Ibid., 206.

abled Williams to strengthen his pastoral ties. By the mid-1850s, over a hundred communicants worshiped regularly at the mission and in a single service in 1855, the Bishop confirmed 148 candidates.[53] In the succeeding years until 1863, the mission experienced steady growth; annually between 32 and 77 slaves were baptized and 30 to 62 confirmed.[54] During his ministry on the Ogeechee, Williams baptized 431 infants and 403 adults, married 227 couples, and buried 400.[55] At the height of his work, war disrupted the mission, and its 423 communicants were widely dispersed. After the war, the former slaves gradually returned to the coastal plantations and services were resumed at the Ogeechee Mission in 1870. According to the Reverend H. Dunlop who revitalized the mission, the old members had been more strongly devoted to Williams than to the church—an observation that can be interpreted as praise of the latter's dedication and perseverance.[56] The Ogeechee Mission survives to the present as St. Bartholomew's at Burroughs, Georgia.[57]

Other Episcopal missions likewise illustrated the soundness of Elliott's strategy. In 1843, the Reverend Jonathan B. T. Smith volunteered to serve a group of plantations in Baker County near Albany in southwest Georgia. After several years of faithful instruction and preaching, he was able to present 42 slaves for confirmation.[58] In the same year, a mission was established for slaves at Hopeton Plantation in Glynn County on the Altamaha where it served about 250 slaves as an isolated extension of St. David's Church.[59] Inspired by the success of the Reverend Williams's Ogeechee Mission, the Reverend Sherod W. Kennerly established a successful mission among the slaves of seven Savannah River plantations in 1851. This was a unique experiment because these plantations lay within the dioceses of Georgia and South Carolina. In the first years, Kennerly baptized 125, prepared 69 for

---

[53]Ibid., 207-11.

[54]Ibid., 211.

[55]Hoskins, *Black Episcopalians*, 40.

[56]*The Spirit of Missions* (March 1881) 131.

[57]St. Bartholomew's was consecrated 26 April 1896. Hoskins, *Black Episcopalians*, 78.

[58]*Journal*, Diocese of Georgia (1844) 11; ibid. (1851) 15; also Lines, "Slaves and Churchmen," 271-72.

[59]*Journal*, Diocese of Georgia (1850) 32.

confirmation, and reported 200 children in sabbath school. Kennerly assumed the ministry of St. Stephen's Chapel in Savannah in 1856, a mission devoted entirely to the blacks of that city. St. Stephen's showed promising growth from the start, and by 1861 it had 78 communicants.[60] The freedmen of this parish church, named in honor of the bishop rather than the Christian martyr, served as pallbearers at Elliott's funeral in December 1866.

Stephen Elliott's stature lies not in his outmoded racial doctrines nor in his championship of a dying social order, but rather in his dedication and submission to what he considered to be God's providence and judgment. An ardent defender of the South and a leader in the formation of the Episcopal Church in the Confederacy, he wrote in 1866 that "no people had ever labored more faithfully, more devotedly, with more self-denial, than have Southern Christians to do their best for the slaves committed to their trust."[61] In his last address to the convention, he announced that he held no regrets about the abolition of slavery. "For myself and my race," he remarked, "I rather rejoice in it, but for them . . . I sincerely believe it the greatest calamity which could have befallen them. . . ." He continued, "I have loved them and do love them, and have labored for them all my life."[62] Because he believed that the existing institutions of society reflected the divine order, Elliott defended slavery as long as it was a pillar of Southern society and, after defeat, acquiesced in its demise. He perceived the fall of the Confederacy, like the abolition of slavery, as a tribulation to test and chasten God's people.[63]

C. C. Jones and Stephen Elliott were among the foremost Southern evangelicals of the antebellum era. Jones agonized and labored for a lifetime to devise a model for the whole of Southern society; his was the most intensely personal encounter with plantation slavery during the age. Elliott, though less zealous, was nonetheless committed to promoting the evangelization of slaves by his church. Both came out of the coastal aristocracy, were well educated, and had experienced vivid conversion experiences. Jones was an Old Presbyterian whose Calvinism was tinged by Old Testa-

---

[60]Ibid. (1852) 49; Hoskins, *Black Episcopalians*, 38.

[61]*Journal*, Diocese of Georgia (1866) 25-29.

[62]Ibid.

[63]Hanckel, *Sermons*, 527, 552-53; Pennington, "Stephen Elliott," 251-56.

ment austerity and duty that he tried to urge upon both master and slave. Elliott did not conform to the traditional stereotype of an Episcopal bishop; rather he, too, was motivated by an evangelistic impulse. Both attacked the problem of slavery as liberal reformers within the framework of their respective denominations. As bishop of an Episcopal diocese, Elliott ordained and assigned ministers, created new missions, consecrated new churches, and exercised pastoral duties. His many responsibilities precluded long-term personal service with communicants, whether free or bond. Hence, he relied on others like the Reverend Williams to implement his strategy of Episcopal outreach. As bishop, he could criticize and chastise subordinates and church members without incurring hostility. By contrast, Jones did not hold sacramental authority and was thus forced to appeal to his flock by persuasion, example, and the commands of the Bible. Jones's mechanism was the voluntary association of laymen who supported his personal mission in the limited area of coastal Liberty County. To insure support from the planters, he felt compelled to appeal to their religious and economic interests. Jones and Elliott had to rely upon good will and enlightenment which were not sufficient to transform Southern society. They struggled to change people without changing institutions and laws.

Planters were surely affected by the strictures of the clergy, but if practice scarcely ever matched the ideal, it was no wonder. It has been estimated that only a fifth to a third of all antebellum Southern whites were churchgoers. But no one, faithful disciple or not, could escape the coercive power of legal and community sanctions that regulated the social order and condoned slavery.

Although neither Jones nor Elliott viewed slavery as a positive good, no doubt their efforts gave credence to the institution. They were Christians who loved their native South but were trapped in the defense of slavery. Blinded by racism and by their cultural and sectional loyalties, they either could not or would not address the fundamental injustice of humans treated as property and denied freedom and dignity. Their noble intentions thus seem futile and misdirected. But they did provide a modicum of religious care for their flocks and formulate a theory for Southern churchmen. Who would argue that their response was not more humane than to deny religion to the slaves or more courageous than to flee the South? They knew well the limits imposed upon them by their social order; their dilemma was fraught with irony.

FOUR

The Scourge
of Sherman's Men
In Liberty County, Georgia *

THE CIVIL WAR apparently has a unique and enduring appeal for the American imagination. If sheer volume of writings was the measure, one might readily conclude that this tragic and fratricidal conflict was the greatest single event in U.S. history. Professional historians and amateurs alike have probed every phase and event of the Civil War from seminal beginnings in the Constitutional Convention to Lee's surrender at Appomattox. It has enlisted not only the interests of successive generations, but also their passions and loyalties. Georgians have never been allowed to forget the depredations their ancestors suffered at the hands of Sherman's "marauding hellhounds." Indeed, every white family that encountered Yankee soldiers during Sherman's march has its own stock of sorrowful tales.

After more than a century of controversy in interpreting Civil War issues, however, partisan diehards who proclaimed the righteousness of section and cause have essentially been refuted. In recent years more dispassionate revisionists have focused on questions raised by the war that relate to contemporary life. Many of the problems of the modern South appear to have their origins in the traumatic defeat of 1865 and in the disruption of Reconstruction. To complete the mosaic of portraying our most private and destructive war, there remains a need for historians to direct their attentions to the local scene—away from battlefront and statehouse to

*Another version of this essay was published in *Georgia Historical Quarterly* 60 (Winter 1976): 356-69. Material from that article is reprinted here with permission.

the homefront—to depict the impact of war on the lives of the women, children, and other noncombatants who were left behind the lines.

Liberty County, though not directly in the path of Sherman's march, was subjected for some six weeks to the presence of Union troops. This area whose early Puritan settlers were in the vanguard of the Revolutionary movement in Georgia had contributed numerous leaders in religion, government, education, and science. Owners of large rice and cotton plantations worked by slave labor enjoyed a life-style that cultivated religious devotion, civic responsibility, education, military honor, productive farming, and paternalism toward slaves and poor whites.[1] Among the foremost examples of this class were the Joneses, LeContes, Varnadoes, Bacons, Ways, Kings, Quartermans, and others.[2] It is reported that they feared only malaria and a decline in the price of rice and sea-island cotton.

The ordeal of Liberty Countians under Union occupation in December 1864 and January 1865 can be understood only as it relates to Sherman's objectives of his march to the sea. His strategy depended not only on defeating Confederate troops but on breaking the morale of the civilian population as well. "We are not only fighting hostile armies," he contended, "but a hostile people, and we must make old and young, rich and poor, feel the hard hand of war as well as their organizied armies."[3] In more picturesque language, he wanted "to make Georgia howl."

Sherman's concept of "total war" challenged the chivalric notion of a romantic age and ushered in warfare as twentieth-century humanity has come to know it. How hollow the bellicose speeches of Confederate sena-

---

[1]For accounts of early history of Midway community, see James Stacy, *History of the Midway Congregational Church* (Newnan GA: S. W. Murray, 1951); J. Edward Kirbye, *Puritanism in the South* (Boston: The Pilgrim Press, 1908); C. C. Jones, Jr., *The History of Georgia* (Boston: Houghton, Mifflin and Company, 1883) 1: ch. 30; Josephine Martin, *Midway, Georgia in History and Legend* (Savannah: Southern Publishers, 1936); Paul McIlvaine, *The Dead Towns of Sunbury, Ga. and Dorchester, S.C.* (Asheville: Groves Printing Co., 1975); Orville A. Park, *The Puritan in Georgia* (Savannah: Georgia Historical Society, 1929); Allen P. Tankersley, "Midway District: A Study of Puritanism in Colonial Georgia," *Georgia Historical Quarterly* 32 (September 1948): 149-57.

[2]Dr. W. P. McConnell, a Liberty County wit, coined the following couplet of names during a depression period in 1843: "We have Hams and Dun-hams, Bacons and Greens, Manns and Quartermans, plenty of Ways, but no Means." Stacy, *History*, 356-57.

[3]William T. Sherman, *Memoirs of General W. T. Sherman* (New York: Charles L. Webster and Co., 1891) 2:227.

tors in Montgomery must have sounded as they urged: "Georgians, be firm! Never have you had so good a chance to destroy the enemy; remove all food from the invader's path; destroy the roads, rise in arms. Death is preferable to the loss of liberty."[4] Departing Atlanta with a troop strength of 60,000, Sherman issued a special order commanding that "The army will forage liberally on the country during the march." However, soldiers were forbidden to enter the dwellings of inhabitants; they were to refrain from abusive or threatening language; and were instructed to leave each family enough food for its subsistence.[5] In spite of strict regulations, it soon became evident that the victorious invaders had made their own rules of conduct.

Sherman planned to march for a base on the coast at Savannah, Port Royal, or if necessary, Pensacola. To confuse his opponents, he feinted toward Macon and Augusta and it was not clear until his columns pivoted at Millen that Savannah was his objective. Encountering only feeble harassment by General Joseph Wheeler's cavalry, the skirmishers swarmed across the heartland of Georgia like a horde of locusts. Wheeler, a daring commander who "warn't afraid of nothing and nobody," disclaimed that his men stole horses and destroyed private property in spite of the fact that General Howell Cobb forwarded evidence to General P. G. T. Beauregard of approximately 40 documented cases of depredations. Writing to Governor Joseph E. Brown, Burke County planter Alexander C. Walker called Wheeler's men a "plundering band of horse-stealing ruffians" who had destroyed plantations outside the path of the invaders. An investigation of Wheeler's conduct, however, essentially vindicated the general, but recommended he should be relieved from his command.[6]

After a few minor skirmishes along his route, Sherman advanced to Fort McAllister, which was located on Genesis Point on the right bank of the Great Ogeechee and blocked his access to the Union fleet and fresh supplies. The fort, the "back door" to Savannah, was captured after a ten-min-

---

[4]Fletcher Pratt, *A Short History of the Civil War (Ordeal by Fire)* (New York: Pocket Books, Inc., 1962) 350-51.

[5]Sherman, *Memoirs*, 2:175.

[6]*War of the Rebellion: A Compilation of the Official Records of the Union and Confederate Armies*, 1st ser., 53 vols. (Washington, 1880-1898) 44:410, 899, 979 (hereafter referred to as *Official Records*); T. Conn Bryan, *Confederate Georgia* (Athens: University of Georgia Press, 1953) 170-71; for a biography of Wheeler see John P. Dyer, *"Fightin' Joe" Wheeler* (Baton Rouge: Louisiana State University Press, 1941).

ute bombardment by General W. B. Hazen's Fifteenth Corps on 13 December. Sherman shared the sentiments of a junior officer who wrote that evening: "Take a big drink, a long breath, and yell like the devil."[7] For the most part, the march to the sea was over. Savannah was occupied on 21 December 1864. Sherman's campaign through Georgia proved to be one of the most successful of the entire Civil War.[8]

This march brought the war to the edge of Liberty County. Actual fighting in the county was extremely limited and consisted mostly of mopping-up operations by General Judson Kilpatrick's cavalry. Kilpatrick, eager for recognition and promotion, was anxious to erase from his record the memory of his disastrous raid on Richmond with success in the Georgia campaign. His Third Cavalry Division was composed of seasoned midwesterners who had rendered invaluable service to Sherman's columns at Macon, Milledgeville, Waynesboro, and Buckhead Church.[9] Liberty County was poorly defended by the Twenty-ninth Battalion, Georgia Cavalry, under the command of Lieutenant Colonel Arthur Hood, and by members of a Remount Detachment of the Liberty Independent Troop. On 13 December, Colonel Olive L. Baldwin, commanding a brigade of the Fifth Kentucky Cavalry (USA), marched to Midway and Sunbury; a separate battalion was dispatched to Dorchester.

A short distance from Midway, the cavalry encountered approximately 40 defenders and the Federal troops charged them. It was reported that "The rebels broke in all directions, leaving their guns, hats, blankets, and in fact everything which could impede them in their progress, behind

---

[7]George Ward Nichols, The Story of the Great March (New York: Harper & Brothers, 1865) 89-92; Sherman, Memoirs, 2:196-201; Official Records, 1st ser., 44:27, 72, 698, 704, 708-709. For sketch of forts and troop movements, see ibid., 112.

[8]Lloyd Lewis, Sherman, Fighting Prophet (New York: Harcourt and Brace, 1932) is still the best biography of Sherman. Besides Sherman's Memoirs, a personal narrative of the general's march through Georgia is found in Mills Lane, ed., War Is Hell (Savannah: The Beehive Press, 1974). The march to the sea is also treated in E. Merton Coulter, "Sherman and the South," Georgia Historical Quarterly 15 (March 1931): 28-45; Tom S. Gray, Jr., "The March to the Sea," Georgia Historical Quarterly 12 (June 1930): 111-38; C. C. Jones, Jr., "Sherman's March from Atlanta to the Coast," Southern Historical Society Papers 12 (July-August-September 1884): 294-309; F. Y. Hedley, Marching Through Georgia (Chicago: Donohue, Henneberry and Co., 1890); Henry Hitchcock, Marching With Sherman (New Haven: Yale University Press, 1927).

[9]James Moore, Kilpatrick and Our Cavalry: Comprising a Sketch of the Life of General Kilpatrick (New York: Hurst & Co., 1866) 176-98.

them."[10] A small skirmish took place at Hinesville on 16 December in which one Confederate cavalryman was killed.[11] Most of the men in the Remount Detachment were later captured in or near the Cay and Quarterman homes where they had gone for food and rest. An official report states that Colonel Hood was "greatly discomfited by our presence" and that his men were "demoralized and fled, reckless of organization, to the Altamaha bridge, whenever attacked."[12] An unpublished account by Raymond Cay, a member of the Remount Detachment, reports "If Hood's Battalion ever fired a shot at a Yankee in Liberty County, I have never been able to find out where it was." According to Cay, they were outnumbered 50 to one. Hood's retreat left the area between the Ogeechee and Altamaha Rivers undefended, prey to the daily incursions of Kilpatrick's cavalry. The South had spent itself and was now sending old men and boys to fight its battles. Defeat was in the air; all hope was gone.[13] In the totality of the war, these actions and casualties counted for little, however painful they might have been to local troops and noncombatants.

Contrary to popular belief, not all residents south and west of the Ogeechee River supported the Confederate cause. Some time before 28 December 1864, Sherman received a set of resolutions from a group of Liberty and Tattnall Countians, who professed to be old men or deserters from the Confederate Army. They renounced loyalty to the Confederacy and proclaimed their firm allegiance to the United States. Sherman replied on 28 December, assuring them of his support and protection and urging them to bring their produce to Savannah. One can only speculate that these men formulated their resolutions out of fear, war weariness, or maybe because of surviving Union sentiments.[14] Antisecession attitudes had been significant in Tattnall County during the debates over secession. In the election of delegates to the Milledgeville convention of 1861, only antisecession candi-

---

[10]*Official Records*, 1st ser., 44:385.

[11]Ibid., 147.

[12]Ibid., 372.

[13]Raymond Cay, "Capture Remount Detachment of the Liberty Troop" (unpublished). Episode is corroborated in Joseph LeConte, *'Ware Sherman* (Berkeley: University of California Press, 1937) 28.

[14]*Official Records*, 1st ser., 64:827-28.

dates were put forward in Tattnall County. The delegates from Liberty County, W. B. Fleming and S. M. Varnadoe, had favored secession.[15]

Liberty County was to experience military action in other ways: destruction of the railroad from Savannah to the Altamaha, systematic foraging to replenish the army's supplies, and pillaging forays by "bummers." General Sherman ordered the destruction of the Savannah, Albany, and Gulf Railroad on 16 December. The First, Second, and Third Brigades of the Fifteenth Army Corps were to destroy the road by segments. The First Brigade was assigned the track from the Ogeechee to the Medway River; the Second Brigade from Walthourville to a point two miles east of McIntosh; and the Third Brigade was to proceed from a point two miles east of McIntosh to the crossing of the railroad over the Medway River. A division of General J. A. Mower's Seventeenth Corps was commanded to complete the destruction to the Altamaha. Five days were allotted for the mission.[16]

By "liberal and judicious foraging," Sherman's army had arrived in Savannah in "splendid flesh and condition." Writing to General U. S. Grant on 16 December, he reported that he had abundant forage and provisions and needed only bread. He left Atlanta with 5,000 head of cattle; he arrived in Savannah with 10,000 beeves and plenty of horses.[17] Colonel James S. Martin, Second Brigade, Illinois Infantry, wrote that the march to Savannah was almost without hardships and could be termed a pleasure trip.[18] Sergeant Rufus Mead, Jr. of the Connecticut Volunteers described the march as a "glorious old tramp" through the heart of central Georgia. A rich and overflowing country was left a barren waste. He wrote more prophetically than he realized that "they will long remember the Yankees' raid."[19] The productive farms in the environs of Savannah offered an abundance of supplies. Continuing the practice of living off the land, each bri-

---

[15]I. W. Avery, *The History of the State of Georgia from 1850 to 1881* (New York: Brown and Derby Co., 1881) 149; *Journal of the Public and Secret Proceedings of the Convention of the People of Georgia, Held in Milledgeville and Savannah in 1861 Together with Ordinances Adopted* (Milledgeville, 1861) 15-39.

[16]*Official Records*, 1st ser., 64:27, 115, 146, 366, 372, 729-32, 845.

[17]Sherman, *Memoirs*, 2:107-10.

[18]*Official Records*, 1st ser., 64:114.

[19]James A. Padgett, ed., "With Sherman through Georgia and the Carolinas: Letters of a Federal Soldier," *Georgia Historical Quarterly* 33 (March 1949): 55-56.

gade was expected to send out foraging parties to gather food supplies and to procure horses and mules. Major Ruel M. Johnson, 100th Indiana Infantry, reported to his superiors on 24 December that he had escorted a forage train composed of 160 wagons with corn and sweet potatoes from the area across the Ogeechee toward the Altamaha without loss of men or wagons.[20] According to official reports, Sherman's army headed northward into South Carolina in mid-January 1865 with 35,000 animals, 2,690 wagons, and 503 ambulances, slowed only by a shortage of axle grease.[21] Sherman later defended his "bummers" by acknowledging that without doubt there had been acts of pillage, robbery, and violence. He commented, "I have since heard of jewelry taken from women and the plunder of articles that never reached the commissary; but these acts were exceptional and incidental. I never heard of any case of murder or rape; and no army could have carried along sufficient food and forage for a march of three hundred miles; so that foraging in some shape was necessary."[22]

The activities of Union soldiers in Liberty County brought the realities of "total war" to the home front. Extant accounts of personal encounters with Sherman's men depict them as undisciplined pillagers, quite a contrast to Sherman's "skillful foragers." According to these accounts, Yankee soldiers stripped the inhabitants of all subsistence and reduced them to poverty. John Stevens's personal narrative describes the indiscriminate pillaging of whites and blacks near Midway and Riceboro, in what the raiders described as "the richest county that they had struck on their march from the mountains." So successful were their raids that "there wasn't left a rooster to crow in ten miles square of Midway Church." Conducting themselves as "nothing more than a band of thieves," "the scruff of creation," Stevens recalled how they raided Captain Abiel Winn's plantation: "They took all of his provisions, . . . stole every horse and mule, and carried off carriages loaded down with articles. Cattle, hogs, and sheep that they could not drive they would kill, and probably leave the greater part for the buz-

---

[20]*Official Records*, 1st ser., 53:27-31; Theodore F. Upson, *With Sherman to the Sea* (Baton Rouge: Louisiana State University Press, 1943) 143-44, probably describes this same foraging expedition.

[21]*Official Records*, 1st ser., 53:44-46; 47:1, 17-18, 220-21, 857.

[22]Sherman, *Memoirs*, 2:182-83.

zards; the County was one continued stench for weeks after."[23] Not even churches were spared. The Baptist Church at Sunbury was burned to signal a Union gunboat in the nearby sound. The sanctuary and grounds of Midway Church were desecrated; horses and cattle were penned in the cemetery, the church was transformed into a slaughterhouse, the melodeon was used as a chopping block; and the building's cornerstone was plundered.[24]

Joseph LeConte, returning to Halifax Plantation to rescue relatives in the midst of Union occupation, was greeted with a recital of his family's sufferings and losses and the sight of "everything topsy-turvy just as the Yankees had left them." Raiders had entered the house every day for nearly two weeks.[25] Cornelia Jones Pond, daughter of William and Mary Jane Roberts Jones of Tokoah Plantation and Jonesville, recorded that the winter of 1864-1865 was a nightmare. For three weeks squads of soldiers came and took whatever they wanted—silver, firearms, jewelry, money, and food. Smokehouse, storeroom, dairy, hog pen, and chicken coop were robbed of their contents.[26] R. Q. Andrews tells of similar hardships, how the enemy had taken all food from whites and slaves except "rice in the rough." All livestock was either killed for food or shot and left. He considered it a "wonderful Providence" for the destitute families of the county that the blue-clay district escaped these ravages. This section harvested good crops and thus saved many from starvation.[27]

The journal kept by Mary Sharpe Jones, widow of Dr. C. C. Jones, and her pregnant daughter, Mary Jones Mallard, wife of the Reverend Robert Q. Mallard, also a Presbyterian minister, vividly recounted the trials they experienced on Montevideo Plantation. Unlike most inhabitants of the county who fled across the Altamaha, they remained at home to protect their property. With them were Mrs. Kate King and her two children who

---

[23]John Stevens, "Personal Narrative of Sherman's Raid in Liberty County, Georgia," (unpublished), Stevens Papers, Georgia Historical Society, Savannah; Haskell Monroe, "Men Without Law: Federal Raiding in Liberty County, Georgia," *Georgia Historical Quarterly* 44 (June 1960): 154-71.

[24]Stevens, "Personal Narrative." The fate of Midway Church is reported in Robert M. Myers, ed., *The Children of Pride* (New Haven: Yale Univesity Press, 1972) 1440-45.

[25]LeConte, *'Ware Sherman*, 30.

[26]Cornelia Jones Pond, *Life On a Liberty County Plantation*, ed. Josephine Martin (Darien: The Darien News, 1974) 111-14.

[27]R. Q. Andrews, "Recollections of War Times" (unpublished).

had sought refuge at Montevideo after their plantation houses were burned. According to Mrs. Jones, who had wanted to "illuminate the mansion" back in 1860 when she learned that South Carolina had seceded from the Union, they were visited daily by marauders in bands of two to forty who entered her home. In violation of Sherman's orders, they ransacked every room, trunk, chest, closet, and surrounding outbuilding. Valuables including furniture, household effects, clothing, silver, and jewelry were seized or destroyed. In spite of entreaties to the soldiers to spare enough food for her household and guests, little was left. Suffering insults like "You deserve to starve to death. . . . You have no right even to have water or wood. We will humble you in the dust," Mary Jones defied the raiders. The marauders threatened to burn Montevideo and to disinter the remains of her husband who was buried in Midway cemetery. Arcadia, her inland plantation, was burned, crops were destroyed, foodstuffs, carriages, wagons, carts, harnesses, even the well chain, were taken. Mrs. Jones lamented in the depths of her despair, "Do the annals of civilized, and I may add, savage warfare, afford any record of brutality equaled in extent and duration to that we have suffered? . . . For one month our homes and all we possess on earth have been given up to lawless pillage. Officers and men alike engaged in this work of degradation. I scarcely know how we have stood up under it."[28]

Several Liberty County families left their homes to the "mercy of Yankees, Negroes, and Crackers" and fled to southwest Georgia or elsewhere. Upon return, they found their homes either stripped of furnishings or in ashes. William Jones's summer house in Jonesville was burned without his ever knowing who fired the torch. Mrs. John Barnard returned to find her Walthourville residence in ashes. Mrs. Harriet Quarterman's home, located in the same village, was robbed of furnishings. Mrs. Leonora McConnell, more fortunate, recovered her furniture that had been carried off by a former overseer.[29]

<hr>

[28]Mary Sharpe Jones and Mary Jones Mallard, *Yankees A' Coming: One Month's Experience During the Invasion of Liberty County, Georgia, 1864-1865,* ed. Haskell Monroe (Tuscaloosa AL: Confederate Publishing Co., 1959) 33-84 passim; Myers, *Children of Pride,* 1220-48, 1284-86 passim.

[29]Pond, *Life On a Liberty County Plantation,* 129-30; Bird and Paul Yarbrough, *Taylor's Creek* (Pearson GA: Press of the *Atkinson County Citizen,* 1963) 39-40. Mrs. Terence Rustin Martin, youngest daughter of Thomas J. and Serena Way Sheppard, also wrote memoirs of this period.

Mary Jones's writings also reveal serious concern about the reaction of her slaves to Sherman's men. Some remained on the plantations while others left to straggle behind Union columns. "Many servants have proved faithful," Mrs. Jones wrote in January 1865, "others false and rebellious against all authority and restraint."[30] Mary Jones Pond was disappointed in the conduct of faithful slaves who led Union soldiers to her father's horses and mules that had been penned in the woods. One servant, Fortune, had stolen the family's valuables and papers that were buried for safekeeping. After the departure of Kilpatrick's men, Mrs. Pond, alarmed by armed blacks who roamed the road, commented, "Now for the first time we began to know fear of those who had formerly been our protectors."[31] Joseph LeConte recounted that his slaves remained "extremely kind and considerate, even affectionate." However, his overseer reported that the blacks refused to do any work at all.[32]

Before leaving Savannah, Sherman drafted a special order that set aside a zone for the newly freed blacks. It stretched from Charleston south to the St. John's River, including the coastal islands and the abandoned rice fields, for 30 miles deep. The order appointed General Rufus Saxton as Inspector of Settlements and Plantations and charged him with full responsibility to carry out the terms of the order and to provide the head of each black family in such settlements with a possessory title.[33]

In attempting to resolve the contradictions between Sherman's reports and the personal accounts by Liberty Countians who experienced "Yankee depredations," one faces a dilemma in trying to determine how extensive the losses were and to what degree they retarded economic recovery. Unfortunately, there is a paucity of plantation account books available to researchers. One writer explained this deficiency by surmising that planters were simply not very business-like in the operation of their plantations.[34] Likewise, it is difficult to get accurate census data for coastal Liberty County

[30]Myers, *Children of Pride*, 1241.

[31]Pond, *Life On a Liberty County Plantation*, 124-25, 134.

[32]LeConte, *'Ware Sherman*, 32.

[33]Sherman, *Memoirs*, 2:250-52.

[34]Ralph B. Flanders, "Planter Problems in Ante-Bellum Georgia," *Georgia Historical Quarterly* 14 (March 1930): 17.

because the county stretched so far into the sparsely populated and less productive piney woods that county averages are distorted.[35]

"We are a desolated and smitten people," Mary Jones wrote in her journal after the departure of the last enemy troops. Sustained only by her deep Christian faith, she despaired, "At present the foundations of society are broken up. What hereafter is to be our social and civil status, we cannot see."[36] Sherman's men had brought the war home to Liberty County and disrupted the lives of its people. Native sons who had rallied to defend the Confederacy in the early months of the war by enlisting in the Liberty Independent Troop, Liberty Mounted Rangers, Altamaha Scouts, and the Liberty Volunteers, were fighting on other fronts while their homes were left defenseless. Because Liberty County escaped the main thrust of Sherman's army and experienced only minor military skirmishes, there were few casualties. Residents did witness a sizable number of their compatriots captured as prisoners.

The mission of the Federal troops in Liberty County was essentially twofold: to destroy the Savannah, Albany, and Gulf Railroad to the Altamaha River, and to forage for supplies during occupation in preparation for the invasion of South Carolina. The railroad was thoroughly demolished, leaving behind a wreckage of "Sherman's Neckties," and depriving the area of its main artery of transportation. The emancipation of over 6,000 slaves wiped out lifetime investments and destroyed the reliable labor force that supported the plantation economy.[37] Some freedmen were undoubtedly torn between loyalties to former masters and the opportunities promised by their newly gained freedom. Foraging and pillaging raids by Union soldiers did strip local farms and plantations of much of their wealth. Granted that personal accounts of the depredations caused by Sherman's men might well have been exaggerated, agricultural census data reveal drastic reductions in the production of rice and wool for the decade 1860-1870, and significant depletions of cattle, mules, and sheep. However, by 1880, crop yields, with the exception of corn and cotton, had either returned to or surpassed 1860

[35]Roland M. Harper, "Development of Agriculture in Lower Georgia from 1850 to 1880," *Georgia Historical Quarterly* 6 (June 1922): 97-121.

[36]Myers, *Children of Pride*, 1244.

[37]Aggregate slave population in Liberty County numbered 6,083; *Population Of The United States In 1860; Compiled From The Original Returns Of The Eighth Census* (Washington: Government Printing Office, 1864) 66-67.

levels of productivity. Livestock was replenished within the same period, save for horses and mules.[38]

The deplorable and senseless burning and desecrating of churches deeply wounded the religious feelings of many Liberty Countians. The psychological injury caused by personal humiliation, the demoralization brought on by military defeat and occupation, and the affronts suffered to pride and tradition, though impossible to measure quantitatively, left deep and lasting scars. For those Liberty Countians who endured the hell of war during the six weeks from December 1864 into January 1865, sufficient bitterness and anguish were sown to inflame several generations. Perhaps the sentiments expressed by a Yankee corporal in a letter written from Savannah in 1864 revealed the remorse shared by many of his comrades. "The cruelties practiced on this campaign towards citizens have been enough to blast a more sacred cause than ours. We hardly deserve success."[39]

---

[38]*United States Census:* 1860, 1870, 1880, Agriculture.

[39]Cited in Robert Penn Warren, *The Legacy of the Civil War: Meditations on the Centennial* (New York: Random House, 1961) 89.

FIVE

Private Benjamin Wright Darsey's "War Story"

IF ONE CAN ACCEPT the accounts of scholars like Bruce Catton, the grievous inhumanities of Civil War prisons, both North and South, were never deliberately perpetrated. Rather they were the unintentional, albeit tragic, wrongs that resulted from the blinding passions born of a bewildering war. How futile and wasted then were the lives of 50,000 Northern and Southern inmates who, at best, were the victims of logistical failures, human blunders, and the tangles of administrative red tape. Andersonville, the most notorious of the lot, differed from Elmira and Camp Chase only by degrees of deprivation. Debate on the administration of Civil War prisons is not likely to end at this juncture since no refinement of statistics has been able to vindicate the record of either section.[1]

Any reassessment of the treatment of prisoners, however, must come to terms with the credibility of the voluminous literature written by both Northern and Southern veterans who published their memoirs in the postwar decades. Their accounts, often sensational, biased, and self-serving, inflamed and clouded the issues. Over the 60 years from 1862-1922, at least 240 books and articles were written that recounted the sufferings that

[1]Bruce Catton, "Prison Camps of the Civil War," *American Heritage* 10 (August 1959): 4-13, 96-97. William B. Hesseltine, "Civil War Prisons—Introduction," *Civil War History* 8 (June 1962) 117-20. Major source used to document Confederate abuse of Union prisoners: *Report on the Treatment of Prisoners of War by Rebel Authorities During the War of the Rebellion* (Shanks Report), 3rd Session, 40th Congress (Washington: Government Printing Office, 1869). Confederate defenses and countercharges found in "The Treatment of Prisoners During War Between the States," *Southern Historical Society Papers* (March 1876) 1:113-327.

Northern survivors experienced at the hands of their rebel captors. Although fewer Southerners wrote prison memoirs, their polemics were nonetheless virulent and likewise revealed a uniformity of testimony. They
denied charges of a Southern plot, shifted blame for the failure of the pris-
oner-release cartel upon Secretary of War Edwin M. Stanton, and ascribed
the casualties and deprivations of Southern prisons to shortages within the
Confederacy.[2]

The "war story" of Private Benjamin Wright Darsey, in contrast to ac-
counts such as *Three Hundred Days in a Yankee Prison, Reminiscences of War,
Life, Captivity, Imprisonment at Camp Chase, Ohio* by John H. King, another
Georgian, is remarkably judicious and believable.[3] Private Darsey of Liberty
County, a member of Company D, Fifth Georgia Cavalry, was captured
near Woodbury, Tennessee, on 6 September 1864 by troops of the Ninth
Pennsylvania Cavalry. Darsey, along with several other members of his unit,
was imprisoned at Camp Chase, Ohio, where he remained for the duration
of the war. He was paroled on 11 June 1865. In 1901, some 36 years after the
end of the war, Darsey, then a farmer and Methodist preacher in the Eureka
community of Bulloch County, published his war story. He claimed that he
had kept notes during the war years, but since these had been lost, he wrote
mostly from memory. Although he suffered severely at the hands of his captors, Darsey vowed that he would not "deal in fiction, seasoned with rhet-
oric, but would give only plain facts." A true story of his experiences, he
trusted, "would be interesting to the older heads and profitable to the young
and rising ones."[4] This memoir of Camp Chase describes deprivation in a
land of plenty, intense loneliness amidst teeming crowds, occasional sadistic

---

[2]William B. Hesseltine, *Civil War Prisons, A Study in War Psychology* (Columbus: Ohio
State University Press, 1930) 247-55.

[3]King charged that federal reports and "ex parte investigations" of "so-called horrors" of
Andersonville and the "inhuman treatment of Union prisoners were inspired by enmity, par-
tisanship, and vindictiveness." He believed that the real cause of suffering among prisoners
was the refusal of the Federal government to carry out the cartel and to abide by the rules of
civilized warfare. "Let those who still harp on the cruelties of Andersonville read the other
side of the wretched story and then . . . the wonder will be that they have not sooner discovered the beam in their own eyes." John H. King, *Three Hundred Days in a Yankee Prison,
Reminiscences of War, Life, Captivity, Imprisonment at Camp Chase, Ohio* (Atlanta: James P.
Davis, 1904) 3-12.

[4]B. W. Darsey, "Introductory," *A War Story, or My Experiences in a Yankee Prison* (Statesboro GA: News Print Co., 1901).

acts tempered by humanitarianism, and suffering and death in the persistent struggle for human survival.

According to family tradition, the Darseys of Liberty County are of Irish descent. Joseph Darsey, after settling first in Maryland, migrated to North Carolina and then to Georgia about 1775. Arriving in Burke County on the eve of the Revolution, Joseph and his four sons, Joel, James, William, and Benjamin, joined the patriot cause. The elder Darsey was captured during the war by the British and died while confined aboard a prison ship in Charleston harbor. After the war, the brothers received land grants in Burke, Liberty, Washington, Franklin, and Columbia Counties. William Darsey, the great-grandfather of Benjamin Wright Darsey, received 200 acres in Burke County; his son, James Darsey, was the progenitor of the Liberty County Darseys. In 1799, this James Darsey and his wife, Amelia Strother Darsey, settled first on Canoochee Creek and later moved to a frontier homestead ten miles northwest of Hinesville on the Taylors Creek and Glennville Road. James Darsey was conscripted to enforce the quarantine of Savannah in the yellow fever epidemic of 1800; he also served in the War of 1812. He was a charter member of the Taylors Creek Methodist Church that was organized in 1807, and he later selected the site and helped start the Liberty Camp Meeting in 1812. The Darseys had two sons, William Bailey and Benjamin, and three daughters. The old patriarch died in 1879 at the age of 102.

William Bailey Darsey, born in 1800, grew up in Liberty County. He, like his father before him, was a farmer in the Taylors Creek community. He married first Naomi Smart by whom he had eight children. Benjamin Wright Darsey, their sixth child, was born 21 September 1838. William Bailey Darsey's second wife was Lurany Baxter who bore him three more children.[5]

Benjamin Wright Darsey—likely named for his uncle, Squire Ben Darsey, a justice of the Inferior Court, member of the County Commission, examiner of schools, and steward in the Methodist Church—grew up in the

---

[5]For a genealogy of the Darsey family, see Mary Effie D. Smith, ed., *The Willie Community* (Reidsville GA: The *Tattnall Journal*, 1973) 63-93; Bird and Paul Yarbrough, ed., *Taylors Creek* (Pearson GA: Press of the *Atkinson County Citizen*, 1963) 166-76. Extra details were furnished by Mr. Henry Quattlebaum (Statesboro GA), Mrs. Mary Effie D. Smith (Claxton GA), and Mrs. Lanie Clemmons (Tequesta FL). Land grants listed in *Index to the Headright and Bounty Grants of Georgia, 1756-1909* (Vidalia: Georgia Genealogical Reprints, 1970) 145.

pine barrens of Liberty County where folks were hard-working and proud
of their lineage, neighborly, religious, and supportive of education. Taylors
Creek was a community of fertile farms and dense pine and oak forests. Unlike coastal Liberty County where large rice and sea-island cotton plantations were worked by slave labor, Taylors Creek was predominantly a
settlement of independent, family-sized farms worked by owners and their
families. They produced cotton, corn, rice, peas, sweet potatoes, and
raised livestock and poultry. Sawmills, turpentine stills, grist mills, blacksmith shops, and general mercantile stores supplied needed goods and services, supplemented farm incomes, and made the small community
almost self-sufficient. Local doctors, dentists, lawyers, ministers, and teachers formed the professional class. The Methodist Church, the Camp
Ground, and the Taylors Creek Union Academy, incorporated by the General Assembly in 1833, were the centers of social and cultural life in Taylors
Creek. Benjamin Wright Darsey's family was among the most respected,
and the Darsey men were leaders in the church and community.[6]

Young Darsey, as a member of a large family, shared the farm chores,
learned to plant, tend and harvest crops, shear sheep, butcher, rob bees,
make syrup and wine, hunt and fish. Although work was steady, he joined
the other youth in "home-style" fun and frolic. They enjoyed the swimming
hole, cane grindings, peanut boilings, candy pullings, Sunday school pic-
nics, and the excitement of the Camp Meeting that usually began the third
Friday in October and continued through the next Tuesday. Still there was
time for school and study. Ben Darsey's literate diary exemplifies the high
quality of basic education he received at the local academy.[7]

Liberty County, created under the Constitution of 1777, has a military
tradition that predates the American Revolution. In 1941 the Taylors Creek
and Canoochee River regions were consolidated into the 400,000-acre re-
servation of Fort Stewart; consequently a military presence still pervades
the entire county. From the Indian wars of the 1760s to the Vietnam con-

[6]Smith, The Willie Community, 8-34, 279-99; Yarbrough and Yarbrough, Taylors Creek, 7-100; "Diary of Squire Ben Darsey, 1887-1901," unpublished, now in possession of Mrs. Mary Sue Ginter, Midway GA.

[7]For daily life and routine in Taylors Creek see Julia E. Harn, "Old Canoochee Back-wood Sketches," Georgia Historical Quarterly 22 (1938): 77-80, 192-99, 292-93, 395-97; 23 (1939): 80-81, 203-204, 387-93; 24 (1940): 84-86, 158-62, 272-77, 382-85; 25 (1941): 77-79, 172-80, 286-91; Julia Harn, "Old Canoochee—Ogeechee Chronicles," Georgia Histor-ical Quarterly 15 (1931): 345-60; 16 (1932): 47-55, 146-51, 232-39, 298-312; Smith, The Willie Community, 29-34; Yarbrough and Yarbrough, Taylors Creek, 21-34.

flict of the 1960s, the young men of Liberty County have rallied to fight for their homes, section, and nation. The Liberty Troop, the oldest militia unit in the county and perhaps the oldest cavalry company in the state, was organized in July 1789 as the Second Troop of Horse Militia, Liberty County Battalion, under the command of Captain Simon Fraser. Although the unit was known as the Troop of Horse, Liberty County Battalion (1790), and the Liberty County Blues (1800), in 1807 it was designated the Liberty Independent Troop. It was activated during the War of 1812 and sent to Darien to block a British attack on Savannah from Point Petre. The Liberty Independent Troop was the only coastal horse unit that did not disband after the War of 1812.[8] The troopers continued to hold drills and musters during the antebellum period that commonly featured tilts at the ring and head, competitions that tested both horsemanship and dexterity with the sword. These popular social events attracted large crowds that came to enjoy the pageantry and fellowship, and the picnic that usually followed the tournaments. Young belles and matrons vied for the title, "Queen of Love and Beauty," sewed banners, baked cakes, and cheered their beaux and favorite contestants.[9]

The brilliant record of the cavalry units from coastal Georgia in the Civil War can be attributed to the courage of the soldiery and the decades of military training they had received in the First Squadron, Georgia Cavalry. The Liberty Guards, organized in 1845 under the command of Enoch Daniel(s), grew out of the Liberty Troop and drew its membership largely from the western section of Liberty County.[10] Liberty Countians raised five separate units that served the Confederacy; obviously their devotion to the

---

[8]Richard Cohan, *History of the Liberty Independent Troop* (unpublished manuscript) Hinesville GA; Gordon B. Smith, Unit History Work Sheets, "Liberty Independent Troop" and "First Squadron Georgia Cavalry, 1758-1861," Georgia Historical Society, vertical files; Charles C. Jones, "The Liberty Independent Troop" (Savannah, 1856), filed in Charles Colcock Jones Papers, Box 43, Tulane University, and Capt. William A. Fleming, "History of the Liberty Independent Troop" (unpublished manuscript, 1896), Midway Museum, Midway GA.

[9]Cohan, *History of the Liberty Independent Troop; Minutes of the Liberty Independent Troop*, located in museum, National Guard Armory, Hinesville GA.

[10]H. B. Fraser, comp., "The War Record of the Five Military Organizations from Liberty County, Georgia in the Confederate Army" (unpublished manuscript in possession of Mrs. Eliza Martin, Hinesville GA). Also see Smith, *The Willie Community*, 309-10; Yarbrough and Yarbrough, *Taylors Creek*, 37-56; James T. Lambright, "The Liberty Independent Troop," address to the members of Clement A. Evans Chapter, United Daughters of Confederacy, Brunswick GA, 1910 (pamphlet).

military ideal was conditioned by the continued vitality of the military tradition, the principle of loyalty and command, the hierarchical structure of their society, and the belief in chivalry and honor.

The Liberty Independent Troop and the Liberty Guards, commanded by Captain W. L. Walthour and Captain William Hughes, Jr., respectively, became companies G and D in the Fifth Georgia Cavalry. They remained closely associated throughout the Civil War. Both units under the command of Captain Abiel Winn were mustered into service for six months in October 1861 and were stationed at South Newport and Riceboro where they patrolled the Georgia coast. Ben Darsey, age 24, enlisted in the Liberty Guards at South Newport on 25 April 1862 for three years, or the duration of the war.[11] In October 1862 the Liberty Independent Troop, the Liberty Guards, and two other units were joined to create the First Battalion, Georgia Cavalry in the Department of Georgia under the command of Brigadier General H. W. Mercer. The Department of Georgia was a division of the Department of South Carolina, Georgia, and East Florida under Major General P. G. T. Beauregard. Ten horse companies, including the Georgia Hussars, Chatham Light Horse, Blue Caps, Liberty Guards, Bulloch Troop, Screven Troop, Liberty Independent Troop, Lamar Rangers, Effingham Hussars, and the McIntosh Troop were organized into the Fifth Georgia Cavalry in January 1863. Colonel Robert H. Anderson of Savannah, a graduate of West Point, class of 1857, commanded the regiment of approximately 2,000 men. From their headquarters at Isle of Hope they patrolled the coast and defended the river and coastal batteries.

The Liberty Guards, encamped at Riceboro, routinely performed guard and picket duty, drilled in cavalry tactics, went on details, and attended to the duties of daily camp life. Besides their endless struggle against the weather and mosquitoes, they occasionally hunted runaway slaves, went fishing, visited home, attended church, pulled pranks on their comrades—like putting a jackass in the huts with the boys while they were asleep—and went courting. Private James S. Warnell recorded in his diary, 13 July 1862, that he, Hatch Leplus, and Ben Darsey "went to see the girls." Again on

---

[11]Confederate military record of Private B. W. Darsey, "Compiled Service Records of Confederate Soldiers from Georgia," Microfilm, Georgia Department of Archives and History, Atlanta GA.

Sunday, 12 April 1863, he and "B. W. Darsey went to see the girls, met with several disappointments but things worked out right."[12]

Colonel Anderson, apparently restless for action, requested that his regiment be assigned to General Jeb Stuart, Army of Northern Virginia, since his troops were not needed along the Georgia coast. If this request were denied, he planned to seek transfer of his unit to Tennessee.[13] The Liberty Guards, along with the Liberty Independent Troop, left Liberty County in April 1863 to join headquarters command at Fort Devant on the Isle of Hope; their routine, again, was one of drill, guard duty, and general details. Generals Beauregard and Mercer inspected the troops and camp on 10 June 1863. In October the Fifth Georgia Cavalry was ordered to South Carolina, and during the next six weeks they camped at Coosawatchie, Pocotaligo, Green Pond, and at "Camp Dismal" near Adam's Run. Beginning in the spring of 1863, the Federals attacked by sea and land the fortresses that guarded Charleston harbor. General Beauregard's troops, concentrated on the forts and islands around Charleston, were dispersed as far south as the Savannah River. Although enemy gunboats controlled the waters around Hilton Head and Port Royal, they failed to advance inland. In March and October of 1862, Federal troops attempted to cut the Charleston and Savannah Railroad and burn the bridges over the Pocotaligo, Tulifinny, and Coosawatchie Rivers. Both engagements, fought near old Pocotaligo resulted in disaster for the invaders who were forced to retreat back to the coast. The mission of the inexperienced Fifth Georgia Cavalry from October 1863 through February 1864 was to defend the vital communication links between Charleston and Savannah.[14]

During the winter of 1863-1864, Union forces suspended active campaigning in the East, except for an invasion of northern Florida by Major

[12]Lambright, "Liberty Independent Troop," 2-4; *The War of the Rebellion: A Compilation of the Official Records of the Union and Confederate Armies*, 1st ser., 14:487-576, 591-92, 624-25, 822-25, 929-31 (hereafter cited as *Official Records*). For personal narrative of the Liberty Independent Troop and the Liberty Guards while serving along Georgia coast from Ft. McAllister to South Newport, see "The Diary of James Smart Warnell, 1862-63," unpublished, microfilm copy, Georgia Department of Archives and History, Atlanta GA.

[13]*Official Records*, 1st ser., 25:738, 740-41; 1st ser., 32:763.

[14]Activities of Fifth Georgia Cavalry in South Carolina, 1863-1864, can be traced in "John H. Ash, Confederate Diaries (1860-1865)," Keith M. Read Confederate Collection: Special Collections Dept., Woodruff Library, Emory University, Atlanta GA.

General Truman Seymour. Florida, a critical state for the Federals, was a major source of Confederate foodstuffs, cotton, and naval stores. Likewise the strength of Florida's Unionist faction afforded the Federals an opportunity for reconstructing a loyal state government and recruiting black troops. Union troops landed at Jacksonville and began their drive inland toward Tallahassee when they were checked near Olustee by Confederate forces under the command of Brigadier General Joseph Finegan on 20 February 1864. The Fifth Georgia Cavalry was ordered to Florida on 14 February for temporary service to relieve Colonel Harrision's Thirty-second Georgia Regiment. An advance party of two squadrons composed of Companies A, D, F, and I was sent ahead of the regiment to Valdosta via the Atlantic and Gulf Railroad. General Finegan, writing to General Thomas Jordan on 23 February, announced that the Fifth Georgia Cavalry had not yet arrived. They reached Florida on 24 February, four days after the major clash at Olustee. After the arrival of the other squadrons, the Fifth Georgia finally encountered the retreating enemy on 1 March and drew fire as they pursued them to the coast. Missing most of the action, the regiment began its return march to Savannah on 3 May 1864.[15]

Shortly after its arrival in Savannah on 23 May, Colonel Anderson's regiment was ordered to proceed without delay to join General Joseph Wheeler's cavalry corps, under the command of General Joseph E. Johnston, Army of Tennessee. The Fifth Georgia marched along the east side of the Savannah River to Augusta where they boarded a train for Atlanta and Brush Mountain near Kennesaw. General Johnston, attempting to check General William T. Sherman's advance toward Atlanta, extended his lines across the Marietta and Ackworth Roads, along the south bank of Noonday Creek to the base of Brush Mountain. Colonel Anderson's brigade, composed of two Alabama and two Georgia regiments, formed the flanks of General Johnston's army and protected the rear in all retrograde movements. They experienced constant combat from 7 June to 18 June, and at the Battle of Noonday Church, Companies D and I, the Liberty Guards, and Effingham Hussars led the charge and sustained heavy casualties. Captain Hughes incurred serious injuries when his horse was shot from under him. Lieutenant John E. Zoucks then assumed command of Company D. After the Confederate forces retreated across the Chattahoochee River and

[15]*Official Records*, 1st ser., 35, part 1:327-28, 368-74, 542, 558, 607, 612, 635. 1st ser., 35, part 2:457-59, 488; Evans, *Confederate Military History*, 6:283-84; Ash, "Diary."

General Johnston was replaced by General John B. Hood on 17 July, Anderson's Brigade fought in numerous battles around Decatur, Stone Mountain, Lithonia, Conyers, Covington, Jonesboro, Fayetteville, and Newnan.
Anderson's Brigade was also with General Wheeler when Stoneman's Raiders were captured near Macon on 29 July 1864.[16]

With Sherman closing in on Atlanta, Hood sent Wheeler's cavalry to
cut Union supply lines between Chattanooga and Nashville. The grand
strategy was for Wheeler to move between Marietta and Chattanooga, then
cross the Tennessee River and break the two rail lines running to Nashville.
He planned to leave 1,200 men to operate against these roads, return and
strike the lines south of Chattanooga, before rejoining the main command
in the environs of Atlanta. Wheeler ordered his subordinate officers to select the best-mounted men from their commands for a raid on the rear of
the Federal army.

General Anderson, recently commissioned brigadier general (26 July
1864), had been seriously wounded near Newnan, so Brigadier General Fe-
lix H. Robertson commanded the brigade of about 600 cavalrymen who began their march toward Chattanooga on 11 August 1864. Ben Darsey
recorded that they made a circuitous route around the left wing of Sherman's army and marched all night, halting only to rest and feed. After destroying the railroad above Marietta, at Cassville and Calhoun, Kelly's and
Hume's commands captured Dalton on 14 August, where they took possession of a large supply of stores, government property, 200 horses and mules,
200 prisoners, and feasted on "Yankee army supplies." After spending the
night ripping up railroad track, Darsey's brigade moved on to Spring Place
where they rested a day and a night before crossing over into Tennessee. In
addition to their operations against the railroads, they pursued "bush-
whackers" and foraged in east Tennessee, a stronghold of unionism. Wheeler's cavalry destroyed the railroad from Cleveland to Charleston, crossed
the Hiwassee River, captured Athens, and ripped up the line from Charleston to Loudon. Thence they marched to the environs of Chattanooga
where they exchanged a few shots with the Yankees, but decided not to at-

---

[16]Ash, "Diary"; *Official Records*, 1st ser., 35, part 2:503; 1st ser., 38, part 2:820-23;
1st ser., 38, part 4 and part 5 for operations 10 June–3 July 1864. Evans, *Confederate Military
History*, 4:151; 6:301-42; Franklin M. Garrett, *Atlanta and Environs* (Athens: University of
Georgia Press, 1954) 1:580-85, 595-644; Darsey, *A War Story*, 1; *The Union Army, A History
of Military Affairs in the Loyal States*, 1861-1865 (Madison WI: Federal Publishing Co., 1908)
6:650.

tack since the enemy was too strongly entrenched. Instead, they resumed their march toward the Cumberland Mountains where they struck camp and went recruiting and foraging. Darsey, starved after several days on green apples, had memories of sumptuous evening meals of roasted mutton and a stack of slapjacks "about knee high." The next day Robertson's brigade passed through the Cumberland Gap into middle Tennessee in search of smithies to reshoe the horese that were showing lameness from having crossed the rocky terrain.[17]

Colonel George G. Dibrell, a native Tennesseean who commanded the other regiment in General J. H. Kelly's brigade, allowed a couple of days for his troops to visit before their prearranged rendezvous at Lebanon. Captain William Brailsford, commander of Company H, Fifth Georgia Cavalry (Lamar Rangers), was left in command. Ben Darsey, managing to exchange his lame horse for a mule, was disappointed when the owner appeared to recover the animal. Even though he claimed that he had already given 14 horses to the Confederate army, Darsey observed that the owner did not wear a uniform and still had a fine horse and two mules. Private Darsey reminded the man that he had given more—his only horse and himself. Colonel Dibrell arrived at Lebanon on schedule with more than 20 new recruits that increased Darsey's squadron to between 150 and 200 soldiers. Enroute to Murfreesboro that same afternoon a courier informed Colonel Dibrell that the main force had engaged the enemy between Murfreesboro and Nashville and that General J. H. Kelly had been killed. Dibrell was ordered to hasten with relief.[18]

On 31 August, a company of Pennsylvania cavalrymen had begun stalking Dibrell's brigade. The next day they learned that Dibrell's forces had left for McMinnville several days before. On 3 September, the Union cavalry rode hard for 40 miles to overtake Dibrell, reaching McMinnville only three minutes after the rebels had departed. The Ninth Pennsylvania Cavalry then marched westward to Woodbury and on 5 September rode into Murfreesboro. Dibrell, planning to cross the railroad near the town, had camped near Readyville. He reported that his force numbered between 1,000 and 1,200 men, many of whom were unarmed or raw recruits. At day-

---

[17]Darsey, *A War Story*, 1-4; Ash, *Diary* (10 August 1864); *Confederate Military History*, 6:343-45; Lambright, "The Liberty Independent Troop," 4-5.

[18]Darsey, *A War Story*, 5-7; Evans, *Confederate Military History*, 6:305-307; Lambright, "The Liberty Independent Troop," 5.

light on 6 September, the Confederates were completely surprised and surrounded. There was little gunfire as the Yanks attacked the rebels with
sabers. Dibrell reported that "I used every effort to rally the men, but owing
to the large number unarmed, quite a stampede took place and it was with
difficulty that they could be rallied and checked." Fleeing toward Woodbury
five miles away, the Confederates left behind 200 horses and a large number
of Enfield rifles. In the disastrous skirmish, they also suffered 74 casualties
and lost 130 prisoners.[19]

Although Ben Darsey, Robert and Taylor Walthour, and an Alabamian
named Abbott were fatigued from a long ride and the loss of sleep, they were
detailed for picket duty when the regiment struck camp on the evening of
5 September. Darsey had drawn the first watch and had then fallen asleep
on the ground with his bridle reins in hand when he was awakened by the
alarm, "Yankees, boys!" The Walthours, already mounted, dashed into
camp ahead of the raiders; Darsey and Abbott, separated from their command, hid in a steep ravine along Duck River. Concealed behind a large
boulder, they anxiously watched and waited while the enemy stormed the
camp and scoured the woods. "Our condition was evidently a critical one,"
Darsey recalled. "What was best to do was a question hard to decide . . . a
thousand thoughts revolved in my mind. . . . I could see no way or hope of
reaching home or our main command even if we escaped. . . . In all prob-
ability we would be captured and condemned as spies. I was in favor of sur-
rendering and risk our fate with them." As two Union cavalrymen came
near to recover their horses, Darsey and Abbott laid down their carbines
and surrendered. They were taken into Murfreesboro, along with about 75
or 80 other prisoners, where they were temporarily secured in an open shed
or lumber house. Darsey, probably too scared to remember, forgot his blanket and haversack. In addition to Darsey and Abbott, the roll of prisoners
included Captain William Brailsford, Lieutenant J. E. Zoucks, I. T. Grice,
S. H. Zoucks, T. F. Linder, F. Williams, J. S. Kicklighter, Math Miller, W.
P. Merritt, D. R. McIntosh, W. H. Thompson, F. Roe, D. H. Bailey, W.
Maney, and E. J. Zeigler, all members of the Fifth Georgia Cavalry.[20]

After six days in Murfreesboro where they were fed sparingly on hardtack and "old ned" (bacon), the prisoners were loaded on rail cars and sent

---

[19]John W. Rowell, *Yankee Cavalrymen, Through the Civil War with the Ninth Pennsylvania Cavalry* (Knoxville: University of Tennessee Press, 1971) 188-91.

[20]Darsey, *A War Story*, 7-9.

to Camp Chase near Columbus, Ohio. Darsey, still a proud Southerner even though he was now a prisoner, had a "jangle" with a guard who called him a "Jonnie Reb." Darsey, after learning that his captor was from Tennessee, retorted with epithets "blue-bellied Yankee" and "traitor of the deepest dye." After a change of guards at Louisville, Kentucky, they arrived in Columbus and marched to the prison about a mile away. Darsey and his colleagues were processed, searched, given blankets, and then placed in Prison No. 2.[21]

Camp Chase, a square enclosure of 100 acres of farm land, was named for Secretary of Treasury Salmon P. Chase, a former governor of Ohio. The camp had served primarily as a training center for federal troops until July 1861. The need for secure prison facilities, however, prompted the construction of a prison in the southeast corner of the camp. Prison No. 1, designed to accommodate 450 inmates, was a half-acre enclosure surrounded by a 10-foot high plank wall with towers on two sides. Inside were three crude frame buildings, two being 100-by-15 feet, the other 70 feet by 20 feet, that were partitioned into rooms about 18 feet in length. Each room housed a mess of 18 men. From July 1861 until February 1862, the majority of inmates at Camp Chase were political prisoners from Virginia and Kentucky whose major crime was fidelity to the Confederacy.

In November 1861, Secretary of War Simon Cameron ordered the construction of Prison No. 2, an additional unit of three more barracks 100 feet by 15 feet, to provide for the growing numbers. When Confederate General Simon B. Buckner surrendered his army of 12,000 men at Fort Donelson in February 1862, Camp Chase was inundated by captives. By March 1862 the stockade held more than 1,200 prisoners. Prison No. 3, built to hold 1,100 captives, was a three-acre enclosure erected near the center of the camp. The new prison contained four rows of huts arranged in clusters of six and separated from the rest of the camp by a 12-foot board fence. Cheaply constructed, each hut was 20 feet by 14 feet and was equipped with a stove and six bunks. The huts were approximately two and one-half feet apart, and the clusters were separated by narrow dirt streets. Two uncovered sinks, five feet by ten feet, were the only sanitary facilities in the stockade. Since they were located above the cisterns, the water supply was quickly polluted and became the major cause of sickness. Because of the physical conditions in-

[21]Ibid., 9-10.

side the stockade, poor drainage and overcrowding, President H. W. Bellows of the U. S. Sanitary Commission advised General William Hoffman to abandon the location. He considered Chase "enough to drive a sanitarian mad." By late April 1862, Prison No. 3 had nearly 1,000 inmates.[22]

Camp Chase was the focus of controversy almost from the outset. Unionists charged that prisoners were treated too leniently, that rebel prisoners were allowed to frequent Columbus bars, restaurants, and hotels, and that prisoners were served inside the stockade by their personal slaves. Complicated by a conflict of responsibility between state and military authorities, even a federal inspection did not resolve the confusion. The Ohio Senate undertook its own investigation and Senator John Sherman of Ohio introduced a resolution in the U. S. Senate that condemned laxity at Camp Chase. The Secretary of War finally decided in April 1862 to remove all remaining officers to Johnson's Island; thereafter Camp Chase would receive enlisted men, non-commissioned officers, political prisoners, paroled Union prisoners, and serve as a training camp for new recruits. By the end of 1863, the prison population reached 2,763; capacity became a meaningless term in the following month. A rebellion against the draft, the open activities of Copperheads, and General John Hunt Morgan's spectacular raid and escape caused a major revision of prison regulations. Colonel William Wallace, the prison commandant, established a dead line and sent spies, "razor backs," among the prisoners. Prisoners were told that those who stepped over the dead line, placed some 20 feet within the stockade walls, would bring fire from the guards. Those caught trying to escape were suspended by their thumbs, ordered to hard labor with a ball and chain attached to their ankles, "bucked and gagged," or confined to the dungeon, a windowless, unheated cell designed to take the rebellion out of any rebel's mind in 48 to 72 hours. Censorship of mail was instituted, the sutler's store was closed, salt was no longer issued, and rations were reduced to three-fourths of the original allowance. To enforce the stricter disciplines the Eighty-eighth Ohio was recalled to replace the Veteran Recovery Corps de-

---

[22]For stories on Camp Chase, see Hesseltine, *Civil War Prisons*, 37, 45-54; Philip R. Shriver and Donald J. Breen, *Ohio's Military Prisons in the Civil War* (Columbus: Ohio State University Press, 1964) 7-29; William H. Knauss, *The Story of Camp Chase* (Nashville: Publishing House of the Methodist Episcopal Church, South, 1906) 4, 115; for lithographs of Camp Chase, 6-8, 114-39.

tachment. To add to these hardships, January 1864 was insufferably cold with temperatures reaching 30 degrees below zero.[23]

When Colonel William F. Richardson assumed command of the prison in February 1864, he relaxed the stringent policies of his predecessor. The sutler's trade resumed, guards were restricted, and the prisoners were allowed to establish their own daily newspaper and camp government.[24] Two days after his arrival at Camp Chase, Ben Darsey, generally tolerant of his captors, drew his first rations, eight hardtacks and a piece of salty mackerel which were subsequently stolen. "As to suffering," he wrote, "no human speech could express my feelings at times. . . . We had plenty of soap and water, but food and fire were scarce articles." In order to share their blankets, three men slept in the narrow bunks. Darsey chose the middle but found it necessary for all three to turn simultaneously whenever one changed positions. In December 1864, a stove was installed in his barracks, but with several hundred men crowding around, those on the periphery got little heat. Besides cold and hunger, Darsey also acknowledged he suffered psychologically during the confinement, "not knowing when, if ever, I could get out of that miserable place." Even though all mail was censored, he and Sam Zoucks wrote their families soon after imprisonment. Some three weeks later Darsey received a letter from his father. "Never before had I received a letter that gave me such joy," he remembered. Occasionally someone would receive a little box of food from home, a welcomed treat.[25]

Instead of individual issues of rations, prison officials divided the barracks into messes of 24 men each. Each mess elected its own cook who received the rations and served meals twice daily. Darsey was elected cook of his mess in May 1865. He confessed he was anxious for the job because the cook could skim the pots and pick up the extra crumbs. Admitting that he suffered less from hunger, he stated that he always treated his men honestly and divided the rations equally. Tin plates, cups, and knives were issued each member of the mess. Rations usually consisted of beef, hardtack, flour, and light bread. As Darsey put it, "We could have eaten one day's rations at one time and quit hungry." After making "coffee," a drink concocted from parched crusts of bread, only a mouthful of bread and two of meat re-

[23]Shriver and Breen, *Ohio's Military Prisons*, 12-18.

[24]Ibid., 19-20.

[25]Darsey, *A War Story*, 11-12.

mained. Darsey remembered the greasy mush made by boiling beef and meal as their most palatable fare.[26]

Beginning in January 1865, a sutler's shop was again established with a window that opened into the prison. Prison officials issued checks in denominations from five to fifty cents to those whose money had been confiscated when they entered the stockade. Some few received U.S. currency from home. A check for five cents could purchase a quart of meal or a few potatoes. Ingenious prisoners who had no credit upon which to draw manufactured items that could be bartered to the sutler for meal. Toothpicks made of beef bones and rings made from guttapercha buttons were salable items to guards and visitors until the market became glutted. Except for their Confederate issue, warm clothing was scarce and only distributed when prisoners could convince officials that they were nearly naked. Darsey observed how comical his fellow inmates appeared when garbed in their altered, second-hand frock coats.[27]

Time weighed heavily for the inmates inside Camp Chase. Prisoners whiled away their time by reading, carving and fashioning items from scraps scavenged about the camp, playing cards, chess, and checkers. To escape boredom they improvised amusement like louse races and street dances where some of the prisoners were selected by lot to assume the role of female partners. Darsey, an avid reader, longed for the Testament his sister had given him when he left home that had been left in his knapsack. He was elated when a young Marylander gave him a Bible which he read several times. Sometimes they sat around on their bunks and sang hymns and popular songs like "Dixie," "Bonnie Blue Flag," and "When this Cruel War Is Over."[28] Forced to remain inside during the long, severe winter of 1864-1865, Darsey suffered homesickness as he fondly recalled the happy days of the past. He remembered his school days, the black friends with whom he had played and gone raccoon hunting, and the abundance of food on his father's table. Especially vivid was the memory of the young ladies who had flattered him and the Guards when they left their homes in Liberty County. He had pledged his loyalty to their interest and the Confederate cause. Years later when recalling the three long years of his life as a soldier, Darsey

---

[26]Ibid., 16, 22.

[27]Ibid., 17-18.

[28]Ibid., 13, 21; Shriver and Breen, *Ohio's Military Prisons*, 20-21.

proudly stated that he could recall no act of which he was ashamed. "I had kept my vow and my conscience was clear."[29]

Encountering every class and manner of men imaginable inside the prison, Darsey lamented how the deprivations and cruelties of camp and prison life contributed to the moral and religious degradation of the unfortunate inmates. He was shocked by men who gambled and stole each other's rations and clothing, even in the presence of death. Although Darsey was neither prudish nor sanctimonious, he could not escape his strict Methodist upbringing. He was pleased, however, that the "U.S. government got away with the devil when it excluded whiskey and fiddles from the Yankee prisons. . . . " Just as prison life brought out the worst in human nature, it likewise inspired compassion and nobility of character. Darsey risked the danger of being shot when he violated prison rules to procure medicine for Tim Grice, a sick bunkmate.[30]

Ungrounded rumors of exchange constantly circulated through the prison pen, repeatedly leading to false hopes. On 2 February 1865 General U. S. Grant ordered the resumption of parole exchange at the rate of 3,000 prisoners per week. Priority was given to prisoners from states where union sentiment was strongest and to parolees least likely to reenlist in rebel forces. A few days later two Union officers came to the prison to call out the first names. Out of the first 800 called for exchange, only 300 agreed to go. The others apparently chose to remain in the North and take the oath of allegiance to the Federal Constitution rather than return to active duty. Colonel Richardson wrote his superior in March 1865 that there were nearly 3,000 rebels at Camp Chase who refused to be exchanged. Anxiously waiting to hear his name called, Darsey saw his spirits sag when he learned the exchange had been broken off. A new proposal for parole, however, was soon offered to inmates who would "Swallow the eagle"—take an oath to the U.S. Constitution and agree to remain north of the Ohio River. According to Ben Darsey's account not a single Georgian, and in fact very few from any state, accepted the proposition. Those who accepted were moved to Prison No. 2; the remaining were crowded into Prison No. 3 where Darsey and most of the inmates from his old regiment occupied the

---

[29]Darsey, *A War Story*, 14.

[30]Ibid., 14-15.

same barracks.[31] Occasionally guards would throw them an old newspaper that contained news of Confederate defeats on the battle field. Darsey believed this was done to induce them to take the oath of allegiance.[32]

The prison population at Camp Chase rose from 2,015 at the end of June to 5,610 by 31 October 1864. Filled to overflowing with the survivors of the Battle of Atlanta, trainloads of prisoners continued to arrive daily. Rations were reduced again as pork and beef all but disappeared from the diet. Some inmates were so starved they resorted to eating rats. During January 1865, more than 11,000 prisoners were confined at Camp Chase. By 1 February, there were still 9,045 prisoners on hand; 1,503 had been transferred, 126 released, and 499 had died.[33] Many prisoners, already weak and ill when committed to Camp Chase, succumbed to pneumonia, typhoid fever, and/or dysentery. Smallpox, the dread and scourge of every inmate, broke out in the fall of 1864. Commandant Richardson reported 168 cases isolated in the pesthouse in mid-October. All incoming prisoners were vaccinated upon admission. "Volunteers" recruited from among the prisoners served as attendants in the pesthouses, which were little more than way stations to the prison cemetery. Death statistics mounted from 113 in September to 293 in November; during the first four months of 1865 they totaled 1,233. Fred Williams and T. F. Linder, both members of Darsey's company, were casualties of smallpox. Darsey noted that smallpox raged during the coldest months and that proportionately more men died in prison than in the army. "At least 30 or 40 dead," he remembered, "were carried out of prison some days from various diseases." Mass burials in trenches instead of individual graves became the common practice.

During these months, Richardson's reports continued to echo shortages of vegetables, clothing, and straw for bunks. Even the weather seemed to conspire against the hapless prisoners as they endured snow, rain, sleet, and mud.[34] When General Lee surrendered to General Grant on 9 April 1865,

---

[31]Ibid., 18-20; Shriver and Breen, *Ohio's Military Prisons*, 27-28.

[32]Darsey, *A War Story*, 20.

[33]Shriver and Breen, *Ohio's Military Prisons*, 15-16, 25-27. For prison statistics see Appendix, Table 1. Camp Chase had an aggregate prison population in excess of 26,000 between July 1861 and July 1865, and a maximum of 9,045 prisoners on 31 January 1865. *Official Records*, 2d ser., 8:986-1003.

[34]Shriver and Breen, *Ohio's Military Prisons*, 25-26; Darsey, *A War Story*, 13.

5,339 inmates were still confined in Camp Chase. A month later Secretary Stanton directed that all prisoners, except officers above the rank of colonel, were to be released upon taking the oath of loyalty. Transportation was to be provided for their return home and in the next few weeks Camp Chase was emptied. From 5,539 who were counted on 30 April, the number had declined to 3,353 by 31 May; by 30 June, only 48 invalids remained. On 3 July, the Eighty-eighth Ohio Volunteer Infantry Regiment was discharged from guard duty. Camp Chase, after nearly four years of use, was now deserted. Nearby in the prison cemetery, the remains of 2,229 Confederate dead lay buried.[35]

Sorrow and disbelief were the responses of Darsey and his fellow inmates when they realized that the failure of the Confederacy was inevitable. Although others had misgivings, Darsey was truly glad when he learned that President Lincoln had been assassinated. For him, Lincoln merited hatred. Convinced to the bitter end of the righteousness of the Southern cause, he rationalized that "right does not prevail everytime." "If a big man jumps on a little fellow and gives him a whipping," Darsey stated, "it is no proof that the big fellow was right and the little was wrong."[36] Suspense and anxiety about their release mounted daily; finally on 11 June 1865 two Union officers appeared on the parapet and announced that all prisoners would soon be set free. Ben Darsey's name was almost the first one to be called, followed by those who had been captured on the same date. After filing through the prison office where they were measured and given their papers, they drew two days' rations of bacon and hardtack from the commissary. They then walked to Columbus where they procured their tickets to Cincinnati. Two weeks later Ben Darsey reached Savannah from whence he walked to Liberty County. "My home was just 44 miles."[37]

Upon returning home to Liberty County, Darsey discovered that Taylors Creek had experienced first hand the horrors of war. From their encampment at Midway Church, General Judson Kilpatrick's Cavalry had conducted forays in the region between the Ogeechee and Altamaha Rivers for more than a month. They had terrorized, pillaged, and burned plantations

---

[35]Shriver and Breen, *Ohio's Military Prisons*, 28-29.

[36]Darsey wrote that "some clever fellow had cut President Lincoln's throat." *A War Story*, 21.

[37]Ibid., 22-23.

and homesteads left in the care of women, children, and the aged.[38] Although the Methodist Church at Taylors Creek was spared, the invaders moved the pulpit furniture to their camp on the Canoochee River. According to local tradition, only the Masonic emblem displayed over the church door had saved it from the torch. Besides ruin and desolation, many of Liberty County's finest young men either never returned from the war or came home as invalids. The history of the heroism and suffering of the non-combatants remains to be written.[39]

Ben Darsey, age 27, began life anew in Bulloch County. On 28 March 1866 he married Lanie E. Miller (1839-1906), daughter of John R. and Nancy Miller, large landowners in the Eureka community, Forty-eighth Georgia Militia District.[40] Ben Darsey's brother, W. O. Darsey, married America (Mackey) Miller, the sister of Ben's wife. In 1873 Ben Darsey purchased 340 acres of farmland that had formerly been part of his father-in-law's estate, and ten years later he bought another tract of 250 acres nearby.[41] In addition to his farming interests, Darsey was a Methodist preacher for more than 50 years. The Eureka Methodist Church, near his farm, was his home church. He was an ardent advocate of temperance and widely known throughout the region as a monument salesman. From 1916 until his death he received a Confederate pension.[42]

---

[38]For discussion of Yankee raiders in Liberty County, see George A. Rogers and R. Frank Saunders, Jr., "The Scourge of Sherman's Men in Liberty County, Georgia," *Georgia Historical Quarterly* 60 (1976): 356-69 (another version appears elsewhere in this publication), and Haskell Monroe, "Men without Law: Federal Raiding in Liberty County, Georgia," *Georgia Historical Quarterly* 44 (1960): 154-71.

[39]Yarbrough and Yarbrough, *Taylors Creek*, 37-40.

[40]Marriage Records, Book A-J, Part 1, p. 78; Bulloch County Probate Records, Statesboro GA.

[41]Indenture dated 23 January 1873, Darsey purchased 340 acres in the 48th GMD from J. E. C. Tillman for $500, Deed Book FQ, p. 182, Clerk's Office, Bulloch County Courthouse, Statesboro GA; Indenture dated 10 October 1883, Darsey purchased 250 acres in the 48th GMD from I. V. Simmons for $1,500, Deed Book FP, p. 535; in 1901, Darsey bought two lots on North College Street in Statesboro GA, Book 13, p. 133 (5 February 1901).

[42]In 1879 Ben Darsey owned 355 acres, with fences and buildings, valued at $400. He owned 14 cows, 32 swine; planted seven acres of corn, ten acres of oats, 11 acres of cotton, and planted another acre in cane and sweet potatoes. The estimated value of his farm production, including six bales of cotton was $340. Bulloch County Agricultural and Manufacturing Census Record, 1880; reel 112, 48th district, p. 38. *Pensions for Civil War Soldiers and Widows*, Pension Roll, New Roll 1910 Account, p. 3. Bulloch County Probate Records, Statesboro GA.

Ben Darsey is remembered by his family and friends as a kindly gentle-man, a pillar of his church and community. Deeply religious and serious-minded, he was proper in manner, dress, and speech. He enjoyed a wide circle of friends, children, and books. A devoted family man, he had five children—two sons and three daughters—four of whom survived him. Lanie M. Darsey, his wife of 40 years, died in 1906.[43] Having disposed of his farm property, he lived among his children in his last years. Ben Darsey died suddenly at the residence of his son, B. M. Darsey, in Claxton on 18 March 1921, at age 84.[44] Benjamin W. and Lanie M. Darsey were buried in the Macedonia Baptist Church Cemetery.

---

[43]His children: Oriana who married B. P. Porter, Bulloch County; Amanda who married Dr. John P. Holmes, Dublin; Carrie who married Col. G. W. M. Williams, Bamberg SC; F. M. Darsey who settled at Oliver; and B. M. Darsey who moved to Claxton. Family records furnished by Mrs. Lanie Clemons (granddaughter), Tequesta FL. Population census, Bulloch County GA, 1880. Tombstone inscription of Lanie M. Darsey, Macedonia Baptist Church, Bulloch County GA.

[44]Obituaries of B. W. Darsey, *Bulloch Times*, Statesboro GA (24 March 1921) 8; *Savan-nah Morning News* (20 March 1921) 10.

SIX

Camp Lawton Stockade,
Millen, Georgia, C.S.A.*

EVEN AFTER 118 YEARS there remains no subject in Civil War history that is more controversial than the administration of Southern prisons. Who has not heard of the horrors of Andersonville, the atrocities of Salisbury, Cahaba, and Lawton, and the alleged venality of Henry Wirz and John H. Winder? Charges of criminal intent to diminish the ranks of the enemy by deliberate deprivation and neglect were brought against Jefferson Davis and the Confederate government almost from the beginning of the conflict. After the war these accusations were supported by letters and published memoirs of former inmates, reports of congressional committees, politicians who waved the "bloody shirt," pensioners of the Grand Army of the Republic, and partisan historians and journalists.[1]

Southerners, equally convinced of the rightness of their cause, countercharged that conditions were worse and casualties higher in Northern prisons. They shifted the blame for shortages of food, clothing, and medicine to the Union blockade and to mounting logistical problems within the Confederacy. Crowded conditions were explained away as the result of

*This paper was prepared for presentation to the Georgia Studies Symposium at Georgia State University, 15-16 February 1980. Research was partially funded by a grant from the Georgia Southern College Research Fund.

[1]The classic example of "bloody shirt" politics was the dramatic confrontation in the U.S. Senate between James G. Blaine and Benjamin H. Hill in 1876. Congressional Record 44th Congress, 1st session (Washington: Government Printing Office, 1876) 4:323-39, 345-51.

Northern refusal to negotiate a cartel for the exchange of prisoners. Before the turn of the century, these defenses became enmeshed in a cult of Southern patriotism that was nurtured by Confederate Memorial Day celebrations, the Daughters of the Confederacy, the fervent oratory of native sons, and sentimental novelists.[2]

The historian who aspires to make objective judgments of Southern prisons soon discovers that the culpability of all parties is clouded by propaganda, emotion, and distortion. Although North and South alike were officially committed to the humane treatment of prisoners, in practice the dehumanizing brutalities of prison life became a part of the greater tragedy of war. Recriminations aside, there was no justification and there can be no apology, either North or South, for the cruelties inflicted on unfortunate captives.

During the war, the Confederacy operated 68 facilities throughout the South for the separate confinement of enlisted men and officers. These prisons were generally of two types: existing buildings such as warehouses, jails, and penitentiaries hastily converted to hold Union prisoners of war, and specially constructed stockades and enclosed camps. Andersonville, in Sumter County, Georgia, often considered the typical Southern prison in its administration and design, held in excess of 52,000 prisoners before the war ended. Camp Lawton, located five miles north of Millen on the Central of Georgia Railroad, was the largest stockade in the Confederacy. It was built, occupied, and abandoned between August and November 1864. Lawton has generally escaped the notoriety and infamy of Andersonville because of its short history and its reputation for better conditions. Nonetheless, one confronts here all aspects in the administration of prisons

---

[2]William B. Hesseltine's *Civil War Prisons, A Study in War Psychology* (Columbus: Ohio State University Press, 1930) remains the best monograph on Civil War prisons. Professor Hesseltine succinctly outlines historiographical problems encountered in studying Civil War prisons in his introductory essay, "Civil War Prisons—Introduction," *Civil War History* 8 (June 1962): 117-20. Northern charges of deliberate mistreatment of prisoners by the Confederates were given a semblance of credibility in two official government publications, *The Trial of Henry Wirz* (Washington: Government Printing Office, 1868), and *Report on the Treatment of Prisoners of War by Rebel Authorities During the War of the Rebellion*, 40th Congress, 3rd Session (Washington: Government Printing Office, 1869), sometimes called Shanks *Report*. Vindication of the Confederate government against charges of mistreatment of Union prisoners may be found in "The Treatment of Prisoners During the War Between the States," *Southern Historical Society Papers* (March 1876) 1:113-327; see also Jefferson Davis, *Andersonville and Other War Prisons* (New York: Belford Co., 1890).

and the treatment of prisoners of war by the Confederacy. It is a reasonable assumption that Camp Lawton's infamy would have likely rivalled Andersonville's had it escaped Sherman's march.[3]

As early in the war as May 1861, the Confederate Congress passed laws regarding the treatment of prisoners. The most important of these laws provided that prisoners should be disarmed and sent to the rear, that the private property of prisoners be respected, and that they should receive one ration per day equal in quantity and quality to the ration furnished enlisted men in the army of the Confederacy.[4] Always hopeful that a cartel for the exchange of captives might be negotiated, prisoners despaired when these negotiations foundered in 1862. Both sides blamed the other for the stalemate. Throughout the war, issues relating to de facto recognition of the Confederacy and the status of black prisoners appeared irreconcilable.[5]

When the war moved closer to Richmond in 1863, Confederate officials became alarmed about the overcrowded and poorly guarded prisons so near the battle front. Union prisoners were soon dispersed deeper into the Confederacy to Salisbury, North Carolina, and Tuscaloosa, Alabama. Andersonville was opened in February 1864. Originally planned to accommodate 10,000 prisoners, by midsummer it had more than 30,000 inmates inside walls that enclosed 26.5 acres. Deficient supplies of food, clothing, shelter, and medicine debilitated even the healthiest prisoners. Poor sanitation, disease, and death stalked the inmates who were also plagued by "marauders" and guards who were either insensitive or incompetent to remedy hardships.[6]

General John H. Winder, Commissary General of all Confederate prisons east of the Mississippi River, moved his headquarters to Andersonville

---

[3]Besides Hesseltine, see Ovid Futch, *History of Andersonville Prison* (Indiantown FL: University of Florida Presses, 1968). Camp Lawton previously has been given summary treatment in published accounts. An unpublished study by Billy Townsend, "Camp Lawton, Magnolia Springs State Park" (prepared by the Recreation and Interpretive Programming Section, Parks and Historic Sites Division, Georgia Department of Natural Resources, 1975), contains interesting data and illustrations.

[4]Hesseltine, *Civil War Prisons*, 55.

[5]Ibid., 23-26.

[6]McKinley Kantor's Pulitzer prize-winning *Andersonville* (Cleveland: World Press, 1955), though a work of fiction, is considered a reliable account of the construction, administration, and conditions of prison life at Andersonville.

in June 1864; a Richmond newspaper noting his departure to Georgia added, "May God have mercy on the Yankee prisoners."[7] While his previous record as provost-marshal and commander of Northern prisons in Richmond hardly commended his benevolence, Winder was sufficiently disturbed by conditions at Andersonville to call for the construction of another prison. On 28 July 1864, Winder dispatched Captains D. W. Vowels and W. S. Winder to select a site for the new prison and to lease all needed land, water, and timber rights.[8] Vowels had formerly served under Winder at Richmond and had recently been transferred to Andersonville at the general's request; W. S. Winder, the general's son, was an assistant adjutant stationed at Andersonville.[9] General Winder instructed his staff officers to confer with the reliable men in the community before choosing a site; a few days later he urged General Samuel Cooper, Adjutant and Inspector General, C.S.A., to authorize the impressment of blacks, teams, and wagons in the preparation for building the new stockade. He also urged: "It is very important to build as soon as possible. We have now 32,232 prisoners of war."[10] Within a week, Vowels and Winder reported to General Cooper that they had selected a site, five miles from Millen on the Augusta railroad.[11] General Winder, anxious to alleviate conditions at Andersonville, again reminded: "It is the greatest importance that the garrison should be built as soon as possible. We are full here to overflowing."[12]

While General Winder was actively promoting the new prison, Dr. C. R. Johnson, a Waynesboro physician, sent a protest to Secretary of War Seddon against the proposed prison site. He argued that the water at the site came from rotten limestone springs and was unfit for human consumption. He added that the new prison would be situated in the very midst of

---

[7]Frank E. Moran, *Bastiles of the Confederacy. A Reply to Jefferson Davis* (Baltimore, 1890) 145.

[8]*The War of the Rebellion: A Compilation of the Official Records of the Union and Confederate Armies* 2d ser. (Washington: Government Printing Office, 1899): 7:509 (hereafter cited as *Official Records*).

[9]For service record of D. W. Vowels, see *Compiled Service Records of Confederate General and Staff Officers and Nonregimental Enlisted Men*, Roll 255, National Archives.

[10]*Official Records*, 2d ser., 7:514.

[11]Ibid., 546.

[12]Ibid., 565.

productive plantations that were manned by large numbers of blacks. According to Dr. Johnson, General Winder had been influenced by "pecuniary purposes," an indictment that could be supported by a petition of the Inferior Court of Burke County.[13] General Howell Cobb, Commander of the Georgia Reserves, also joined the protest. He advised that another prison camp should not be built in Georgia since the state was already exposed to raiding parties and that too many reserves were already employed in guarding prisoners.[14]

Nonetheless, General Winder moved forward with the new prison by sending Lieutenant R. S. Hopkins to Millen with instructions to procure labor by scouring the adjoining counties.[15] General Cooper, also convinced that conditions at Andersonville were deplorable, inquired if a part of Camp Lawton might be prepared for occupancy before completion of the stockade.[16]

Winder first visited Camp Lawton on 18 September. He came to inquire whether he should move his headquarters to the new stockade, and if prisoners were to be removed from Savannah.[17] A few days later, General Winder claimed that the prison was nearly ready and that prisoners could be received the next week, now that 11 guns, an artillery company, and reserves were available for guard duty. Enclosing a plan of the prison to Cooper, he observed that "it is, I presume, the largest prison in the world; it contains forty-two acres."[18] According to the Morning Report Book of Andersonville prison, the first prisoners were sent to Millen on 18 September 1864.[19] General Winder noted that 2,000 more prisoners were yet to be moved from Andersonville, excluding another 3,000 who were too sick to travel.[20] In the jargon of the prisoners, none of the inmates sent to Lawton

---

[13]Ibid., 579.

[14]Ibid., 585-86.

[15]Ibid., 593.

[16]Ibid., 772.

[17]Ibid., 841.

[18]Ibid., 869-70.

[19]Refers to volume 110; Office of the Commissary General of Prisoners, Adjutant General's Office, Papers Pertaining to Federal Prisoners, 1862-1867, Box 137, National Archives.

[20]*Official Records*, 2d ser., 7:955-56.

were "fresh fish"—that is, newly captured prisoners. Instead, they were either "suckers" or "dry cod" who had already spent time in other prisons. Those few lucky enough to be exchanged were called "pickled sardines."[21]

On 15 October, General Winder wrote Cooper that the stockade was finally completed and that prisoners had arrived from Savannah a few days earlier, 700 of whom were in "dying condition." "We can with great convenience accommodate 32,000 prisoners," he added, "and could without inconvenience increase it to 40,000." General Winder, highly dissatisfied with the assigned guards from the First and Second Georgia Reserves, ridiculed them as "the most unreliable and disorganized set I have ever seen." He accused the undisciplined troops of plundering the countryside and blamed their commanders for general dereliction of duty. He requested that the Second Regiment of Georgia State Troops, currently stationed at Augusta, be assigned to replace the unruly crew.[22]

Throughout the brief history of Camp Lawton, Captain D. W. Vowels acted as commander of the stockade. Of the few surviving reports submitted from Lawton, Vowels signed as "commanding." However, in a report to General Cooper, Winder disclosed that Colonel Henry Forno, former commandant of the guards at Andersonville, was named commander at Lawton.[23] Actually, there is no evidence that Forno ever held the post. This problem is further compounded by the testimony of several former inmates before the Shanks Committee who named a Captain Lawton and a Colonel Means as commander at Lawton.[24] Perhaps the inmates confused the commander with the name of the prison. It is believed that the stockade was named for General Alexander R. Lawton, Quartermaster General of the Confederacy, 1864-1865. The only extant returns from Camp Lawton were sent from Commander Vowels to Colonel Forno at Andersonville on 8 November 1864; Vowels reported that 10,229 prisoners had been received, 486

---

[21]Earl Antrim, *Civil War Prisons and Their Covers* (New York: Collector's Club, 1961) 205.

[22]*Official Records*, 2d ser., 7:993. Captain Vowels likewise voiced dissatisfaction with Georgia Reserves in a letter to Secretary of War Seddon, 12 November 1864. See A. and I.G.O. Register of Letters, October 1864-March 1865, vol. 70, chap. 1, National Archives.

[23]*Official Records*, 2d ser., 7:1051.

[24]Shanks *Report*, 162, 824, 1120.

deaths, 349 enlisted in Confederate service, 285 detailed at work, for a total on hand of 9,394 prisoners.[25]

On 10 November, General William T. Sherman and his army of 60,000 began their march to Savannah. Anticipating that both Andersonville and Camp Lawton would be likely objectives, Secretary of War Seddon alerted General Winder to be ready to remove and secure the prisoners if the enemy should threaten.[26] Even before he received this message, General Winder had already forwarded word to Seddon that General William J. Hardee, Commander, Confederate Forces of South Carolina, Georgia, and Florida, had ordered the 20,000 prisoners at Lawton removed to Savannah.[27] On 25 November, General Winder wrote General Cooper that all prisoners had left Lawton, that Captain Vowels remained behind to settle public business and that he would await further orders in Augusta.[28]

When the wings of Sherman's army joined at Milledgeville, Millen was designated as the next major objective. General Judson Kilpatrick's cavalry was commanded to cover the left flank and to rescue the prisoners at Camp Lawton. When passing through Waynesboro a few days later, Kilpatrick learned that the prisoners had already been evacuated. Sherman entered Millen Junction on 3 December, ordered the town burned, and continued the same day on his march to Savannah.[29] Camp Lawton, apparently completely abandoned, was left standing. In late January 1865, Winder notified Mrs. C. M. Jones, who had leased the prison site to the Confederacy, that the stockade was returned to her and that a government agent would be sent to settle outstanding accounts.[30]

---

[25]*Official Records*, 2d ser., 7:113-14.

[26]Ibid., 1144-45.

[27]Ibid., 1145.

[28]Ibid., 1155, 1160.

[29]William T. Sherman, *Personal Memoirs of General William T. Sherman* (New York: Charles L. Webster and Co., 1891) 2:190-93. For Sherman's route and orders of march, see Sherman's Operation Maps, 1-2 December, RG77, N59, National Archives Civil War Map File. For description of campaigns around Waynesboro, Buckhead Church, and Millen, see M. A. DeWolfe Howe, ed., *Marching with Sherman: Passages from the Letters and Campaign Diaries of Henry Hitchcock, Major and Assistant Adjutant General of Volunteers, November 1864-May 1865* (New Haven: Yale University Press, 1927) 120-35; *Official Records*, 1st ser., 44:363-68; and Earl M. Miers, *The General Who Marched to Hell* (New York: Alfred A. Knopf, 1951) 257-58.

[30]*Official Records*, 2d ser., 8:111.

With Union forces in close pursuit, the former inmates at Lawton were sent to Savannah. According to Colonel Henry Forno, commander of the operation to remove the prisoners from Savannah to Waresborough, some of the prisoners were paroled to Savannah, while others were sent to Thomasville. Defense considerations and transport difficulties necessitated that some 2,500 prisoners should be moved to a temporary stockade at Blackshear. Late arrivals in Savannah from Lawton were paroled aboard Union vessels or shipped to Florence, South Carolina. Forno wrongly assumed that Lawton would soon be reoccupied once Sherman's army had reached Savannah.[31]

Both Brigadier General John W. Geary, Commander, Second Division, Twentieth Corps, and Major George W. Nichols, aide-de-camp on Sherman's staff, recorded their visits to the stockade. Their accounts, however, are conflicting and offer little insight about the physical plan of the prison.[32] Camp Lawton was laid out in the customary style of Southern prison architecture, astride a valley through which a small but steady stream flowed. On either side were low sloping hills covered with pine thickets. The rectangular stockade was 1,398 feet on the north and south sides and 1,329 feet on the east and west; it enclosed a little more than 42 acres. The interior was divided into 32 divisions, each designed for 1,000 prisoners. Divisions were subdivided into ten sections that were supposed to hold 100 men, providing an average of 44 square feet per prisoner. Limestone springs furnished an abundant supply of fresh water. Flowing at the rate of about 25,000 gallons per minute, the stream entered the stockade near the center of the north wall and drained out the opposite side. The upper part of the stream near the mouth of the springs was used exclusively for drinking and bathing; near the center of the compound the stream was diverted to flush the camp latrines or sinks, a feature that remedied the disastrous sanitation problems associated with Andersonville. The entire stockade was surrounded by a wall of upright pine logs, approximately 15 to 20 feet high. A narrow catwalk near the top of the wall connected picket huts that were located approximately 50 feet apart. A dead line, marked by scantlings, encircled the inside of the prison. Double gates, wide enough for wagons, were located midway along the eastern wall. On high slopes to the south behind

[31]Ibid., 1st ser., 7:1204.

[32]Ibid., 1st ser., 44:274, and Miers, The General Who Marched to Hell, 258-59.

earthen ramparts, cannons were emplaced to control the stockade and its approaches.[33]

Personal recollections written by former inmates would appear to furnish the most reliable accounts of conditions in Camp Lawton and other Confederate prisons. However, scholars no less reputable than J. G. Randall and William B. Hesseltine have questioned the credibility of these sources. Purporting to be diaries of prisoners of war, many of these narratives followed the same format, recounted the same episodes, and obviously borrowed freely from partisan government publications.

According to these accounts, Camp Lawton resembled Camp Sumter (Andersonville) in its general appearance—a compound enclosed by palisades, with guard huts and a dead line. Unlike Andersonville, however, Lawton was relatively clean, spacious, and supplied by an abundance of fresh water. The absence of a swamp and the use of an innovative sanitation system made Lawton a healthier site.[34] Most inmates mentioned that the prison was constructed in great haste and that the logs, branches, and underbrush left inside were put to good use in building crude huts.[35] John W. Urban, Company D, First Regiment, Pennsylvania Reserve Infantry, ac-

---

[33]Plan of Camp Lawton shown in *Official Records*, 2d ser., 7:882. For description of the stockade, see Hesseltine, *Civil War Prisons*, 156-57; *Harper's Weekly* (7 January 1865); *Leslie's Illustrated Newspaper* (14 January 1865) and *The True Citizen* (Waynesboro GA) (20 April 1961) 12B, 13B. While there has never been an archaelogical study made of Camp Lawton, the site analysis prepared in 1975 by the Parks and Historic Sites Division, Georgia Department of Natural Resources, has estimated the location; See Townsend, "Camp Lawton," Appendix.

[34]Testimony of Alvin S. Graton, Company C, Twenty-first Massachusetts Infantry, Shanks *Report*, 850; testimony of Horace R. Rowe, Company H, Fourth Vermont Infantry, ibid., 840.

[35]W. H. Lightcap, *The Horrors of Southern Prisons During the War of Rebellion from 1861 to 1865* (Lancaster WI, 1902) 55-56; Willard W. Glazier, *The Capture, the Prison Pen, and the Escape* (Hartford: H. E. Goodwin, 1868) 316. Robert H. Kellogg, *Life and Death in Rebel Prisons* (Hartford: L. Stebbins, 1866) 390; H. M. Davidson, *Fourteen Months in Southern Prisons* (Milwaukee: Daily Wisconsin Printing House, 1865) 328-39; John W. Urban, *Battle Field and Prison Pen* (Philadelphia: Hubbard Bros. Publishers, 1882) 437-38; *A Voice from Rebel Prisons; Giving An Account of Some of the Horrors at Andersonville, Milan, and Other Prisons* (Boston: George C. Rand & Avery, 1865) 14-15; Asa B. Isham, et al., *Prisoners of War and Military Prisons, Personal Narratives of Experience in the Prisons at Richmond, Danville, Macon, Andersonville, Savannah, Millen, Charleston and Columbia* (Cincinnati: Lyman and Cushing, 1890) 361-68; John M. Gibson, *Those 163 Days* (New York: Bramhall House, 1961) 59-61.

knowledged that Lawton would have been a "credit to the South," if adequate food had been given to the inmates.[36] Hubert H. Taylor, First New Hampshire Cavalry, recalled that "Had men been in good condition when put in here (Lawton), they would not have suffered much except for hunger."[37] Private George H. Truell, Company A, Thirty-seventh Massachusetts Infantry, concurred that "There (Lawton) we were better off than at any place I was in in the Confederacy."[38]

When Lawton first opened, Robert H. Kellogg claimed that the rations were double those provided at Andersonville.[39] Several others recalled that the ration issue for 24 hours was typically a pint of corn meal, six ounces of uncooked beef, a few tablespoons of rice or beans, and a little salt.[40] According to H. M. Davidson, who worked in the slaughterhouse at Lawton, 35 scrawny cattle were butchered daily. After the officers and guards were fed, the prisoners got what remained.[41] John M. McElroy remembered that in the beginning prisoners were given only the heads or bones of the cattle which they boiled and later charred.[42] Cooking facilities were apparently never completed at Lawton and individuals or groups prepared their own meals.

When beef was in short supply, barrels of molasses were occasionally brought in. Ingenious inmates soon engaged in making taffy candy that was sold to new prisoners.[43] Both John L. Ransom and John W. Urban wrote

---

[36]Urban, Battle Field, 437.

[37]Shanks Report, 830.

[38]Ibid., 899.

[39]Kellogg, Life and Death in Rebel Prisons, 392.

[40]Glazier, The Capture, 318; Urban, Battle Field, 438; S. S. Boggs, Eighteen Months A Prisoner Under the Rebel Flag (Lovington IL: S. S. Boggs, 1887) 15; John McElroy, Andersonville: A Story of Rebel Military Prisons (Toledo: D. R. Locke, 1879) 458-59. John L. Ransom, John Ransom's Diary (New York: Paul S. Erikson, Inc., 1963) 163-64. Testimonies of Herbert H. Taylor, First New Hampshire Cavalry, Edgar Clair, First Vermont Cavalry, Julius H. Marvin, Company C, Fifth Vermont Infantry, Shanks Report, 830, 806, 824.

[41]Davidson, Fourteen Months, 336-37.

[42]McElroy, Andersonville, 458-59; also testimony of James Conway, First Massachusetts Heavy Artillery, Shanks Report, 922.

[43]Davidson, Fourteen Months, 331; Urban, Battle Field and Prison Pen, 444; Ransom, Diary, 163-64, passim.

that anyone with money could buy extras like tobacco and sweet potatoes from sutlers who were allowed to peddle their wares inside the gates.[44] Private James Conway, First Massachusetts Heavy Artillery, and Private Vincent Halley, Company C, Seventy-second New York Volunteers, reported to the Shanks Committee that they were nearly starved at Lawton and that they suffered a repetition of the cruelties of Andersonville, perhaps to a lesser extent.[45]

Prior to their arrival at Lawton, many prisoners were already debilitated by the deprivations of Andersonville. Further weakened by a scant and deficient diet and exposed daily to inclement weather, they frequently suffered and many died. Scurvy, diarrhea, and rheumatism were the most prevalent maladies.[46] W. H. Lightcap remembered that dysentery was the "dread of our lives."[47] Several mentioned that invalids who were strong enough to travel were periodically exchanged. H. M. Davidson recalled that a hospital was established in the southwest corner of the stockade even though it lacked shelter, blankets, and medicines; another hospital was opened outside the pen for the sick and dying. According to Davidson, "pale, haggard wretches starved and froze day by day." While the mortality rate at Lawton did not approach that of Andersonville, Davidson thought that approximately nine percent perished monthly.[48] Others estimated that 15 to 35 died daily.[49] Sergeant Harry R. Breneman, Company B, Fourteenth Pennsylvania Cavalry, testified that "It was a common occurrence to wake in the morning, finding the man next to you had died during the night." Michael Cooley, Fifty-ninth Massachusetts Infantry, compared the cycle to the steps of a ladder: "the men who were sick today . . . would be dead in the morning."[50] Lacking a death house, inmates collected and carried the dead to the

[44]Urban, *Battle Field and Prison Pen*, 445-46. Ransom observed, "A man belonging to the Masonic order need not stay here an hour." Ransom, *Diary*, 167-68.

[45]Shanks *Report*, 922, 945; Michael Cooley, Fifty-ninth Massachusetts Infantry, reported conditions "about the same as Andersonville," ibid., 892; R. C. Fisher, Company A, Fifth Indiana Cavalry, and Jacob I. Over, Company A, 184th Pennsylvania Volunteers, also described suffering at Lawton comparable as to Andersonville. Ibid., 1120, 1156.

[46]Kellogg, *Life and Death in Rebel Prisons*, 391.

[47]Lightcap, *The Horrors of Southern Prisons*, 59.

[48]Davidson, *Fourteen Months*, 332, 333.

[49]Kellogg, *Life and Death in Rebel Prisons*, 391.

[50]Shanks *Report*, 892, 1145.

prison gate daily. The bodies were then buried in shallow trenches near the stockade by a detail of the prisoners.[51] When the trenches were opened in 1867, a vault approximately 12 inches deep was uncovered. Bodies were laid side by side and strips of split logs were laid over them. A low mound of earth topped the shallow trenches.[52]

Many of the recollections described regular musters where recruiters would offer rewards, bounties, and land grants to those who would take an oath to the Confederate government. While their comrades considered enlistment a disgraceful act, several hundred prisoners risked dishonor and accepted rebel inducements that included a suit of clothes, several bushels of sweet potatoes, and $100 in Confederate scrip.[53] Another episode that recurred in several accounts involved a mock election held inside Lawton in November 1864. Ballot boxes were brought in and prisoners were encouraged to vote their choice. According to Robert H. Kellogg, Lincoln received 3,014 votes to 1,050 for McClellan.[54]

Unlike Henry Wirz, Vowels was considered a more humane commandant by his captives. John McElroy called him "the best of his class," and praised him for his "mildness and wisdom."[55] John L. Ransom referred to Vowels as "a sociable commander whose guards were not cruelly strict."[56] Vowels also won the gratitude of the prisoners by dealing effectively with the marauders who had victimized defenseless prisoners at Andersonville. Consequently, this menace never became a serious problem at Lawton.[57]

While serving at Lawton, Vowels requested promotion and sent to Adjutant General Cooper endorsements of his official character from

---

[51]Urban, Battle Field and Prison Pen, 441, 444.

[52]Cemetery Service Historical Records, Roll of Honor, 17:466-67.

[53]McElroy, Andersonville, 466-68; Kellogg, Life and Death in Rebel Prisons, 392-93; Glazier, The Capture, 318-21; Davidson, Fourteen Months, 334-35; James Conway, First Massachusetts Heavy Artillery recalled that Col. O'Neill offered inducements to prisoners at Lawton, Shanks Report, 922, other accounts 750-51, 850, 1050.

[54]Vote totals varied in the several accounts; the election is described in McElroy, Andersonville, 464; Urban, Battle Field and Prison Pen, 449; Ransom, Diary, 166-67; Lightcap, The Horrors of Southern Prisons, 59-60; Kellogg, Life and Death in Rebel Prisons, 393; Davidson, Fourteen Months, 334.

[55]McElroy, Andersonville, 456-57.

[56]Ransom, Diary, 163.

[57]McElroy, Andersonville, 462.

Generals T. A. Harris, J. L. Kemper, and J. H. Winder. Every endorsement attested to Vowels's character and general capability. General Winder submitted that "he would be much gratified if he could be made Lieutenant Colonel," a promotion of two ranks.[58] The only adverse criticism against Vowels involved the charge that he accepted bribes from prisoners seeking to be exchanged.[59] After the war Captain Vowels was listed among those who were charged with alleged cruel treatment of Federal prisoners. In the trials of the so-called "war criminals," Wirz was convicted and hanged; John Gee of Salisbury, James M. Duncan of Andersonville, and Dick Turner of Libby were found guilty and sentenced to prison terms. Captain Vowels, however, escaped trial and disappeared into anonymity.[60]

One of Vowels's last official acts before leaving Camp Lawton involved the removal of the prison records. Presumably, Vowels instructed Captain Cameron, a subordinate, to pack the records and take them to Waynesboro for shipment to General Winder in Columbia, South Carolina. Cameron delivered them in a wine box to the railroad agent at Waynesboro where they disappeared. Perhaps they were burned when Kilpatrick's men set fire to the depot. Strangely, a small box of blank books was later discovered by a Presbyterian minister in Savannah. Inside one of the books was the death register of Camp Lawton. He removed the pages and turned them over to the United States Christian Commission; the Reverend Edward P. Smith, secretary of the commission, forwarded this manuscript in 1865 to General Montgomery C. Meigs, Quartermaster-General of the United States. The list of 488 burials contained 391 names and 97 designated as "unknown." The numbers by the names most probably indicated the order in which the bodies were buried. The recurrence of the names of J. T. Shepherd and J. B. Northrup in the same numerical order on both the list and their respective headboards at Camp Lawton seemed to make the roster authentic.[61]

---

[58]Compiled Service Records of Confederate General and Staff Officers, roll 255.

[59]Ibid., 458. See testimony of Alvin S. Graton, Company C, Twenty-first Massachusetts Infantry, and Edgar Claire, First Vermont Cavalry, Shanks *Report*, 806, 850, and others.

[60]*Official Records*, 2d ser., 8:782-83: Hesseltine, *Civil War Prisons*, 245-46.

[61]*Honor Roll*, 17:466-68; U.S. Christian Commission, *Record of the Federal Dead Buried from Libby, Belle Isle, Danville and Camp Lawton Prisons* (Philadelphia: James B. Rodgers, Printer, 1865) 159-68. Office of Quartermaster-General, Cemeterial Files, Box 137, Reverend E. P. Smith to M. C. Meigs, 29 December 1865.

After the war, the quartermaster-general ordered the inspection of all burial sites where Union soldiers were interred. Lieutenant D. B. Chesley visited Camp Lawton in November 1865 and reported that 1,646 bodies (an erroneous count) were buried nearby in four trenches—three at Hack's Mill and a fourth near Mrs. Jones's mill pond. He reported that the burying grounds were not enclosed and were subject to desecration by livestock. Chesley recommended that the sites should be fenced, provided with head-boards, and that the "slightly buried" graves be re-covered with earth and stone.[62]

Nearly a year later, Colonel E. B. Carling selected a four-acre site for the Lawton National Cemetery at Lawton on the Augusta and Savannah Railroad and arranged for its purchase from Mrs. Caroline E. Jones.[63] Pursuant to orders from the quartermaster-general, the bodies of Union soldiers at Camp Lawton and surrounding sites were to be interred in the Lawton National Cemetery between 10 November 1866 and 23 February 1867. As best as can be determined, the new cemetery contained 748 graves—685 casualties from Camp Lawton and 63 others removed from around Waynesboro, Buckhead Church, and neighboring locations.[64] In late summer of 1867, Robert Wood was appointed superintendent of the cemetery.[65] Lawton National Cemetery was described as follows: "A substantial board fence, well white-washed, encloses the cemetery; and suitable headboards painted white, and lettered in black, have been erected at the graves of those who could be identified."[66]

Apparently, when the cemetery was enclosed, an area greater than that specified in the original deed was fenced, for which Mrs. Jones requested an additional $1,500. Rather than settle with Mrs. Jones, Brigadier General Rufus Saxton recommended the removal of the remains buried at Lawton

---

[62]Records of the Quartermaster-General, Files on Fort Lawton and Millen, Georgia, RG245, National Archives (hereafter referred to as RG245).

[63]F. G. Godbee (Lawtonville GA) to Major General Rucker, n. d., ibid. For plan of Lawton National Cemetery, ibid.

[64]*Statement of the Disposition of Some of the Bodies of Deceased Union Soldiers* (Washington: Government Printing Office, 1868) RG245.

[65]Robert Wood to General M. C. Meigs, 12 August 1867, RG245.

[66]*Roll of Honor* (1867-1868) 3:293.

to a national cemetery to be established near Savannah.[67] Subsequently, General Saxton negotiated contracts with J. P. Low of Charleston for the removal of Union dead from East Florida, Savannah, and Lawton to the National Cemetery in Beaufort, South Carolina. The contract stipulated that Low would remove remains and headboards from Lawton to be reinterred at Beaufort at the rate of $6 per body; the U.S. Government would furnish all rail transportation. This task was completed during February 1868. Lawton National Cemetery existed for approximately one year.[68] Beaufort National Cemetery, the final resting place for the casualties of Camp Lawton, was completed in 1868 and ultimately contained 9,072 Union dead.

A macabre tale relating to the removal of the remains to Beaufort appeared in the *Virginia Free Press* (Charleston, W. Virginia), 7 October 1869. According to accounts which cannot be verified, a local guide told the paper's correspondent that some of the so-called Union dead wore gray jackets or were bodies "snatched" from slave cemeteries. Contractors, anxious to count bodies for which they received $10 per corpse, "dug up men, then divided them, so that a $10.00 job, by separating arms, legs, and head, was made to pay 500 percent." "I should not wonder," the guide continued, "if some bummer's skull was at that gate and a big toe a clean half-mile away down in yonder corner."[69]

Camp Lawton thus passes into history—a Confederate stockade built, occupied, and abandoned during the last half of 1864. During its brief occupancy of ten weeks, more than 10,000 prisoners were confined there. Its cemetery held the remains of 748 Union dead. While most evidence seems to indicate that conditions at Lawton were an improvement over Andersonville, this prison was only a temporary reprieve for the captives who were all too familiar with the deprivations of prison life. Searching for some meaning to the atrocities of Civil War prisons, one returns to the question: What madness drives civilized people to war, fostering the need for places like Camp Lawton, Andersonville, Camp Chase, or Elmira? The tragic ep-

---

[67]General Rufus Saxton, 23 September 1867, endorsement to report submitted by Lieutenant Charles Kelley, 21 September 1867. RG245.

[68]General Rufus Saxton to General D. H. Rucker, 3 January 1868; Abstract of Contracts between General R. Saxton and J. T. Low, Office of the Quartermaster-General, Cemeterial Files, Box 137, National Archives.

[69]*Virginia Free Press* (Charlestown WV) 7 October 1869, Cemeterial Files, Box 137, National Archives.

isodes of unfortunate prisoners illustrate how accepted and humane practices, endorsed as valid by civilized foes, are compromised at the expense
of military necessity. Throughout the Civil War, prisoners were mere pawns
in the power struggle between the Union and Confederate governments.

The site of Camp Lawton is now a part of Magnolia Springs State Park
and except for the eroded earthen ramparts and a few historic markers that
tell the story of the prison, there are no reminders of the days of 1864. Nature has reclaimed its own. Recognizing the natural beauty of the landscape and springs, the state of Georgia has developed the site for recreation.
On the northeast slope stands a national fish hatchery. It is a quiet and
peaceful place—that stillness disturbed only in the minds of those who
know the past.

SEVEN

The American Missionary Association in Liberty County, Georgia: An Invasion of Light and Love*

THE CIVIL WAR HAD hardly begun before neo-abolitionists and philanthropists launched a social revolution to regenerate the South. Inspired with missionary zeal comparable to a religious crusade, they sought to redeem former slaves from ignorance and deprivation. This mission enlisted the support of numerous sectarian and nonsectarian freedmen's aid societies as well as the Freedmen's Bureau.[1] The American Missionary Association, organized in Albany, New York (1846), was actually the first agency to accept the challenge and the last to relinquish it. Established as a protest against the failure of other missionary societies to denounce the evils of slavery, the association was committed to Christian missionary and educational operations at home and abroad from its very inception.[2]

---

*Another version of this essay appeared in Georgia Historical Quarterly 62 (Winter 1978): 304-15, and is reprinted here with permission.

[1]Sources differ widely as to the number of these relief societies. Julius H. Parmelee listed 79 in his "Freedmen's Aid Societies, 1861-1871," Office of Education Bulletin 38 (1916): 299-300. E. Merton Coulter counted 366 separate societies and auxiliaries in The South During Reconstruction, 1865-1877 (Baton Rouge: Louisiana State University Press, 1947) 81. Also see Richard B. Drake, "Freedmen's Aid Societies and the Sectional Compromise," Journal of Southern History 29 (May 1963): 175-86; Henry L. Swint, The Northern Teacher in the South (Nashville: Vanderbilt University Press, 1941).

[2]For general studies of the American Missionary Association, see History of the American Missionary Association (New York, 1886); Augustus F. Beard, A Crusade of Brotherhood: A History of the American Missionary Association (Boston: Pilgrim Press, 1909); Harlan P. Douglass, Christian Reconstruction of the South (Boston: Pilgrim Press, 1909); Clifton H. Johnson, "The American Missionary Association, 1841-1861: A Study of Christian Abolitionism" (Ph.D. dissertation, University of Wisconsin-Madison, 1973); Richard B. Drake,

Originally nonsectarian, the association became the relief agency of the Congregational Church among the freedmen in the early 1860s. Dedicated to the attainment of equality for blacks, the association focused on the twin pillars of church and school. In Georgia, this philosophy led to the establishment of Atlanta University and Storrs School, Ballard Normal School in Macon, Beach Institute in Savannah, and numerous common schools scattered across the state.[3] As late as 1891, the association continued to operate 80 colleges, normal and graded schools in the South. Commonly, it established Congregational churches near its schools, and that same year, 28 Congregational churches for freedmen in the South were reported, the largest of which were the Atlanta First Church and the Dorchester Church near McIntosh in Liberty County.[4] But perhaps in no other place did the association have a more pervasive influence than in isolated, rural, and predominantly black Liberty County. Here Dorchester Academy and the New Midway Congregational Church profoundly affected the social fabric of an entire community.

The rediscovery of old Midway Church by the Reverend Giles Pease, an association missionary in 1868, awakened interest in Liberty County, a remote outpost of Congregationalism since colonial days.[5] The Midway dis-

"The American Missionary Association and the Southern Negro, 1861-1888" (Ph.D. dissertation, Emory University, 1957); James M. McPherson, *The Abolitionist Legacy: From Reconstruction to the NAACP* (Princeton: Princeton University Press, 1976), and Leon F. Litwack, *Been in the Storm So Long* (New York: Alfred A. Knopf, 1979).

[3]*History of the American Missionary Association with Illustrative Facts and Anecdotes* (New York, 1891) 88-95.

[4]Ibid. For broader treatments of black education, see Lance G. E. Jones, *Negro Schools in the Southern States* (Oxford: Clarendon Press, 1928); Horace M. Bond, *The Education of the Negro in the American Social Order* (New York: Prentice-Hall, 1934); Henry A. Bullock, *A History of Negro Education in the South from 1619 to the Present* (Cambridge: Harvard University Press, 1967); Ullin W. Leavell, *Philanthropy in Negro Education* (Nashville: George Peabody College for Teachers, 1930); Edward E. Redclay, *County Training Schools and Public Secondary Education for Negroes in the South* (Washington: John F. Slater Fund, 1935); Louise Ware, *George Foster Peabody: Banker, Philanthropist, Publicist* (Athens: University of Georgia Press, 1951); Doxey A. Wilkerson, *Special Problems of Negro Education* (Washington: Government Printing Office, 1939); Dorothy Orr, *A History of Education in Georgia* (Chapel Hill: University of North Carolina Press, 1950); and Richard R. Wright, *Brief Historical Sketch of Negro Education in Georgia* (Savannah: Robinson Printing House, 1894).

[5]Giles Pease to S. S. Jocelyn, 25 March 1868, American Missionary Association Archives, Georgia (hereafter cited as A.M.A. Archives, GA); C. L. Woodworth, "The Church of the Pilgrims—South: Lost But Found," *The American Missionary* 19 (September 1875): 202-207; "Liberty County, from Rev. James Porter, Savannah, An Old Congrega-

trict was originally settled in 1752 by religious descendants of a Congregationalist band who had migrated from Dorchester, England, to Dorchester, Massachusetts, to Dorchester, South Carolina, and thence to Georgia. About two years later (1754), they built the first Midway meeting house and incorporated the Midway Society. The church as spiritual guardian, aided by a society that managed the temporal affairs of the congregation, was the nucleus of the cohesive community. Although the original church was nominally Congregational, it was so far removed from New England theological centers that all but two of its pastors were Presbyterian.[6] In the decades that followed the Revolution, prosperous rice and sea-island cotton planters formed an indigenous aristocracy in the region. Perhaps the best exemplar of their breed was the Reverend Charles Colcock Jones, a planter-evangelist who dreamed of transforming Liberty County into a model biracial community.

An indication of the rigid moral standards of this community is found in the scarcity of mulattoes as reported in antebellum census returns.[7] However, the prosperity and stability of the society were swept away by the fratricidal conflict of 1861-1865. Before the conflict ended, war came to the home front leaving in its wake a devastated countryside and a demoralized populace.[8] In these troubled times the white membership of old Midway

---

tional Church Reorganized and Recognized, Interesting Services," *The American Missionary* 18 (October 1874): 141-42. *The American Missionary* was published by the American Missionary Association, 1846-1934.

[6]For an early history of Midway community, see James Stacy, *History of the Midway Congregational Church, Liberty County, Georgia* (Newnan GA: S. W. Murray, 1903); J. Edward Kirbye, *Puritanism in the South* (Boston: The Pilgrim Press, 1908); C. C. Jones, Jr., *The History of Georgia* (Boston: The Pilgrim Press, 1883) 1:491-501; Robert M. Myers, ed., *The Children of Pride* (New Haven: Yale University Press, 1972); Josephine Martin, *Midway, Georgia in History and Legend* (Savannah: Southern Publishers, 1936); Orville A. Park, *The Puritan in Georgia* (Savannah: Georgia Historical Society, 1929); Allen P. Tankersley, "Midway District: A Study of Puritanism in Colonial Georgia," *Georgia Historical Quarterly* 32 (September 1948): 149-57.

[7]Donald G. Mathews, "Charles Colcock Jones and the Southern Evangelical Crusade to Form a Biracial Community," *The Journal of Southern History* 41 (August 1975): 299-320. As late as 1922, Secretary Samuel L. Loomis, A.M.A., observed that students at Dorchester were darker and that there were no mulattoes among them. *The American Missionary* 76 (February 1922): 521-25.

[8]George A. Rogers and R. Frank Saunders, Jr., "The Scourge of Sherman's Men in Liberty County, Georgia," *Georgia Historical Quarterly* 40 (Winter 1976): 356-69 (another version of that essay appears in this volume); also Haskell Monroe, "Men Without Law: Federal Raiding in Liberty County," *Georgia Historical Quarterly* 44 (June 1960): 154-71.

Church attended daughter-churches at Walthourville, Flemington, Jonesville, and Dorchester that were affiliated with the Presbytery of Georgia. A new chapter in the history of old Midway Church, involving the American Missionary Association, was soon to begin.

The Freedmen's Bureau, a principal agency of radical Reconstruction, established several schools for blacks in Liberty County. Among these were Lodebar Plantation Schools taught by Mrs. H. A. Newell Hart and Homestead School at Golding's Grove that was under Mrs. Harriet Golding for several years.[9] The latter was the special project of William A. Golding, a black political leader who represented the county for three terms in the state legislature. Born the son of a slave who was a local Congregational minister, Golding led a faction of the black membership in the old Midway Church until the American Missionary Association entered the community. Golding, although poorly educated, was an ardent champion of education for his people. Initially, he secured funds from the Freedmen's Bureau to support Homestead School where his wife conducted classes for two years.[10] When the bureau ceased to operate, he turned to the association for assistance.[11] In April 1870, Golding sold one acre of land to the association for $30 "in trust for the purpose of a site for a school house to be used for the education of freedmen, and children irrespective of race or color."[12]

Miss Eliza Ann Ward from Monson, Massachusetts, a 45-year-old school teacher who had previously taught at Beach Institute in Savannah and Seybrook School on Hilton Head Island, was the first Northern teacher

[9]Mrs. H. A. Hart to Pastor of First Presbyterian Church of New Haven CT, 9 January 1870; Mrs. H. A. Hart to E. P. Smith, 23 February, 18 April and 16 May 1870, A.M.A. Archives, GA; Freedmen's Bureau Records, National Archives, Washington, D. C., Box 29; Letters Received, Orders Received, Reports: Savannah, 1865-1872; Miscellaneous School Reports, 4th District, Sub-district Savannah, Educational Report by Charles R. Holcombe, Agent in Hinesville, November 1868.

[10]Monthly school reports of Harriet R. Golding show 67 pupils in February 1869, 56 pupils in March 1869, and 55 pupils in April 1869; also, monthly school report of Jack Mallard, teacher of Hutchinson School. Freedmen's Bureau Records, Box 29.

[11]W. A. Golding to E. M. Cravath, 3 October 1870; A. N. Niles to E. M. Cravath, 2 December 1870, A.M.A. Archives, GA.

[12]Book Q, Liberty County Deed Records, 12, Liberty County Courthouse, Hinesville GA.

sent to Liberty County by the association. During her first term at Homestead School she reported an average attendance of 27 students in the un-
graded school and nearly 50 in sabbath school. Miss Ward returned for a
second term in 1871-1872 where she served as teacher, preacher, and physician to local blacks before her retirement at the end of the year.[13] After
the school stood empty for two years, the association sent the Reverend
Floyd Snelson of Sumter County, an alumnus of Atlanta University, to
preach and teach in Liberty County. Snelson was described by R. F. Markham, an association agent, as "a good man but overbearing, tyrannical, ob-
stinate, and severe to all who [did] not yield to his plans."[14] He arrived at
Golding's Grove in March 1874, and soon became embroiled in a factional
controversy over the use of the old Midway Church.[15]

In 1868 the Reverend Joseph Williams of Macon, a former slave who
had been ordained by the Hopewell Presbytery, organized a black Presbyterian congregation in the old Midway Church that claimed a membership
of 600 by 1875.[16] Williams was later joined by a white minister, the Reverend J. T. H. Waite, a graduate of Columbia Seminary, who served the
congregation until after the turn of the century. When the Reverend Aaron
Rowe, an association minister, visited Midway in April 1874, he was startled to find the Macedonian Presbyterian Church instead of a Congregational meeting. He wrote to the association that Congregationalism had
been "gobbled up by Presbyterianism."[17] Both Presbyterians and Congregationalists advanced claims for possession of the historic edifice. Pending
settlement of this controversy, Snelson opened school and conducted Congregational services at Golding's Grove. In June 1874, he reported to the
association that 80 persons had united to form a church. Meanwhile, Presbyterians and Congregationalists met in the Midway Church and agreed to
hold services on alternate Sundays. The controversy reached a climax in

[13]Reports of Homestead School, January, February, March 1871; E. A. Ward to E. M.
Cravath, 30 March, 30 November, 31 December 1871, A.M.A. Archives, GA. Also see *The
Twenty-Fifth Annual Report of the American Missionary Association* (1871) 53.

[14]R. F. Markham to M. E. Strieby, 1 December 1875, A.M.A. Archives, GA.

[15]Floyd Snelson to E. M. Cravath, 28 March 1874, A.M.A. Archives, GA.

[16]Stacy, *History of Midway Church*, 233-35; James Stacy, *A History of the Presbyterian
Church in Georgia* (Elberton GA: Press of the Star, 1912) 266.

[17]Aaron Rowe to E. M. Cravath, 18 April 1874, A.M.A. Archives, GA.

August when the Presbyterians locked the Congregationalists out of the building and later disrupted their meeting. The Snelson faction prosecuted the offenders for assault and disturbing a church meeting. The county court, however, refused to hear the case since the Congregationalists were not an incorporated body. Congregational leaders attributed their troubles to the political machinations of local white leaders who sought to divide and control the black vote.[18]

Having withdrawn from old Midway, the Congregationalists decided to build a new church. In December 1874, a notice in the *Hinesville Gazette* that the blacks near McIntosh were starting to erect a large church "with commendable zeal." "The building which is to be fifty feet long, and thirty-five wide, is located near Arcadia, the former residence of Rev. C. C. Jones, D.D. This enterprise, which is under the charge of the Congregationalists, has received material aid from the north."[19] Three months later Snelson reported to the association that the new church's foundation was laid. Progress on the structure was slow and the need for funds always pressing. The endemic poverty of blacks in the area meant that local effort was minimal since the price of every chicken and egg was saved to pay the annual installment for farm land. Northern assistance, however, trickled southward; a notable example was a gift of $308 donated by the Dorchester Church in Boston.[20]

Meeting in the original one-room building at Golding's Grove that would accommodate only 48 students, Snelson's school continued to grow in enrollment and reputation. William Golding, assisted by the local school commissioner, secured $300 from the Peabody Fund in 1875. Proud of this accomplishment, Golding reported to the association that the school was in a "healthy condition" and was accommodating 164 students. Snelson confirmed this growth in a report that his school was so large that about 60 pupils were kept out of doors.[21]

---

[18] Aaron Rowe to E. M. Cravath, 7 September 1874; Aaron Rowe to George Whipple, 11 September 1874; Floyd Snelson to M. E. Strieby, 10 October 1876, A.M.A. Archives, GA.

[19] Hinesville *Gazette*, 1 November 1875, found in A.M.A. Archives, GA.

[20] Floyd Snelson to M. E. Strieby, 13 October 1875, A.M.A. Archives, GA.

[21] W. A. Golding to E. M. Cravath, 23 March 1875; W. A. Golding to M. E. Strieby, 7 August 1875; Floyd Snelson to M. E. Strieby, 13 and 20 October 1875; R. F. Markham to M. E. Strieby, 1 December 1875, A.M.A. Archives, GA.

In those times the state of Georgia had but the merest apology for a common school system, according to an agent of the association. The state provided "no buildings and only half pay for teachers for half the children three months in the year." The Liberty County school commissioner's report for 1880 confirmed these inadequacies. The county supported 34 separate schools for 310 white students, and 32 other schools for 1,071 black students. The average monthly cost of tuition per pupil was 66 cents; the state contributed 47 cents of this amount.[22]

Obviously pleased with Snelson's achievements at Golding's Grove, the association decided to send him to the Mendi Mission in West Africa in 1877.[23] The Reverend E. P. Smith then arrived to serve the church that had grown to 240 members. He began a concerted effort to expand the school's facilities. The completion of the church, an enlarged school, and the hiring of a competent staff, Smith wrote to the association, could make Golding's Grove an "oasis of intelligence in all this dark desert of ignorance."[24] When the school enrollment increased by about 80 students, Smith was authorized by the association to negotiate a contract for $847.54 (without the nails) to build a new school to provide for recent growth.[25]

In late 1878, after little more than a year in Africa, Snelson returned to Liberty County to resume the pastorate and to build the school adjacent to the partially completed church on the old Sunbury Road. Snelson named the new school Dorchester Academy in honor of its Puritan lineage. The completed structure cost $1,100, most of which was contributed by the association. It was dedicated on 13 April 1879.[26] At the sixth anniversary of the "New" Midway Church that same year, Snelson reported that, including

---

[22]Thomas N. Chase to M. E. Strieby, 10 May 1878, A.M.A. Archives, GA; Liberty County, Minutes of the Superior Court (1876-1888) 338.

[23]"Reinforcement of the Mendi Mission," *The American Missionary* 1 (September 1877): 11.

[24]Seaborn Snelson to M. E. Strieby, 15 October 1877; Joseph E. Smith to M. E. Strieby, 4 and 19 February 1878, A.M.A. Archives, GA.

[25]Joseph E. Smith to M. E. Strieby, 8 and 11 November 1878, A.M.A. Archives, GA.

[26]R. F. Markham to M. E. Strieby, 26 November 1878, A.M.A. Archives, GA.; Floyd Snelson, "Midway Church—Dorchester Academy—New Church at Cypress Slash," *The American Missionary* 33 (June 1879): 172-74. For an interesting account of building a new church, see Thomas F. Armstrong, "The Building of a Black Church: Community in Post Civil War Liberty County," *Georgia Historical Quarterly* 66 (Fall 1982): 346-67.

those who had formed the original church, 337 persons had joined the congregation, 10 had been dismissed, 15 excommunicated, and 28 deceased, leaving 284 members "to continue the Christian warfare."[27]

During the decade of the 1880s, the association sent 12 Northern "school marms" to the Dorchester Academy. The teaching staff never numbered more that four for any year prior to 1890. Tenure was generally brief since few were willing to endure for very long the hardships and isolation associated with the assignment. Miss Elizabeth Plimpton from Walpole, Massachusetts, remaining longer than most others, taught at Dorchester Academy from 1884 to 1889.[28] When a Congregational evangelist visited Dorchester at Christmas in 1886, he was surprised to discover that Miss Plimpton had 72 students under her charge; Miss Bertha Robertson, 74; and Miss Minnie Dox, 84. "They are taxed to the utmost of their strength," he wrote, "and have turned away between 50-60 children."[29] The enrollment for January 1887 was 250; again 60 pupils were turned away.

For those Northern teachers and missionaries who sought a challenge, Dorchester Academy provided a unique opportunity. Most Liberty County blacks lived in crude log cabins located on small farms which they tilled in a "thriftless and slipshod fashion." Isolation, uncertain seasons, poor markets, low prices, and a vicious credit system combined to produce a "race needing and deserving all that Christian philanthropy [could] render." Poverty, ignorance, and superstition generated more of the same. With only the rudiments of agricultural technology, black farmers utilized all hands, young and old, to tend their patches of rice, corn, and sweet potatoes. Children were needed at home to drop the seeds, hoe the crops, do the chores, and to "scare off the rice birds," leaving little time for school from early spring to late fall. Some were kept away from school because of distance; many others could not afford decent clothing or tuition. Yet,

---

[27]Floyd Snelson, "Anniversary of Midway Church," *The American Missionary* 34 (October 1880): 304.

[28]Abstracted from field appointments printed in *The American Missionary* 35 (February 1881): 45; 36 (February 1882): 42; 37 (February 1883): 43; 38 (February 1884): 46; 39 (February 1885): 43; 40 (February 1886): 38; 41 (February 1887): 42; 42 (February 1888): 36; 43 (February 1889): 38; 44 (February 1890): 43. See also the *Annual Report* of the A.M.A. for respective years. *The Forty-Fourth Annual Report* 53 (1890) is the first to list five teachers.

[29]James Wharton, "Christmas at McIntosh, Georgia," *The American Missionary* 41 (February 1887): 51-52.

hundreds came from their cabins in the rice fields, turpentine swamps, and sawmill quarters. Some walked six miles morning and night to attend Dorchester Academy.[30]

The forty-second annual report of the association affirmed the need for expanded facilities at Dorchester.[31] The *American Missionary* described conditions at Dorchester as so crowded in 1889 that 119 pupils were crowded in a single room with one teacher while scores were turned away.[32] Snelson entreated the association to establish a boarding department at Dorchester to offer normal training for teachers. The need for teachers in the area was so urgent, he contended, that 28 of their students had been licensed to teach.[33] The association responded with a new building program at Dorchester and when school closed in May 1890, facilities had been expanded to include a new girls' hall, principal's home, and renovated school rooms for 250 students.[34]

During the summer of 1889 the "Christ craze" swept through the rice-growing district of Liberty County causing widespread social and economic disruption. Jacob Orth, alias Dupont Bell, a demented white drifter from Ohio, first appeared in June. Prophesying that the "day of Canaan" was coming on 16 August 1889, he convinced several hundred credulous followers that he had ordered a "cyar load of wings" for their ascension on the appointed day. Since wings would be distributed only to those who reserved them at $5 per pair, believers abandoned their families, farms, and jobs and joined Bell at his campground near Walthourville. Before the hysteria subsided, Bell and his immediate successor, Edward James, were committed to the state lunatic asylum. A new leader, Shadrack Walthour, who called himself "King Solomon," died under mysterious circumstances in the county jail in Hinesville. Ellen Roberts, the self-styled "Queen of Sheba," changed the craze into an innocuous voodoo cult. The Reverend James

[30]Fred W. Foster, "Dorchester Academy," *The American Missionary* 55 (May 1902): 231-33.

[31]"Forty-Second Annual Report of the Executive Committee," *The American Missionary* 42 (November 1888): 305.

[32]"Voices From the Field," *The American Missionary* 43 (June 1889): 152.

[33]*The American Missionary* 37 (October 1883): 307.

[34]Payson E. Little, "Dorchester Academy, McIntosh, Georgia," *The American Missionary* 44 (July 1890): 216.

Stacy, shocked by the excesses of the craze, namely, communal living, human sacrifice, assaults on non-believers, and phallic worship, chose to "draw the vail" over these activities in his popular *History of the Midway Congregational Church.*[35]

The association apparently exerted little influence in restraining the craze, mainly because the vast majority of local blacks were not associated with either Dorchester Academy or the "New" Midway Congregational Church. Instead, they attended independent churches that encouraged the expression of fervent emotionalism. Although Snelson opposed the craze, he had already resigned as pastor of the church to accept the principalship of Waycross Branch Institute in Ware County. Besides Snelson, Samuel McIver was the most influential black leader in the community, but as a state legislator he was so closely associated with the conservative white power structure that he exerted little influence among the alienated and politically apathetic blacks who followed the craze. William A. Golding, prominent black leader in earlier days, had moved to Savannah in the mideighties; he died in Liberty County in 1889. Since the Northern teachers were away during the summer, they exercised no constraint on the blacks. The Reverend Stacy, although never a supporter of the association, acknowledged that he knew of no pupils from the academy who participated in the craze.[36]

As Dorchester Academy entered the new century, its reputation as a "seat of learning" and "the college of Liberty County" spread throughout

[35]Stacy, *History of Midway Church*, 244-51; *The Savannah Tribune*, 15 June, 22 June, and 20 July 1889; *The Atlanta Constitution*, 24 July, 25 July, 27 July, 29 July, 31 July, 1 August, 7 August, 13 August, and 17 August 1889.

[36]Stacy, *History of Midway Church*, 251; *The Savannah Tribune*, 22 June, 6 July, 20 July, 7 September 1889, and 29 April 1893. The Reverend Floyd Snelson attended Atlanta University and preached at Andersonville, Georgia, before coming to Liberty County in 1874. Dorchester Academy and the Congregational Church nearby were fitting monuments to his labors for the next 15 years. In 1889 he moved to Waycross, Georgia, where he achieved new distinction as a school principal. During the 1880s, he was active in Republican Party politics, serving as chairman of the Liberty County Republican Party and as his party's nominee for Congress in 1888. He was one of Georgia's delegates to the National Republican Convention in 1888. During that same year he served as a county commissioner in Liberty County. Snelson's interest in politics continued on a less active level after he moved to Ware County. For notice of William Golding's death, see *The Savannah Tribune*, 3 August 1889; for McIver, *Brunswick Daily Advertiser*, 9 October 1889, *Darien Timber Gazette*, 3 August 1889, and *Thomasville Daily Times Enterprise*, 25 September and 26 October 1889.

coastal Georgia. The building program begun in 1890 continued and by 1917 the school, located on 105 acres of land, owned eight frame buildings, employed 13 teachers and workers, and enrolled 500 pupils.[37] Regular tuition was $4 to $6 per year.[38] Enrollment stabilized at 250 to 300 students for the next two decades.

While it was unlikely that the A.M.A. and the other freedmen's aid societies ever formulated a consistent educational philosophy, there appeared to be a general consensus that the cure for black "depravity" could be found in Christianity and the Puritan work ethic. Southern blacks should be taught how to live moral lives and earn the rewards of labor. At the core of what was called industrial education was a deliberate effort to inculcate the virtues of morality, thrift, industry, honesty, cleanliness, racial pride, and order—the essence of character. In addition to the three R's, instruction was given in agriculture to increase productivity, shop-training and domestic arts to promote self-sufficiency, and in religion, cooperative techniques, and community regeneration. The curriculum fostered land ownership and the improvement of rural life so as to create a contented, independent, and self-respecting yeomanry. Samuel Chapman Armstrong, son of New England and founder of Hampton Institute in Virginia, had developed such a program for young blacks that became the model throughout the South.[39]

---

[37]"Negro Education, A Study of the Private and Higher Schools for Colored People in the United States," Department of the Interior, Bureau of Education *Bulletin* 39 (1916) (Washington: Government Printing Office, 1917) 2:230-31.

[38]Ina H. Lewis, "Dorchester Academy, McIntosh Georgia," *The American Missionary* 71 (July 1917): 219-20.

[39]For provocative discussion of the "industrial education myth," see Elizabeth Jacoway, *Yankee Missionaries in the South, The Penn School Experiment* (Baton Rouge: Louisiana State University Press, 1980) 1-22, 252-67; James D. Anderson, "Education for Servitude: The Social Purposes of Schooling in the Black South, 1870-1930" (Ph.D. dissertation, University of Illinois, 1973); Robert C. Morris, "Reading, 'Riting, and Reconstruction: Freedmen's Education in the South, 1865-1870" (Ph.D. dissertation, University of Chicago, 1976); Luther P. Jackson, "The Origin of Hampton Institute," *Journal of Negro History* 10 (April 1925): 131-49; Frances Peabody, *Education for Life: The Story of Hampton Institute* (New York: Doubleday, Page, 1919); Stanley K. Schultz, *The Culture Factory: Boston Public Schools, 1789-1860* (New York: Oxford University Press, 1973); Donald Spivey, *Schooling for the New Slavery: Black Industrial Education, 1865-1915* (Westport CT: Greenwood Press, 1978); and Carter Woodson, *The Mis-Education of the Negro* (New York: AMS Press, 1973). White racial attitudes are discussed in George M. Frederickson, *The Black Image in the White Mind: The Debate on Afro-American Character and Destiny, 1817-1914* (New York: Harper and Row, 1971); August Meier, *Negro Thought in America, 1880-1915: Racial Ideologies in the Age of*

The program of uplift at Dorchester Academy incorporated many of the features of Armstrong's educational philosophy. With the development of a comprehensive program by 1900, educational work began in the kindergarten class and was not completed until the young black man or woman graduated from the normal department. Most students, however, dropped out along the way since few had the means, time, or motivation to complete the course of study. As explained by Professor Fred W. Foster in *The American Missionary*, academic instruction was but one part of the total educational experience that students received at Dorchester. "Everyone who *knows*, realizes that *training* is an equally important part of education and Dorchester students are trained from alpha to omega." Religious and moral training was strongly emphasized through Bible instruction, the Young Men's Christian Association and the Young People's Society for Christian Endeavor activities, a missionary society, weekly prayer meetings, and temperance education. In addition to the intellectual and spiritual training, manual work was required in the industrial shop for boys or in the sewing room for girls. Students were expected to maintain and repair buildings and grounds. Foster reported that a good New England housekeeper would be delighted with the orderliness and cleanliness of the students' dormitories.[40]

A typical day for the boarding students at Dorchester began with breakfast, cleaning of dormitory rooms for daily inspection, followed by manual work. At 8:30 A.M., students prepared for school, which began at nine when everyone assembled in the church for the morning devotional service; students then reported to their classrooms for daily recitations and regular examinations that continued until 3:00 P.M., except for an hour lunch break. After school there was time for manual labor and 45 minutes of recreation. Supper was served at 5:30 P.M.; then came a social hour until 7:00 P.M., which was followed by supervised study halls until 8:30 P.M. All lights were turned out at 9:30 P.M. According to Foster, "The colored folk are pastmasters in unpunctuality and dilatory ways"; he believed that being "com-

Booker T. Washington (Ann Arbor: University of Michigan Press, 1963); Idus A. Newby, *Jim Crow's Defense: Anti-Negro Thought in America, 1900-1930* (Baton Rouge: Louisiana State University Press, 1965); and Claude Nolen, *The Negro's Image in the South: The Anatomy of White Supremacy* (Lexington: University of Kentucky Press, 1967).

[40]Fred. W. Foster, "Dorchester Academy," *The American Missionary* 55 (May 1902): 234-35.

pelled to step to time" during school would correct old habits and encourage students to become prompt and orderly.[41]

During the 1920s the secretary of the association recommended that a department of scientific agriculture with a demonstration farm should be established at Dorchester to show what could be produced when low wetlands were properly drained, fenced, and cultivated. The A.M.A. already supported similar programs in North Carolina and Virginia.[42] Miss Elizabeth Moore, an able administrator and inspiring teacher who became principal at Dorchester in 1925, recognized that programs in scientific agriculture and stock farming were acutely needed to improve the productivity of the poverty-ridden black farmers.[43] Unfortunately these goals were never realized since funds and qualified personnel were always in short supply. The failure to introduce these programs represented a lost opportunity to meet the most basic economic needs of the community.

Perhaps the most significant changes at Dorchester during the 1920s and 1930s came as a result of a new self-help program initiated by Miss Moore. Whereas the school had depended almost exclusively upon A.M.A. assistance during the previous decades, Miss Moore mobilized community support and encouraged all students to contribute something, either money or farm produce, toward their tuition costs. In December 1925, she reported that local women's clubs had raised $56.46 to equip the dining room and kitchen and that local men were raising money to buy a gasoline engine. School patrons from Walthourville, in keeping with the new philosophy, leased a truck to transport 20 children to the academy. Graduates and friends of the academy organized an advisory board in 1928 to plan for future growth. Their first project was to begin a program of extracurricular

---

[41]Ibid., 236-37.

[42]Samuel L. Loomis, "Dorchester," *The American Missionary* 76 (February 1922): 521-25.

[43]Elizabeth B. Moore, "Letter from McIntosh, Georgia," *The American Missionary* 79 (December 1925): 353-54; Miss Moore was the first black as well as the first female to be named as principal, serving from 1925 to 1932. She was succeeded by Dr. J. R. Jenkins, who served from 1933 to 1940 and was successful in obtaining accreditation for the school. According to Mrs. Mary Baggs, who attended the academy in the 1930s, the entire faculty and student body were then black. Teachers and a large number of students boarded on the campus. Mrs. Baggs recalled studying homemaking, cooking, and gardening, in addition to academic courses. There were only ten students in her graduating class. Mrs. Baggs remembered Miss Moore as a strict principal who was obsessed with cleanliness and order. Interview with Mrs. Mary Baggs, Liberty County, Georgia, January 1976.

activities to publicize the academy and to promote community spirit. Mr. and Mrs. Richard Perry donated three and one-half acres adjacent to the school to be used as an athletic field. The advisory board soon raised $500 to pay for grading, fencing, and the construction of grandstands.[44]

When the county built a consolidated public school for black youth in 1940, the association encouraged the people of the community to continue their self-help program. The vacated academy was turned over to the newly formed Dorchester Center, Inc. Organizations that have used the facilities through the years include a credit union that has functioned since 1938, a farmers' union, the Liberty County Political Council, and the Dorchester Improvement Association. In the late 1960s the Southern Christian Leadership Conference and the United Church Board for Homeland Ministries conducted a Citizenship Education Project that was initially directed by the Rev. Andrew Young. Dr. Martin Luther King, Jr. was a frequent visitor to the center. In the 1970s, a summer youth program, a day-care center that served some 60 children and their mothers, and the Midway Nursing Home were organized by Dorchester Center, Inc.[45]

In 1955 the congregation of the New Midway Church, assisted by the United Church Board for Homeland Ministries, United Church of Christ, erected the present brick church located near the center. It is currently served by Dr. James A. Eaton, who is also dean of the graduate school at Savannah State College and Armstrong College. Many of its members are descendants of former slaves and alumni of the academy. Although the church membership is predominantly black, an increasing number of whites from Fort Stewart attend the services. The church choir is considered one of the finest in the region. Conscious of a rich heritage, the church and the autonomous center still embody the philosophy of the American Missionary Association—a mission of light and love.

---

[44]Moore, "Letter from McIntosh, Georgia," 353-54.

[45]United Church Board for Homeland Ministries, "Notes to Our Friends," No. 27 (June 1975).

Pictorial Sketches
of Coastal Georgia

Midway Congregational Church, Liberty County, Georgia. (Photographic collection, Georgia Historical Society.)

Botanist Stephen Elliott (1771-1830) who compiled, wrote, and published A Sketch of the Botany of South Carolina and Georgia. *Photo circa 1823.*

Charles Colcock Jones (1801-1863) was a Presbyterian clergyman, planter, and "Apostle to the Blacks" in Liberty County. (Charles Colcock Jones Papers, Tulane University Library.)

Bishop Stephen Elliott (1896-1866) was elected the first bishop of the Diocese of Georgia, Protestant Episcopal Church in 1840. (Original painting in Georgia Historical Society.)

Mary Jones Jones (1808-1864) was the wife of Charles Colcock Jones and the mother of Charles Colcock Jones, Jr., Joseph Jones, and Mary Sharpe Jones Mallard. (Charles Colcock Jones Papers, Tulane University Library.)

Exterior view of Camp Lawton, located near Millen, Georgia. (Harper's Weekly, 7 January 1865, p. 9.)

Benjamin Wright Darsey (1838-1921), native of Liberty County, who later published the memories of his confinement in Camp Chase, Ohio, as a prisoner of the Union Army.

Prison stockade at Camp Chase, Columbus, Ohio, 1862.

Christian Endeavor Hall, Dorchester Academy, McIntosh, Georgia (Liberty County). Circa 1902. (Photographic collection of The Amistad Research Center, New Orleans, Louisiana.)

Charging at the Head and Ring at speed, with sword in hand.

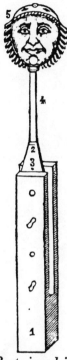 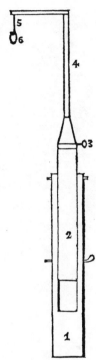

Gage Post viewed in front.

1. The body.
2. The slider.
3. A brass screw.
4. The staff of soft wood.
5. The head.

Ring Post.

1. The body.
2. The slider which can be fixed to any height.
3. A brass screw.
4. A triangle.
5. Hook to place the ring on.
6. The ring.

Head and ring used in cavalry drills, as described by George W. Behn, Concise System of Instruction, Arranged and Adapted for the Volunteer Cavalry of the United States *(Savannah, 1842).*

The flag, saber and scabbard, and block and ring used by the Liberty County Independent Troop, Hinesville Georgia.

"Turning Rice" at Hofwyl-Broadfield Plantation, 1893. (Hofwyl-Broadfield Plantation State Historic Site, Georgia Department of Natural Resources.)

"Picking Cotton." Circa 1900. (Photographic collection, Georgia Historical Society.)

"Dipping Tar." Turpentine production in Chatham County, Georgia. Circa 1920. (Photographic collection, Georgia Historical Society.)

"Uncle Billy's Ox," McIntosh County, Georgia. Circa 1920. (Margaret Davis Cate Collection, Georgia Historical Society.)

"Richmond," winter home of Henry and Clara Ford, Richmond Hill, Georgia. (Photographic collection, Georgia Historical Society.)

Mr. and Mrs. Henry Ford visit the elementary school in Richmond Hill, Georgia. Circa 1940. (Photographic collection, Georgia Historical Society.)

EIGHT

Eliza Ann Ward:
Teacher and Missionary
to the Freedmen*

DURING THE RECONSTRUCTION PERIOD, Americans experi-
mented with the most drastic changes ever attempted in their society. This
abortive revolution drew upon the noblest and basest of human motives and
spawned a myriad of solutions and panaceas. One of the most laudable and
ambitious endeavors undertaken was the attempt to meet the educational
needs of four million freedmen. "New England can furnish enough teachers
to make a New England of the whole South," one enthusiast proclaimed,
"[and] . . . we will not pause in our work until the free school system . . .
has been established from Maryland to Florida."[1] Numerous relief societies
and the Freedmen's Bureau enlisted corps of personnel and expended millions of dollars to accomplish this purpose.[2]

In the vanguard of this crusade was a legion of "Yankee school
marms"—mostly daughters of New England who came to regenerate the defeated South. Armed with Bibles and spelling books, they were earnestly

---

*Other versions of this essay appeared in the *Bulletin of the Congregational Library* 31:1
(Fall 1979): 4-11, and *Furman Studies* 26 (December 1980): 43-54. This material is reprinted
here with permission.

[1]Luther P. Jackson, "The Educational Efforts of the Freedman's Bureau and Freedman's
Aid Societies in South Carolina, 1862-1872," *Journal of Negro History* 8 (January 1923): 28.

[2]E. Merton Coulter, *The South During Reconstruction, 1865-1877* (Baton Rouge: Louisiana State University Press, 1947) 81, counts 366 societies and auxiliaries. Henry L. Swint,
The Northern Teacher in the South, 1862-1870 (New York: Octagon Books, 1967) 3-22, esti-
mates that five to six million dollars were spent during 1862-1870 to support teachers.

committed to free schools, their version of "liberal Christianity," and the Puritan work ethic. For their zeal they were praised by Northern reformers and scorned by Southern whites as meddlers and "nig teachers." These devoted women deserve the attention of historians as pioneers of education among the freedmen. They demonstrated, contrary to the then-popular racial theory, that their charges could be educated. Although the typical teacher taught only one year "at the South," some like Laura Matilda Towne, Elizabeth Botume, Abby Munro, and Martha Schofield gave decades of service.[3] Eliza Ann Ward was quite representative of these Northern teachers. She taught two years in Savannah, one year on Hilton Head Island, and two additional years in Liberty County, Georgia. She published no memoirs, but neither did the majority of her co-workers. Like many others, the record of her experiences lies buried in the records of the American Missionary Association.[4]

The war had hardly commenced when the association launched relief and educational work among General Ben Butler's "contrabands" by sending teachers to Fortress Monroe. The first day school for the freedmen was established there on 17 September 1861 by Mrs. Mary S. Peake, a "free woman of color." Beginning in 1862, this migration of Northern teachers turned toward the deep South. Several of these so-called "Gideonites" were

---

[3]An older study on Northern teachers in the South is Swint, *The Northern Teacher in the South*. For more recent interpretation of Northern teachers in Georgia, see Jacqueline Jones, *Soldiers of Light and Love: Teachers and Georgia Blacks, 1865-1873* (Chapel Hill: University of North Carolina Press, 1980). Jones, however, failed to mention either Liberty County or Dorchester Academy. The most interesting personal accounts by Northern teachers include Rupert S. Holland, ed., *Letters and Diary of Laura M. Towne; written from the Sea Islands of South Carolina, 1862-1884* (Cambridge: Riverside Press, 1912); Elizabeth Hyde Botume, *First Days Among the Contrabands* (Boston: Lee and Shepard, 1893); Matilda A. Evans, *Martha Schofield, Pioneer Negro Educator* (Columbia SC: DuPre, 1916); Mary Ames, *From a New England Woman's Diary in Dixie in 1865* (Norwood MA: Plimpton Press, 1906); Rossa B. Cooley, *School Acres, An Adventure in Rural Education* (New Haven: Yale University Press, 1930); and Elizabeth Ware Pearson, ed., *Letters from Port Royal Written at the Time of the Civil War* (Boston: W. B. Clark Co., 1906).

[4]Major sources on the American Missionary Association are A.M.A. Archives (microfilm, University of Georgia, Athens) and *The American Missionary* (microfilm, Georgia Southern College, Statesboro). Published studies include *History of the American Missionary Association* (New York, 1891); Augustus F. Beard, *A Crusade of Brotherhood: A History of the American Missionary Association* (Boston: The Pilgrim Press, 1909); H. Paul Douglass, *Christian Reconstruction of the South* (Boston: The Pilgrim Press, 1909); Richard B. Drake, "The American Missionary Association and the Southern Negro" (Ph.D. dissertation, Emory University, 1957).

in the first group that began the Port Royal experiment. John Murray Forbes, a Boston businessman who arrived at Beaufort with the first party, described them as "odd looking men with odder looking women." He wondered whether they were "the adjournment of a John Brown meeting or the fag end of a broken down phalanstery." Within the decade, this migration to the South swelled to more than 5,000. Most of these educational evangelists subscribed to the purpose of Charlotte Forten, a young mulatto teacher from Philadelphia, who stated that she had come South for the good she could do for her oppressed and suffering race.[5]

Religious and humanitarian interests were the major motives impelling Yankee teachers to come to the South. Fervent piety was their most singular trait.[6] In an advertisement for prospective teachers, the American Missionary Association emphasized that serious applicants must possess a true missionary spirit. They should be "prepared to endure hardness as a good soldier of Jesus Christ," and none should apply who were influenced by either "romantic or mercenary motives . . . poetry or pay . . . or because they have failed in the North." Since duties would be onerous and living conditions primitive, good health and stamina were essential. "This is not a hygienic association, to help invalids try a change of air, or travel at others' expense," the association bluntly announced. Culture, common sense, and character were qualities given high priority. Undesirable personal habits, such as "moroseness, petulance, frivolity and fondness for society," as well as addictions for "tobacco, opium, or intoxicating drinks," disqualified applicants. Recognizing the special difficulties in teaching freedmen, experienced teachers who were stern disciplinarians were preferred. The association paid male teachers $450 per year; women teachers received much less.[7] These meager salaries were supplemented by an occasional bag of corn or rice, a few eggs, or a squawking chicken brought by an eager student.[8]

---

[5]*History of the American Missionary Association,* 10-12; Willie Lee Rose, *Rehearsal for Reconstruction, The Port Royal Experiment* (New York: Vintage Books, 1964) 45-46. Edward L. Pierce, "The Freedmen of Port Royal," *Atlantic Monthly* 13 (September 1863): 298-307. For more details see Ray A. Billington, ed., *The Journal of Charlotte L. Forten* (New York: Collier Books, 1953).

[6]Swint, *The Northern Teacher,* 35-36.

[7]*The American Missionary* (July 1866) 151-52.

[8]Eliza A. Ward to H. W. Hubbard, 30 December 1877, A.M.A. Archives, Massachusetts.

The association encouraged Northern churches and organizations to sponsor and provide monetary support for a teacher. Individuals were solicited for contributions. Young women who were eager for an assignment understood that their chances were improved if they agreed to loan their salary to the association during their term in the South. Often the monthly salary was slow in coming and teachers complained about the delay.[9]

About 80 percent of these "missionary teachers" were women; half of them were under 30 years of age. Typically, they came from small-town or rural, middle-class families in New England or the Middle West. Their father was most commonly a clergyman, a farmer, or a skilled tradesman. More came from Massachusetts than from any other state. Nearly all had some training in a normal school, female seminary, or college, and many were experienced teachers. Except for her age, Eliza Ann Ward fitted this pattern. Most stayed only one year in the South, but some returned again and again. A few made it their life work.[10]

Excited by gifts of clothing and food, the novelty and awesome magic of the Three Rs, Bible verses, and hymns, freedmen of all ages flocked to common sabbath schools. One elderly black recalled that any shelter, corn crib, fodder house, or brush arbor served as a school house in those days and that these were filled with black children, packed as tightly as a sardine box. Laura Matilda Towne despaired over the limited cultural experiences of her students when she reported their answers to the following questions: "Who wrote the Ten Commandments?" "General Saxby"; "Who is Jesus Christ?" "Massa Linkum."[11] Elizabeth Botume, teacher at the Old Fort Plantation School, Beaufort County, became convinced that "needle and thread and soap and decent clothing were the best educators and would civilize them sooner than book learning." As Booker T. Washington observed, "It was a whole race trying to go to school. Few were too young, and none too old to make an attempt to learn. As fast as any kind of teacher could be secured, not only were day schools filled, but night schools as well."[12]

---

[9]Jones, *Soldiers of Light and Love*, 37-48; Eliza A. Ward to William E. Whiting, 20 February 1868, A.M.A. Archives, Georgia.

[10]Jones, *Soldiers of Light and Love*, 209-29.

[11]Holland, *Letters of Laura M. Towne*, 5.

[12] Botume, *First Days Among the Contrabands*, 236; John Hope Franklin, *Reconstruction: After the Civil War* (Chicago: University of Chicago Press, 1961) 108.

Sociology and politics were commonly incorporated into daily lessons, much to the consternation of local whites. Southern whites and radical Republicans alike were quick to recognize that the school and the church were vital agencies for controlling the votes of freedmen. Since teachers openly associated with freedmen and urged them to assert independence and equality, the reaction of Southern whites ranged from suspicion to violence. As crusaders for the new order who were both intolerant of and unfamiliar with Southern culture, teachers became prime targets of white frustration and hostility. While some few had their schools burned or experienced Klan-type violence, nearly all were subjected to social ostracism. One teacher observed that "Gentlemen sometimes lift their hats to us, but the ladies always lift their noses."[13]

Soon after the surrender of Savannah in December 1864, the initial plan to educate Georgia freedmen was developed by General William T. Sherman, Secretary of War Edwin M. Stanton, and a local committee of black ministers. Pursuant to their decision, the Savannah Education Association opened schools at Bryan's Slave Mart and Oglethorpe House in January 1865. According to an agent of the American Missionary Association, approximately 500 students appeared "like untrained animals, . . . without any idea of order or application." The association dispatched the Reverend S. W. Magill, a native Georgian who resided in Connecticut, and a number of white teachers to Savannah; thus the first Northern "school marms" came to Georgia. Within the year, eight schools supported by Northern relief societies and several private schools were in operation.[14]

The Freedman's Bureau, organized in March 1865, soon became involved in educational work. General Oliver O. Howard, head of the bureau, believed that education was the only effective and permanent means for establishing a free society in the South. Before its stormy career ended in 1872, the bureau founded more than 4,000 schools. While most historians either exaggerate the bureau's weaknesses or minimize its strengths,

---

[13]For Southern reaction see Swint, *The Northern Teacher*, 94-142; Jones, *Soldiers of Light and Love*, 78, 183, 188; and Jackson, "The Educational Efforts of the Freedmen's Bureau," 29.

[14]Willard Range, *The Rise and Progress of Negro Colleges in Georgia, 1865-1949* (Athens: University of Georgia Press, 1951) 3-7; Robert E. Perdue, *The Negro in Savannah, 1865-1900* (New York: Exposition Press, 1973) 72. John W. Blassingame, "Before the Ghetto: The Making of the Black Community in Savannah, Georgia, 1865-1880," *Journal of Social History* 6 (1973): 471.

they generally concede that education was its most successful venture. Closely collaborating with relief societies and local groups, the bureau supplied books, teachers, and funds. A good example of this cooperation occurred at Beach Institute in Savannah. On land acquired by the American Missionary Association, the bureau constructed the school building, and the Savannah Education Association erected a home for teachers. As the bureau recognized that Northern teachers could supply only a fraction of the number needed, it employed local teachers of both races and founded normal schools. Ballard Normal School in Macon, Storrs School in Atlanta, and Beach Institute in Savannah in time began to send black teachers into schools across the state.[15]

From its inception in 1867, Beach Institute was staffed by teachers sent South by the American Missionary Association. Among them was Eliza Ann Ward, who, inspired by missionary zeal, came to teach and save the freedmen. Her ancestry can be traced back to William Ward who migrated from England in 1639 and settled in Sudbury, Massachusetts. He soon became a prominent leader in the Congregational Church and a well-to-do citizen.[16] Nearly two centuries later, a descendant, Samuel Nichols Ward, married Betsy Pepper on 15 October 1822. The first child of this marriage was Eliza Ann, born 30 January 1825 on the Ward farm located on the Palmer road near Monson, Massachusetts.[17] Details of her childhood are lacking but, with a younger sister and four younger brothers, she must have experienced family responsibilities from an early age. She joined the Congregational Church of Monson in June of 1836 when she was 11 years old. Typically, she would have received catechetical instruction prior to joining the church. She probably attended Monson Academy, a local private school, although the records have not been found.[18]

[15]There is no monograph on the Freedmen's Bureau in Georgia. For information on the bureau in South Carolina, see Martin L. Abbott, *The Freedmen's Bureau in South Carolina, 1865-1872* (Chapel Hill: University of North Carolina Press, 1967); Range, *Negro Colleges in Georgia*, 17-18; Perdue, *The Negro in Savannah*, 71.

[16]William Read Cutter and William F. Adams, eds., *Genealogical and Personal Memoirs Relating to the Families of the State of Massachusetts* (New York: Lewis Historical Publishing Company, 1910) 3:1862.

[17]*Ward Family* (Boston, 1851) 11-12, 22, 37, 66, 114, 174, 223.

[18]*Records* of the Congregational Church of Monson cited in letter, Sylvia de Santis to George A. Rogers, 9 March 1977.

Eliza Ann Ward transferred to a different church in 1850 and moved to Newark, New Jersey, in 1853. She may have married since an "Eliza Ward, widow of Henry," was listed in the Newark City Directory for that year. She taught as Miss E. A. Ward at a "young ladies' school" in 1853-1854. From 1854 to 1858 she taught in Newark; at least two years were at the orphan asylum. She then left Newark and probably worked in Brooklyn and the New York City area. In 1861 she returned to Monson and rejoined her old church.[19] In the latter part of October 1867, she agreed to go south as a teacher for the American Missionary Association. Sponsored by the Congregational Church of Monson, she was a fervent Congregationalist, a staunch abolitionist, and an experienced teacher. En route she visited friends in New York, Brooklyn, and Newark, and arrived in Savannah late in November of 1867. Within a fortnight she discovered that it was difficult "to keep the colored children orderly." Eliza Ward was designated as a "Primary A" teacher who taught in both common and sabbath schools for a cash salary of $15.00 per month. The local teachers, excluded from white society, comprised a closely knit group that she called "the family." At the end of her first year, she returned to Monson for the summer.[20]

With the approach of a new school year, she requested that the association reassign her to Beach Institute. She added that the ladies of her church had already raised $100 to send her south for another year.[21] She returned to Savannah in November 1868 and joined the faculty at Beach Institute. Six monthly reports, meticulously completed, show an enrollment of 68 students in November, with a high of 76 in January, declining to 49 in May. Besides regular day classes, she taught night classes for adults and two mission sabbath schools.[22] Such was the normal load for most teachers. Undoubtedly, this caused many to complain and not a few to abandon the field. During the term, a squabble involving petty rivalry and charges of incompetence disrupted "the family." The superintendent, commenting on

---

[19]Letter, Sylvia de Santis to George A. Rogers, 9 March 1977; Newark City Directories, 1852-1858, cited in letter, Charles F. Cummings to George A. Rogers, 15 November 1977.

[20]E. A. Ward to E. P. Smith, 8 November and 12 November 1867, A.M.A. Archives, Massachusetts; 30 November 1867, A.M.A. Archives, Georgia.

[21]E. A. Ward to E. P. Smith, 16 July and 23 September 1868, A.M.A. Archives, Massachusetts.

[22]E. A. Ward, Monthly School Reports, Beach Institute, November, December 1868; January, March, April, May 1869; A.M.A. Archives, Georgia.

the fracas to the field agent of the association, noted that "there is a type of piety in our New England life, which I do not regard as the most natural and healthful, nor as the most genuine and useful." Exhausted and ill, Eliza Ward recuperated that summer in Monson.[23]

Five members of "the family" did not return to Savannah the next fall. Much to her disappointment, Eliza Ward was sent to Seybrook School on Hilton Head Island. Arriving at Port Royal Sound in the dead of night, she and her baggage were literally dumped at the landing. She soon learned that a school did exist, but also that there was no place for her to live. After the resident overseer ordered her from his house, she moved into a dilapidated building, mostly without doors and windows, no stove, and meager furniture. Except for the few necessities that were supplied by friends in Monson, she walked 12 miles to purchase common needs such as kerosene. Isolated among some of the most deprived blacks in the entire South, she had as her only white associate another teacher in a neighboring school.[24] Sufficient penance, one might assume, for excessive piety shown while at Beach Institute! Her monthly reports from Seybrook School showed 39 students in November, 81 in December, and a sharp drop in March as field work began. Her sabbath school, however, steadily averaged more than 40. During the winter she complained that "the children will not bring wood." She became so discouraged after 14 students withdrew that she wrote "they might about as well all leave." Again, she returned to Monson for the summer.[25]

Eliza Ward's next assignment was in Liberty County, where William Golding, a local black leader and member of the Georgia legislature, was struggling to maintain Homestead School at Golding's Grove. When support from the Freedmen's Bureau ceased, Golding turned to the American Missionary Association for support. The association responded by sending a reluctant Eliza Ward. A. N. Niles, principal at Beach Institute, observed that "Miss Ward . . . after two days sojourn here has gone on her way. I can't

---

[23]C. W. Sharp to E. P. Smith, 19 January, 3 March, 16 April, 30 April 1869, A.M.A. Archives, Georgia; E. A. Ward to E. P. Smith, 30 August 1869, A.M.A. Archives, Massachusetts.

[24]Ibid., 15 November 1869; 1 April, 7 April 1870, A.M.A. Archives, South Carolina.

[25]E. A. Ward, Monthly School Reports, Seybrook School, November, December 1869; January, February, March 1870; A.M.A. Archives, South Carolina.

say rejoicing and must not say muttering. I may say that dames so *Ancient* and honorable ought not to go so far from home in mid-winter."[26]

Arriving at Golding's Grove in mid-December 1870, she immediately opened her one-room school. Her highest enrollment that year was 39 students; sabbath school averaged about 50. Late in the term she suggested closing the school to escape the fevers and insects that drove local planters to inland retreats. Unlike the discouraged spirit who had passed that way in the fall, she was described by A. N. Niles upon her return to Savannah as "all smiles and sunshine . . . she thinks she has done good service in her field."[27]

Golding petitioned the association for Eliza Ward's return in 1871 and for the fifth year she returned to the South. She opened school in November and was amazed at the considerable reading ability of many of her children. She reported that in her absence four schools had been taught by students and that one of them had been granted a certificate to teach in Bryan County. Recognizing the tremendous religious and educational needs of the community, she urged the association to send a black missionary from "the Atlanta school" to show the people "the true light."

Eliza Ward retired that spring to Monson in poor health. In her declining years she continued to collect clothing, raise funds, and to solicit letters from Golding's Grove, a school obviously dear to her heart. She died 6 September 1900 at age 75 and was buried in the Monson cemetery.[28] Two years after her departure, the association sent the Reverend Floyd Snelson, an alumnus of Atlanta University, to Liberty County. Under his leadership the small one-room school grew into Dorchester Academy. By 1917 the school,

---

[26]W. A. Golding to E. M. Cravath, 3 October and 22 November 1870, A.M.A. Archives, Georgia; A. N. Niles to E. M. Cravath, 3 October 1870, and A. N. Niles to Miss Minnie _____, 16 December 1870, A.M.A. Archives, Georgia.

[27]E. A. Ward, Monthly School Reports, Homestead School, January, February, March 1871, and E. A. Ward to E. M. Cravath, 30 March 1871; A. N. Niles to _____, 3 May 1871; A. N. Niles to E. M. Cravath, 8 May 1871, A.M.A. Archives, Georgia. Also see *Twenty-Fifth Annual Report of the American Missionary Association* (1871) 53.

[28]W. A. Golding to E. M. Cravath, 1 August 1871; E. A. Ward to E. M. Cravath, 21 November, 30 November, 23 December, 31 December 1871; 29 February 1872, A.M.A. Archives, Georgia. E. A. Ward to Dear Friends, 11 May 1874; E. A. Ward to E. M. Cravath, 10 July 1874; E. A. Ward to H. W. Hubbard, 30 December 1877, A.M.A. Archives, Massachusetts; obituary notice in *Springfield Republican* (9 August 1900) 8; Sylvia de Santis to George A. Rogers, 9 March 1977.

now located on 105 acres of land, owned eight frame buildings, employed 13 teachers and workers, and enrolled 300 students.[29]

Northern reformers and Republican politicians, as well as Southern whites and freedmen, recognized that social progress, economic change, and the establishment of political power in the South would ultimately depend on who controlled the schools of the freedmen. Altruistic Northern teachers, expecting sudden and dramatic transformation, entered the fallen South to stamp out ignorance, racial prejudice, and poverty. Their presence added another element to an already crowded field of reformers, opportunists, and pragmatists. In spite of noble intentions, the promises of a great social revolution were thwarted. Freedmen were not given land, social equality, or political rights. Instead, they were abandoned to Bourbon regimes that left despairing blacks "to root hog, or die." As early at 1875 the leaders of the American Missionary Association acknowledged that "the joy that was felt . . . in the emancipation of the slaves, dazzled the imagination and blinded the mind to the immense complications involved in the new order of things." The president of a Baptist freedmen's school, realizing that a few years had not produced miraculous results, wrote that at first they "thought that the school and the mission might almost vie with the sword in the rapidity and completeness of their work." "These illusions have been dispelled," he admitted, "and the real nature of the work has become manifest. . . . A hurrah and a rush cannot effect anything permanent."[30] In his retirement, General Oliver O. Howard wrote that the educational work of the Freedmen's Bureau and the relief societies was merely the beginning.

It would be spurious to contend that Eliza Ward's five years of service significantly affected the plight of freedmen in Georgia and South Carolina. Nonetheless, she and hundreds like her launched a crusade of light and love to elevate former slaves. What they did was a noble representation of that common battle against ignorance and racial prejudice. Viewing the freedmen from a paternalistic and neo-Puritan perspective perhaps they did

---

[29]Floyd Snelson, "Midway Church—Dorchester Academy—New Church at Cypress Slash," *The American Missionary* 99 (June 1879): 172-74. See *Annual Reports* of A.M.A. for 1872-1875. Also "Negro Education, A Study of the Private and Higher Schools for Colored People in the United States" (Washington: Government Printing Office, 1917) 2:230-31. Department of the Interior, Bureau of Education, Bulletin no. 39.

[30]James M. McPherson, *The Abolitionist Legacy, From Reconstruction to the NAACP* (Princeton: Princeton University Press, 1975) 53.

contribute toward establishing the "Sambo" image. Because they were so rigidly culture-bound and convinced that blacks were universally corrupted by slavery, they were unable to recognize any positive values in black culture. Northern teachers as a group apparently were less racist than most of their generation since they believed that freedmen were inherently equal to whites. They were environmentalists who explained racial differences by citing the cultural deprivation of slavery. While they attempted to measure the progress of their students by "white standards," unlike the vast majority of Americans of their generation, they believed that freedmen were both capable and worthy of meeting those same standards. For them the best evidence for the validity of this philosophy was the performance of their students in freedmen's schools.

Even conservative historians of the Reconstruction era like Francis Butler Simkins and E. Merton Coulter, while conceding that these Northern teachers were both sincere and self-sacrificing, concluded that they reached only a small percentage of school-age freedmen, that support for their mission was inadequate and temporary, that many of the teachers were fanatics who contributed to the growth of racial prejudice, and that oftentimes the type of education they offered was abstruse and unsuitable for a people just emerging from slavery.[31] Critics have emphasized that freedmen soon lost their original zeal for education when exposed to rigorous classroom discipline. Teachers recognized this tendency among their students and often despaired over what they called "plantation bitters."[32]

Many of the makeshift schools started by Northern teachers soon closed. Several, however, were consolidated into the newly emerging state common school systems, along with their material assets in land, buildings, and equipment. Especially significant were the normal schools that continued to train several generations of teachers and ministers who became the leaders of the black race in the brutal decades of Jim Crow, lynching, and second-class citizenship. Beach Institute in Savannah, Eliza Ward's first assignment, continues today as an important unit in the Chatham County school system. Dorchester Academy, the lineal descendant of Eliza Ward's one-room school at Golding's Grove, was esteemed as the "college of Lib-

---

[31]Francis B. Simkins and Robert H. Woody, *South Carolina During Reconstruction* (Chapel Hill: University of North Carolina Press, 1932) 431-34; Coulter, *The South During Reconstruction*, 82.

[32]Rose, *Rehearsal for Reconstruction*, 366.

erty County" by local blacks. Graduating several hundred through the years, it served blacks of the region until it was superseded in 1940 by a public, segregated high school. The buildings and grounds are now owned by Dorchester Center, Inc. and serve as a day-care and community center for local blacks.

Perhaps the Northern teacher was praised excessively when she was called the "tutelary goddess of American freedom," but these pioneers of black education, in the true spirit of Christianity and humanitarianism, brought New England's finest gifts to the Southern freedmen. Their shortcomings stemmed not from want of zeal but from their failure to understand the culture and needs of Southern blacks. Many of their charges were too preoccupied with survival to benefit from instruction or naively believed that exposure to the classroom would transform their lives.[33] In an eloquent tribute, Dr. W. E. B. DuBois praised the Northern teachers for not trying "to keep the Negroes in their places," and for raising them "out of the defilement of the places where slavery had wallowed them."[34] Eliza Ann Ward shares this legacy.

---

[33]Ibid., 229. John H. Franklin, *From Slavery to Freedom, A History of Negro Americans* (New York: Alfred A. Knopf, 1974) 246.

[34]W. E. B. DuBois, *The Souls of Black Folk, Essays and Sketches* (Chicago: A. C. McClurg & Co., 1903) 100.

NINE

Black Dirt
and High Ground:
Agriculture in Nineteenth-Century
Liberty County, Georgia

LIBERTY COUNTY AGRICULTURE in the last century was characterized by two distinctive systems of farming. Prior to the Civil War a prosperous plantation-slave economy devoted to the culture of rice and sea-
island cotton thrived in the lowlands and swamps and along the tidal creeks
of the narrow coastal district. Subsistence farming and the raising of livestock prevailed in the pine barrens of the interior region. Reconstruction
ushered in a new era in labor-management relations, land tenure, and
credit that caused the demise of staple crop productions. Upland cotton,
turpentine, and sawmill operations took on a new significance as the majority of residents, both white and black, lapsed into marginal farming. Poverty and cultural deprivation replaced the prosperity and aristocratic life-
style of the old "slaveocracy."[1]

---

[1]Although there are standard works on Southern and Georgia agriculture, there are no
published studies of Liberty County agriculture. This essay is based primarily on U.S. Census schedules, courthouse records, and private collections. Especially useful works include
Lewis C. Gray, *History of Agriculture in the Southern United States to 1860* 2 vols. (Washington: Carnegie Institute of Washington, 1933); Roger L. Ransom and Richard Sutch, *One
Kind of Freedom, The Economic Consequences of Emancipation* (London: Cambridge University Press, 1977); Robert Higgs, *Competition and Coercion, Blacks in the American Economy
1865-1914* (London: Cambridge University Press, 1977); Charles L. Flynn, Jr., *White Land,
Black Labor, Cast and Class in Late Nineteenth Century Georgia* (Baton Rouge: Louisiana State
University Press, 1983); Gilbert C. Fite, "Georgia Agriculture Since the Civil War" (paper
presented at teachers institute, "Elites and Common Folks: A Comparative Study of Georgia
History and Culture, 1733-1983," Georgia Southern College, Statesboro GA, summer,
1983); James C. Bonner, *A History of Georgia Agriculture, 1732-1860* (Athens: University of

152 / Swamp Water and Wiregrass

Liberty County, like the rest of coastal Georgia, was heir to an agricultural legacy that combined the crops and farming methods of the American Indians, west Africans, northwestern Europeans, and transplanted settlers from neighboring colonies who were already seasoned to the new-world environment. From the Indians came crops such as corn (maize), tobacco, sweet potatoes, beans, squash, and pumpkin; slaves from west Africa brought peanuts, okra, and indigenous varieties of melons and squash. Europeans introduced their small grains—wheat, rye, oats, and barley. Rice may have existed as a wild plant along the coast, but the cultivated varieties were brought in from South Carolina.

Beginning in 1752, the settlers of the Midway district who migrated to Georgia from Dorchester, South Carolina, drastically changed Georgia agriculture by expanding commercial rice production and plantation slavery. Whereas the struggling colony had previously lacked both a staple crop and a cheap, dependable labor supply, it now adopted the plantation-slave system. Attracted by the virgin rice lands along the coastal rivers, South Carolina planters continued to expand their farming operations into Georgia after 1763. Indigo, the second major staple crop in colonial South Carolina, was never a significant crop in coastal Georgia. Sea-island cotton, however, was uniquely adapted to the soil and climatic conditions of the region. Other crops like corn and sugar cane were important locally, but rice and cotton were the premier cash crops throughout coastal Georgia in 1800.[2]

Rice culture in Georgia was concentrated along the Savannah and Ogeechee Rivers, in the Midway-Riceboro area of Liberty County, and

Georgia Press, 1964); Willard Range, A Century of Georgia Agriculture, 1850-1950 (Athens: University of Georgia Press, 1954); Robert P. Brooks, The Agrarian Revolution in Georgia, 1865-1912, bulletin 639 (Madison: University of Wisconsin, 1914); Enoch M. Banks, The Economics of Land Tenure in Georgia (New York: Columbia University Press, 1905); Ralph B. Flanders, Plantation Salvery in Georgia (Chapel Hill: University of North Carolina Press, 1933); Milton S. Heath, Constructive Liberalism: The Role of the State in Economic Development in Georgia, 1733-1860 (Cambridge: Harvard University Press, 1954); Ronald L. Davis, "Good and Faithful Labor: A Study in the Origins, Development and Economics of Southern Sharecropping, 1860-1880," (Ph.D. dissertation, University of Missouri, 1974); Frederick L. Olmstead, A Journey in the Seaboard Slave States, with Remarks on Their Economy (New York: G. P. Putnam's Sons, 1904) and Robert F. Myers, ed., The Children of Pride (New Haven: Yale University Press, 1972).

[2]Bonner, History of Georgia Agriculture, chs. 1 and 2; David R. Chestnutt, "South Carolina's Expansion into Colonial Georgia, 1720-1765" (Ph.D. dissertation, University of Georgia, 1973); Gray, History of Agriculture, 1:3-6, 95-104, 182-84, 277-97; 2:593-94, 721-39.

along the Altamaha River and its delta. Smaller centers were located on the Satilla and St. Marys Rivers to the south. Before the American Revolution, much of the rice was grown in the alluvial soil of the inland cypress swamps where the rice fields could be flooded as needed by releasing river water that had been impounded upstream during the high-water cycle. This gravity-flow system, involving an ingenious network of dams, sluice gates, and canals, was the common technique used in Liberty County until 1860. The shift to tidal swamplands along the Savannah, Ogeechee, and Altamaha Rivers that was already underway by the time of the Revolution harnessed the rhythm of the tides to flood and drain the fields. However, in Liberty County, the small rivers limited the use of this tidal-flow system. The basic cultivation techniques were the same, however, whether fields were flooded and drained by gravity or by tidal-flow.[3]

For the twentieth-century observer, it is difficult to comprehend the enormous investment in capital and labor to establish and operate a rice plantation. One can still observe the rectangular pattern of the fields at Woodmanston, a plantation laid out by Louis LeConte in the 1820s. A bank or levee, constructed to hold freshets out and retain the water during flooding operations, surrounded the fields. Inside the protecting bank, a ditch approximately eight feet wide and four feet deep was excavated for drainage and use as a waterway. A network of smaller ditches subdivided the enclosed field.

Commonly, crop rotation was practiced in rice culture. Cotton was grown between rice crops, or between rice and sugar cane. The preparations for planting rice thus depended on the preceding crop. If it had been

---

[3]James M. Clifton, ed., *Life and Labor on Argyle Island* (Savannah: Beehive Press, 1978); Virginia Reeves Gunn, *Hofwyl Plantation* (Georgia Department of Natural Resources, 1976); Hugh F. Grant, *Planter Management and Capitalism in Antebellum Georgia* (New York: Columbia University Press, 1954); E. Merton Coulter, *Thomas Spalding of Sapelo* (Baton Rouge: Louisiana State University Press, 1940); James E. Bagwell, "James Hamilton Couper, Georgia Rice Planter" (Ph.D. dissertation, University of Southern Mississippi, 1978) 164-200; Dale E. Swan, "The Structure and Profitability of the Antebellum Rice Industry" (Ph.D. dissertation, University of North Carolina, 1972); T. Addison Richards, "The Rice Lands of the South," *Harper's New Monthly Magazine* 19 (November 1859): 721-38; George K. Holmes, "Rice Crop of the United States, 1712-1911," U.S. Department of Agriculture, Bureau of Statistics, circular 34 (Washington, 1912); Arthur H. Cole, "The American Rice-Growing Industry: A Study of Comparative Advantage," *Quarterly Journal of Economics* 41 (August 1927): 595-643; James M. Clifton, "The Rice Industry in Colonial America," *Agricultural History* (July 1981): 266-83; Douglas C. Wims, "The Development of Rice Culture in Eighteenth Century Georgia," *Southeastern Geographer* 12 (May 1972): 45-57.

cotton, which was grown on raised beds, the field was leveled and cleared of debris and then flooded. If rice was planted successively, the fields were flooded after the harvest to float the loose debris which was removed and burned. Fields were generally kept dry during winter to allow birds to gather the pesky, volunteer "red rice." Early in March, fields were flooded briefly and then drained to germinate the remaining "red rice" that needed to be destroyed before the spring planting.

After the soil was prepared, trenches for sowing the rice were dug about four inches wide and 15 to 17 inches from center to center. Seeding ranged from one-and-one-quarter to three bushels of seed per acre. As soon as sowing was completed, the field was flooded. This flooding, known as the "sprout flow," lasted from three to six days or until the seed pipped. Water was then removed and the tender rice shoots were hoed. Fields were sometimes flooded again for several days to control weeds and grass. This was called the "point flow" and was avoided when possible. When the rice plants had put forth their fifth or sixth leaves, the fields were hoed again and flooded in the the the "long" or "stretch" flow. This flooding was done to kill grass and weeds, soften the earth, and protect the young plants from the birds. The water was then lowered until the rice tops barely showed. It was held at this level for 10 to 20 days and then drained. This was the most important of the flows and tested the expertise of the overseer. When the fields dried, two more hoeings followed. The final flooding, the "harvest" or "lay-by" flow, came when the fruiting shoots had formed on the stalks. For six to eight weeks, water was gradually raised to support the ripening grain. A week before harvest, the fields were drained. The ripened heads were then cut with a hook and stacked in the fields until they were hauled to the threshing area. A good yield was 70 bushels per acre, although continuous rice cropping on the same plot might reduce the yield to 45 or 50 bushels.

Preparing rice for market involved threshing, winnowing, grinding and pounding, and a final grading. Threshing removed the rice from the plant; winnowing separated the grain from the chaff; and grinding and pounding removed the hulls from the kernels. A final grading separated large kernels, small kernels, and flour. Most of these processes were done by hand, even though pounding machines were invented about 1787 and threshing machines became practical in the 1850s. When the costs of expensive machines were added to the value of the land, slaves, buildings, and draft animals, a minimal investment of $100,000 was easily reached; a capital value of $500,000 was not uncommon for large operations.[4]

Managing a rice plantation was a business enterprise that required constant attention to gates and dikes and the myriad problems associated with labor management and the natural hazards. Weather, crop diseases, insects, and rice birds (bobolinks) were anticipated risks. On large plantations, particularly where the owner was often an absentee landlord, the experience and efficiency of the overseer was a crucial factor in determining the success or failure of the crop. Whites tended to believe that blacks were physically adapted to working long hours under the scorching summer sun in the swampy rice fields. Although some slaves possessed a partial genetic protection against malaria, fevers, and flux, accidents took their toll in lost work hours.[5]

During the antebellum decades, sea-island cotton ranked second only to rice in commercial production in Chatham, Bryan, Liberty, McIntosh, Glynn, and Camden Counties. Although some cotton was grown in Georgia as early as 1734, sea-island cotton was introduced in 1786. The first seeds were sent from the Bahamas to Governor Josiah Tattnall, William Spaulding, Richard Leake, and Alexander Pisset. They planted the long-staple variety which subsequently spread throughout the coastal district.[6]

---

[4]For detailed descriptions of rice culture, see George A. Rogers and R. Frank Saunders, Jr., "The Impact of Rice Culture upon Antebellum Georgia," *An Introduction to LeConte-Woodmanston* (Institute of Community and Area Development, University of Georgia, 1978) 19-23; Clifton, *Argyle Island*, vii-xlvi; S. A. Knapp, "Rice Culture," U.S. Department of Agriculture, Farmers Bulletin 417 (Washington, 1910) 5-25; Alexander Gordon, "An Account of an Agricultural Excursion Made into the South of Georgia in the Winter of 1832," *The Southern Agriculturist and Register of Rural Affairs* 6 (1833): 298-304, 413, 416; Amory Austin, "Rice: Its Cultivation, Production, and Distribution in the United States and Foreign Countries," U.S. Department of Agriculture, Report 6 (Washington, 1893) 15-25.

[5]Albert V. House, Jr., "The Management of a Rice Plantation in Georgia, 1834-1861," *Agricultural History* 13 (October 1939): 208-17; Albert V. House, Jr., "Labor Management Problems on Georgia Rice Plantations, 1840-1860," *Agricultural History* 28 (October 1954): 149-55; Dorothy S. Magoffin, "A Georgia Planter and His Plantations, 1837-1861," *North Carolina Historical Review* 15 (October 1938): 354-77; James M. Clifton, "The Rice Driver: His Role in Slave Management," *South Carolina Historical Magazine* 82 (October 1981): 331-53; Sir Charles Lyell, *A Second Visit to the United States of North America* (New York: Harper and Brothers, 1849) 1:262-73.

[6]Charles W. Dabney, Jr., *The Cotton Plant: Its History, Botany, Chemistry, Culture, Enemies, and Uses* (Washington: Government Printing Office, 1896) 35-36.

Prior to the Civil War, the growing of sea-island cotton was essentially a hoe culture. Since the crop required good drainage, cotton was planted on raised beds in fields and bordered by shallow ditches. If cotton had been planted on the field the previous season, stalks and litter were collected and burned. Furrows were opened between the old beds in February; manure, marsh, mud, and guano in the later decades of the nineteenth century were distributed in the furrows that were then ridged and compacted in preparation for planting. In late March and early April, seeds were planted in hills at intervals of 12 to 18 inches. Germination took eight to 12 days and necessary replanting followed. The young cotton plants were gradually thinned through four hoeings until only one stalk was left in each hill. "Middle busting" and "hauling" gradually worked the soil around the base of the growing plants. Regular cultivation continued into July and occasionally into August.

Cotton plants commonly grew to a height of four to five feet; the first blooms appeared in mid-June and matured into "squares" and bolls in the intense heat of August. Picking commenced soon afterwards and continued into the late fall or until the entire crop was harvested. After weighing and temporary housing, the cotton was spread out in the sun to air and dry. Dust, sand, dirt, and leaves were then removed by hand or by a machine called the whipper, after which the cotton was ready for ginning. An average production was 300 pounds per acre.[7] Always able to command a higher price than upland cotton, sea-island cotton sold for 30 cents per pound while upland cotton brought 22 cents in 1805. A decade later, prices were 47 and 27 cents, respectively. The highest price on record for sea-island cotton was two dollars a pound in 1828. Production fluctuated erratically throughout the antebellum period; Georgia produced 13,729 bales in 1829; 4,225 bales in 1839; 1,560 bales in 1849; and 10,352 bales in 1859.[8]

---

[7]Ibid., 228-31; Gray, History of Agriculture, 2:675-80, 731-39; William H. Capers, "On the Culture of Sea Island Cotton," Southern Agriculturist 8 (August 1835): 401-12; John Couper, "On the Origin of Sea Island Cotton," Southern Agriculturist 4 (May 1831): 242-45; Thomas Spalding, "Cotton—Its Introduction and Progress of Its Culture in the United States," Southern Agriculturist 8 (January 1835): 35-46, 81-87; Thomas Spalding, "On the Introduction of Sea Island Cotton into Georgia," Southern Agriculturist 4 (March 1831): 131-33; U.S. Department of Agriculture, "The Sea Island Cotton of the South, Its History, Characteristics, Cultivation, Etc.," De Bow's Review series 3 (January 1867): 84-89; Alexander Gordon, "Account of an Agricultural Excursion Made into the South of Georgia in the Winter of 1832," The Southern Agriculturist and Register 6 (1833): 144-47, 159-62, 167-69, 243-48, 366, 460-66.

[8]Dabney, The Cotton Plant, 230-31.

Liberty County was one of the wealthiest rural communities in the antebellum South and farming supported virtually everyone. In 1850, only 24 persons earned their livelihood from manufacturing, which was valued at $4,737. Liberty County farms, farm machinery, and livestock were assessed at $985,564, or $492.34 per white resident. Much of the wealth in the county was invested in land and slaves. Jacob Walburg, owner of St. Catherines Island, was the largest landowner in Liberty County in 1860 with 19,000 acres. William B. Gaulden ranked second with 9,533 acres, and George Walthour was third with 9,000 acres. Two other planters owned acreages between 5,000 and 9,000 acres; seven held estates of 2,000 to 5,000 acres. Of those remaining among the 28 largest landowners, 12 owned from 1,000 to 2,000 acres, and four others had between 650 and 1,000.[9]

Although the white population of Liberty County grew slightly from 1,303 in 1790 to 1,705 in 1820, and upward to 2,284 in 1860, the slave population always exceeded that of whites and increased more rapidly. In 1790 the slave population for the county was 4,025 which increased to 4,973 by 1820; this count grew to 5,908 in 1850 and rose to 6,083 by 1860.[10] Of the 362 white families enumerated in the census of 1850, nearly 70 percent owned slaves; 23 percent of these, however, owned five or fewer chattels. Fewer than ten slaves were owned by 41 percent. Those owning 50 or fewer accounted for 90 percent of all slaveholders. Seven percent of the total slaveholders owned 51 to 100 slaves; nearly 4.5 percent owned more than 100. The five largest slaveholders in Liberty County in 1850 were George W. Walthour with 206; Roswell King, 141; John B. Barnard, 124; Joseph Jones's estate, 120; and Jacob Walburg with 118. C. C. Jones ranked seventh with 107 slaves. Liberty County, second in this category only to Chatham among the coastal counties, had 32 slaveholders in 1850 owning 50 or more slaves.[11]

---

[9]James W. Berry, "Growing Up in the Old South: The Childhood of Charles Colcock Jones, Jr." (Ph.D. dissertation, Princeton University, 1981) 54-56; Joseph K. Menn, "The Large Slaveholders of the Deep South, 1860" (Ph.D. dissertation, University of Texas, 1964) 2:739-42.

[10]*Ninth Census, The Statistics of the Population of the United States* (Washington: Government Printing Office, 1872) 1:21-22; *Compendium of the Tenth Census* (Washington: Government Printing Office, 1882) Part 1, p. 342; unpublished Slave Schedules, Seventh U.S. Census, 1850: Liberty County, Georgia; Berry, "Growing Up in the Old South," 61-62.

[11]Unpublished Slave Schedules, Eighth Census, 1850: Liberty County, Georgia.

A decade later (1860), 58 percent of the white families in Liberty County were slaveholders. Of these nearly 33 percent held five or fewer slaves; 47 percent owned ten or fewer. Planters owning 50 or fewer slaves constituted 88 percent of all slaveholders. Twenty-six families, nearly ten percent, had 51 to 100 slaves and seven families owned more than 100. George Walthour remained the largest slaveholder with 300, having added 94 slaves to his plantation labor force; Jacob Walburg increased his to 255; John B. Barnard, 132; Charlton Hines, 130; and William B. Gaulden had 122.[12]

Besides slave labor, Liberty County planters used horses, mules, asses, and oxen as beasts of burden. On the average, the 32 largest slaveholders in the county owned 8.4 horses, 5 mules/asses, and 8.5 oxen. Livestock raised for food included milk cows, other cattle, sheep, and swine. These large slaveholders averaged owning 33 milk cows, 73 head of other cattle, 41 sheep, and 31 swine. Plantations were nearly self-sufficient in producing food crops; production of corn averaged 1,511 bushels; sweet potatoes, 1,484 bushels; peas and beans, 385 bushels. Poultry, fish, game, and garden produce supplemented the basic diet of corn bread, grits, rice, salt pork, syrup, and yams.[13]

This plantation-slave system was an integral part of a complex and hierarchical socio-economic structure. At the top was a small privileged and aristocratic class composed of planters and their families. This was the smallest class. Alluding to this elite class, Mary Jones, wife of Charles Colcock Jones, remarked to her daughter in 1857, "Equality of rank and fortune prevails more generally in Liberty County than in any place I have seen."[14] Their commodious plantation houses hardly matched the popular image of antebellum Greek Revival mansions. Planters generally owned summer retreats at Dorchester, Walthourville, Flemington, or Jonesville where they resided from early May until the first frost to escape the insects and fevers of the swampy district. Others summered at the seashore or traveled in the North and abroad. Members of this class interacted socially with extensive visiting, letter-writing, and intermarriage. Literacy was high among both

---

[12]These statistics were calculated from data on the 32 largest slaveholders in Liberty County, 1860, found in Menn, "Large Slaveholders," 2:739-42.

[13]Ibid.

[14]Mary Jones to Mrs. Mary S. Mallard, 10 July 1857, in Myers, *Children of Pride*, 346-47.

sexes of this class and many of its members published treatises on agricul-ture, politics, religion, or literature. [15]

Perhaps the most renowned member of this local aristocracy was Dr. Charles Colcock Jones, owner of Arcadia, Montevideo, and Maybank Plantations and more than 100 slaves. A leading Presbyterian clergyman, Dr. Jones devoted his life to the moral and religious improvement of South-ern slaves, earning the reputation of "Missionary to the Blacks." He found time to write sermons, catechisms, pamphlets, *The Religious Instruction of the Negroes in the United States,* and *The History of the Church of God.* Another Liberty County planter, Louis LeConte, studied chemistry, mathematics, and botany. One of his sons became a physicist, another a geologist. Ste-phen Elliott, father of the first Episcopal Bishop of Georgia, owned plan-tations along the Ogeechee River in Chatham County and "The Desert" along Bull Town Swamp in Liberty County near Woodmanston. He and his nephew, William, managed about 5,000 acres on the Satilla River. Elliott served as president of a bank in Charleston and as a college trustee. He pub-lished two volumes of original botanical research and many articles for a lit-erary review. Other elite Liberty Countians distinguished themselves as pastors, educators, and public officials. [16]

Almost without exception this class controlled the political scene. They served in the state legislature, held local offices, and controlled both the grand and trial juries. George Walthour, whose public career spanned two decades, 1821-1841, served five terms in the Georgia House of Repre-

---

[15]Berry, "Growing Up in the Old South," 43-48; Myers, *Children of Pride,* 9-10; James Stacy, *History of the Midway Congregational Church, Liberty County, Georgia* (Newnan GA: S. W. Murray, Printer, 1951) 286-90.

[16]For biographical data on Charles C. Jones, see Myers, *Children of Pride,* 1567; Stacy, *Midway Congregational Church,* 145-46, 212-33; Berry, "Growing Up in the Old South," 17-30; Virginia F. Evans, comp., *Liberty County, Georgia, A Pictorial History* (Statesville NC: Brady Printing Co., 1979); R. Q. Mallard, *Plantation Life before Emancipation* (Richmond: Whittet and Shepperson, 1892); R. Q. Mallard, *Montevideo-Maybank,* or *The Family Life of the Rev. Charles Colcock Jones, D.D.* (Richmond: Presbyterian Committee of Publication, 1898); on the LeContes, see Myers, *Children of Pride,* 1592; Stacy, *Midway Congregational Church,* 135-36; Richard L. Anderson, *LeConte History and Genealogy* (Macon GA: R. L. Anderson, 1981); Stephen B. Barnwell, *The Story of An American Family* (Marquette MI, 1969); George A. Rogers, "Stephen Elliott, A Southern Humanist," in *The Humanist in His World,* ed. by Barbara W. Bitter and Frederick K. Sanders (Greenwood SC: The Attic Press, 1976) 116-33. For other distinguished Liberty Countians, see Stacy, *Midway Congregational Church,* 112-91.

sentatives and four terms in the Georgia Senate. Charlton Hines, founder of Hinesville, represented Liberty County nine terms in the state senate between 1828 and 1845. Three members of the Quarterman family collectively served seven terms in the lower house of the state legislature and one term in the upper house. Five members of the Baker family represented the county eight times in the legislature between 1819 and 1841. Among the relatives of C. C. Jones, Jr., his grandfather, two uncles, a great-uncle, and two cousins served in the state legislature. County offices were dominated by family names like Hines, Fleming, Quarterman, Baker, Bacon, and Way.[17]

Liberty County also had a sizable class of small landowners who engaged in general farming. In 1850, 30 percent of all white families in Liberty County owned no slaves; their number had increased to 42 percent by 1860. Utilizing family labor, these farmers grew corn, sweet potatoes, sugar cane, and patches of rice and cotton. These subsistence farms were most commonly located in the pine barrens of the interior. Among those who owned no slaves were the poor whites whom Joseph LeConte described as a "pale cadaverous people." These "pine knockers" or "crackers" squatted on wild lands where they planted small patches, supplementing their meager produce by fishing and hunting, sometimes even poaching their neighbor's cattle. Fanny Kemble called them the "most degraded race of human beings claiming an Anglo-Saxon origin that can be found on the face of the Earth."[18]

Fortune continued to favor Liberty County planters until the coming of the Civil War. Joining other Georgians, Liberty Countians supported secession and sent their finest sons to fight for the Confederacy. Safe behind the homefront until late in 1864, they experienced the scourge of Sherman's men for six weeks. Kilpatrick's cavalry foraged and plundered across the county leaving desolation in its path. After the departure of Yankee troops, Mary Jones perceived that the old order had passed; she despaired, "we are

[17]Berry, "Growing Up in the Old South," 70-75.

[18]Ibid., 58-59; William D. Armes, ed., The Autobiography of Joseph LeConte (New York: D. Appleton & Co., 1903) 17; Frances A. Kemble, Journal of a Residence on a Georgia Plantation in 1838-1839 (New York: Harper and Brothers, 1863) 182.

a desolate and smitten people." Agriculture, the foundation of Liberty County prosperity, was left prostrate after Sherman's destructive visit.[19]

Immediately after the war, the Freedmen's Bureau attempted to alleviate the suffering of blacks and whites and to bring order to the disorganized conditions. In addition to its relief work, the bureau also supervised labor contracts between the races. Confronted with local regulators and the united efforts of white conservatives, blacks in Liberty County struggled to survive and maintain their newly won freedom. Blacks, in spite of promises, had received no freedom dues—land, money, tools, or work animals. Legally, they enjoyed mobility and held property rights over their own bodies and such services as they might produce. The economic institutions of the post-emancipation era, however, operated to keep blacks dependent and landless, working as farm laborers or tenants. The little income that was generated beyond the bare essentials was siphoned away by a monopolistic credit system.

Blacks, in spite of their vulnerability, were never passive victims of exploitation and racial coercion. Liberty County blacks engaged in competitive processes under adverse conditions and were able to acquire land and protect themselves from some of the worse abuses of racism. Their trump cards were always the demand for black labor and their agricultural expertise, as well as their production. Profits could be made by mercantile operators who specialized in serving the needs of the blacks. In 1875, a field agent of the American Missionary Association noted that "The rice lands would all have to be given up if the colored people refused to work the land." An Ogeechee planter confided to the same agent that "if the Negroes knew their power, they could make the rice land not worth a dollar, and then buy them at their own price." Such was especially vital in a county where blacks outnumbered whites. During the abnormally bad crop years of 1865-1867, bureau agents decried the shortage of labor, the poverty of the area, and the

---

[19]George A. Rogers and R. Frank Saunders, Jr., "The Scourge of Sherman's Men in Liberty County, Georgia," *Georgia Historical Quarterly* 60 (Winter 1976): 356-69 (another version of that essay appears in this volume); Haskell Monroe, "Men without Law: Federal Raiding in Liberty County," *Georgia Historical Quarterly* 44 (1960): 154-71; also see Joseph LeConte, *'Ware Sherman* (Berkeley: University of California Press, 1938); Haskell Monroe, ed., *Yankees A'Coming* (Tuscaloosa AL: Confederate Publishing Co., 1959); Armes, *Autobiography of Joseph LeConte*; Mrs. Mary Jones in her journal, Montevideo, 3 January 1865, in Myers, *Children of Pride*, 1244.

flight of freedmen to Florida. Frances Butler Leigh of neighboring McIntosh County observed that there was scarcely a planter whose plantation was not mortgaged and whose crop was not the property of his factor; they planted on sufferance and lived from hand to mouth as best they could.[20]

The United States Commissioner of Agriculture reported in 1871 that the "rice planters were driven from the Carolina and Georgia shores during the war, labor was in a disorganized and chaotic state, production had ceased, and at its close, dams, floodgates, canals, mills, and houses were either dilapidated or destroyed, and the power to compel laborers to go into the rice swamps utterly broken." Coastal planters had their life-savings wiped out when Confederate money and bonds were declared worthless; their investments vanished with the emancipation of their slaves. In the long run, the physical destruction of the Civil War, as devastating as it was, proved less ruinous than the irreparable damage to the financial and merchandising system wrought by the disruption of credit and commerce. During the antebellum era, the success of the highly specialized staple system depended upon the effective management of slave labor and a profitable market for rice and cotton. Survival in the new order, however, depended upon the development of a new system of labor-management relations, a unique credit system, an improved technology, and a favorable price structure.[21]

The traditional views found in the standard studies by Banks, Brooks, and Range concerning post-Civil War agriculture held that the large antebellum plantations had been broken up in large measure by 1870.[22] This contention, however, does not appear valid for Liberty County. This assumption was tested by selecting the 18 largest slave-owning planters identifiable in the census of 1860 and then subjecting their holdings to an exhaustive chain-of-title search in the records of the county clerk and the probate judge of Liberty County. Since some of these planters owned several

---

[20]Letter, R. F. Markham to M. E. Strieby, 10 December 1875, American Missionary Association Archives, Georgia; C. Mildred Thompson, *Reconstruction in Georgia* (Savannah: Beehive Press, 1972) chs. 3 and 4; Frances Butler Leigh, *Ten Years on a Georgia Plantation Since the War* (London: Richard Bentley and Son, 1883).

[21]*Annual Reports of the U.S. Commission of Agriculture* (Washington, 1865-1888); Range, *Century of Georgia Agriculture*, 77-89.

[22]Banks, *Economics of Land Tenure*, ch. 2; Range, *Century of Georgia Agriculture*, 83-89; Brooks, *Agrarian Revolution in Georgia*, 41-45, 86, 94.

plantations, the total number of units exceeded 25. Only two of these, Arcadia, containing 1,799 acres, owned by Dr. C. C. Jones in 1860, and the lands of Peter Fleming, totaling 2,545 acres, were completely broken up. In each case, most of the purchasers of the subdivided tracts were black farmers; only two such purchases, however, occurred prior to 1876. Most of the sales date to the period 1876-1890. The heirs of the Thomas Mallard estate sold 11 small holdings ranging from 14 to 80 acres to blacks between 1876 and 1888. From only one other estate, that of B. A. Busby who owned 2,771 acres, is it possible to identify black purchasers. After the Busby heirs divided the family estate in 1873 they sold two tracts totaling 90 acres to blacks in 1881 and 1882.

In all the other holdings, the natural heirs either retained ownership collectively, sold to a single heir, or they sold all or portions of the family estate to outside purchasers who could usually be identified as white. The estates of the other planters adhered to this same pattern: Abiel Winn, 1,103 acres in Stedfield Plantation; Jacob Walburg, 13,000 acres on St. Catherines Island; William B. Gaulden, 5,245 acres in Rice Hope and Millhaven Plantations; Raymond Harris, 9,696 acres in Retreat and Hunter's Hall Plantations and other tracts; Joseph LeConte, 526 acres in Syphax Plantation; C. C. Jones, 2,641 acres in Montevideo and Maybank Plantations. In a statistical context, out of the 50,000 acres that represented the combined plantations of 18 major planters, blacks acquired about 2,300 acres, or less than five percent of the total, a minor part of the lands acquired by blacks in this period.[23]

One is confronted then with an apparent conflict: blacks did not acquire major quantities of land from the partition of the largest plantations, yet blacks had acquired over 45,000 acres in Liberty County by 1900.[24] By what means, then, did this substantial land transfer take place? In seeking an answer to this question, W. E. B. DuBois stated that Liberty County was by far the most interesting black county in Georgia. Perhaps blacks first acquired land in the county when General Sherman issued his celebrated field order that gave hundreds of slaves temporary possession of land on the coast

---

[23]Liberty County Deed Books, 1876-1890, Liberty County Courthouse, Hinesville, Georgia.

[24]W. E. B. DuBois, *Negro Landholder of Georgia*, Department of Labor Bulletin 35, printed in U.S. House Documents, 56th Congress, 2nd Session, 1900-1901 (Washington, 1901): 88:735-36; Banks, *Economics of Land Tenure*, 120.

and sea islands. According to DuBois, many of these holdings became permanent. Under the slave system, vast acreages of swamps and pinelands were considered by white planters to be unproductive or inaccessible, so freedmen were able to acquire these wild lands for nominal payments in money or services.

In an effort to further test the hypothesis that blacks acquired significant holdings from neglected or bankrupt plantations, individual blacks were identified in the census of 1880, and 20 individual black owners were traced in the Liberty County courthouse records. This sample, perhaps too small for a valid generalization, revealed that these 20 acquired land between 1872 and 1892.

One of the largest black landowners in Liberty County, Louis Blue, bought 466 acres at a sheriff's sale in 1880. Prince Stevens bought 33 acres in 1876 in an administrator's sale. Isaac and Maria Pinkney were granted a life estate in a tract by George McConnell in 1897 "in consideration of his love for them." Frank Elliott bought 50 acres from a Chatham County firm in 1878. Plenty James purchased 50 acres in 1888 from the Rev. T. S. Winn of Hale County, Alabama. Primus Jones bought 80 acres from Benjamin F. Allen and Sumner W. Allen who appear to have formed a land buying and selling partnership. Jupiter James bought 50 acres in 1892 from W. A. Fraser for $100. Conclusions from this small sample of black owners must be tentative at best, but it appears that blacks acquired land from land dealers, administrator and sheriff's sales, heirs who left the area, and from the small holdings of white farmers.[25]

Even though the ownership of the large plantations generally remained intact, the plantations ceased to be large commercial operations devoted to rice and sea-island cotton. Owners either reduced their operations, rented for turpentining or cattle grazing, or sold their timber to a sawmill company. Liberty County agriculture rapidly became characterized by small subsistence farms. In 1880 there were 1,209 farmers in Liberty County. Of these 62 percent were owners, 32 percent were renters, and only five percent were sharecroppers. Within these categories, blacks constituted 41 percent of all owners, 90 percent of all renters, and 75 percent of the few sharecroppers. Blacks owned 11 percent of the 225,946 acres of improved land in the county. While the mean for all owners of improved land was 32 acres, the

---

[25]Liberty County Deed Books, 1876-1890, Liberty County Courthouse, Hinesville, Georgia.

mean for black owners only was 14 acres. With the exception of the Louis Blue purchase in 1880, tracts of improved land of 100 acres or more were owned exclusively by whites. One can readily conclude that a majority of farms in 1880 were diminutive; there was a high percentage of ownership by both races; a significant class of renters, and a near absence of sharecroppers.[26]

On large and small holdings, the most widely planted crop was corn. Corn was a subsistence crop, consumed by humans as corn bread or grits, or fed to the draft animals, cattle, swine, and poultry. The most important cash crop in the postbellum period was rice, but it, too, was often produced for subsistence. Contrary to popular belief, rice culture reached a peak about 1880 and then began to decline. In 1880, Liberty County farmers planted 4,291 acres and produced 2,722,596 pounds of rice. In 1890 they planted 3,416 acres of rice to produce 1,842,542 pounds. This harvest exceeded that of 1860 when rice was planted on large-scale plantations and worked by slave labor. Whether planted for sale or home consumption, 75 percent of all farmers planted some rice in 1880. Of those farmers who planted rice, 64 percent were black. Blacks accounted for half of both the acreage and production. The average yield for Liberty County was 634 pounds per acre. Black farmers produced about 12 pounds less per acre. The 15th Georgia Militia District, the major rice-producing area of Liberty County in the antebellum period, continued to be the center of rice farming. This tidewater region, embracing Midway and Riceboro, contained 58 percent of all rice farmers in Liberty County, 61 percent of the acreage, and 72 percent of the total production. The average yield per acre in the 15th G.M.D. exceeded the county average by nearly 18 percent. Liberty County farmers who planted rice averaged 4.7 acres each. But this average is distorted since some farmers planted large acreages. Benjamin F. Allen, a white owner, planted 120 acres of rice and produced 180,000 pounds; Anderson Jones, a white renter, planted 85 acres, produced 144,000 pounds of rice; Louis Blue and William A. Fraser, black renters, planted 40 and 27 acres and harvested 36,000 and 35,000 pounds, respectively. A majority of all farmers who planted rice grew two acres or less.[27]

---

[26]Statistics based on the unpublished Agriculture Census, 1880: Liberty County, Georgia.

[27]Ibid., *Report on the Statistics of Agriculture in the United States at the Eleventh Census: 1890* (Washington: Government Printing Office, 1895) 427.

The elaborate system of canals, dikes, and sluice gates associated with antebellum rice plantations was impractical for small farmers. Instead, natural lowlands and fields on the edge of swamps were commonly planted in rice. The seed bed was prepared in the spring using oxen, and in mid-June seed was planted either in rows or broadcast by hand. Fertilizers were never applied. The crop was hoed during the growing season and watered by the regular rains. Rice was harvested in September, usually by women who used rice hooks. Gathering the stalks into sheaves, the rice was "cooked" in the field for drying; later it was brought to the barn where it was flailed and winnowed, after which it was ready for milling.

The great prosperity of the rice era ended in 1892, the year of the first major crop in the Southwest. The price of rice on the Atlantic coast at the close of the Civil War was about $2 per bushel on the plantations. The higher grades never fell below $1.50 per bushel prior to the 1890s when the price dropped to about 40 cents per bushel. In the same era, a shortage of skilled rice laborers and an accompanying rise in labor costs caused the profit margin to dwindle.[28] Blacks associated working in the rice fields with slavery, which meant that available skilled labor was reluctant to work the rice fields even for pay. The *Southern Cultivator* observed that the labor was too heavy for Cuffy now that he was his own master.

Changing agricultural patterns forced blacks to find new employment opportunities in the lumbering or turpentine industries which gave them credit at the commissary and money in their pockets. A series of devastating hurricanes in 1893, 1896, and two in 1898 sealed the fate of the surviving rice industry. In 1899 Liberty County farmers planted only 2,736 acres of rice to produce 1,125,308 pounds. Milled rice from Louisiana, available at the local store for a few cents a pound, displaced the home grown rice. Many factors, including disorganization of the black labor supply, declining fertility, shortage of capital, the opening of rice production in Louisiana, east Texas, and Arkansas, and losses due to hurricanes, combined to destroy this once profitable business.[29]

---

[28]"Rice Lands," unpublished typescript, Hofwyl Plantation papers, Darien, Georgia; James M. Clifton, "Twilight Comes to the Rice Kingdom," *Georgia Historical Quarterly* 62 (1978): 146-54.

[29]*Twelfth Census of the United States, Agriculture, Part II, Crops and Irrigation* (Washington: U.S. Census Office, 1902) table 56, p. 192.

Sea-island cotton was restricted to the coastal areas and offshore islands until about 1890 by the assumption that the region had the unique combination of suitable soil and climate. In 1860 Liberty County produced 2,405 bales, a yield never to be matched again. Always closely associated with slave labor, sea-island cotton required intensive cultivation from planting to harvest. In 1880, Liberty County farmers planted 2,097 acres to produce only 697 bales. Only two-fifths of all farmers planted cotton and of this number two-thirds were black. The Liberty County average for all farmers was approximately four acres. There was no appreciable difference in size of plantings for either race. For the entire county, the yield averaged about one-third bale per acre; black farmers averaged slightly less. Samuel E. Swindle, a white farm owner, planted 30 acres of cotton in 1880 and produced 15 bales; this was the largest acreage and production of any single farmer. Philip Terry, a white owner, planted 27 acres and harvested six bales; John B. Curry and Henry A. Swindle, white owners, both planted 25 acres and harvested five and nine bales respectively. Samuel Boggs, Sr., a black owner, planted 16 acres and harvested six bales; Dick Dixon, a black renter, planted 16 acres and produced only two bales.[30]

Undoubtedly, the changes in the labor system also crippled the sea-island cotton industry in Liberty County. The development of "Gordon C" or "Gordon Low Bush" seed, a coarser variety of sea-island cotton adaptable to the sandy pinelands of the coastal plains, met the requirements of the textile industry and thus replaced the older variety. In the postwar decades, the price of upland cotton on the New York Exchange dropped from 83 cents per pound in 1865 to as low as seven and two-thirds cents per pound in 1894. While the price of sea-island cotton did not fluctuate so dramatically, it did, however, drop from a high of 32 cents per pound in 1883 to 11 cents per pound in 1898. Liberty County farmers were either too poor or too backward to apply commercial fertilizers to cotton production. Like the rice industry, sea-island farmers suffered severe losses from the hurricanes of the 1890s. In 1900, Liberty Countians planted 913 acres of sea-island cotton and produced only 243 bales. The arrival of the boll weevil in the 1920s wiped out the industry completely.[31]

---

[30]U.S. Census Office, *Agriculture of the United States in 1860* (Washington: Government Printing Office, 1864) 27; statistics on cotton farmers based on unpublished Agriculture Census, 1880, Liberty County, Georgia.

[31]*Twelfth Census Agriculture, 1900*, 436; G. A. Gordon, *Sea Island Cotton*, Transactions, no. 82, National Association of Cotton Maufacturers (Boston, 24-25 April 1907) 9, 21; M.

168 / *Swamp Water and Wiregrass*

Throughout the late nineteenth century an acute shortage of draft animals existed in Liberty County. In the 15 years following the "requisitioning" of draft animals and the destruction of livestock during the Civil War, farmers only partially recovered. By 1880, there were about 2,000 draft animals (horses, mules, and oxen) for some 1,200 farms, averaging about one and two-thirds horse power, or its near equivalent, per farm. Black farmers owned about one-third of the horses and mules. Mules were especially scarce, costing between $120 and $180 each; barely one-eighth of all farmers owned one. Oxen were widely used. The census of 1880 listed 946 of the ponderous beasts, more than twice the count of 1860. Black farmers owned about two-thirds of these. Neal McQueen, a white owner, had eight oxen, the largest number owned by any single farmer; one ox was the most common. Presumably, oxen were cheaper and perhaps more efficient in the boggy lowlands of the county.[32]

Diversification, neglected by most Georgia farmers in this era, is demonstrated by the balance between livestock and crop production even on small farms in Liberty County. The swine population was replenished by 1880; four-fifths of all farmers had at least one pig. Black farmers owned an average of six head compared with 22 head for white farmers. Major swine growers in 1880 were William Shave, a white owner, with 99 head, and Samuel Monroe, Sr., a black renter, with 80 head. Cattle, cheaply maintained on wild lands, numbered 21,890 by 1880. Two of the largest cattle owners were Jacob Rauers of St. Catherines Island with 430 and William Shave with 330. Racial disparity was also pronounced in cattle ownership, since whites averaged owning ten times as many. Sheep raising, also widely prevalent in the county, supplemented the income of only a few farmers. There were 12,155 sheep in the county in 1880, more than double the number in 1860. While a few blacks owned sheep, the majority of sheep owners and all of the major producers were whites. Among these were William

---

B. Hammond, *The Cotton Industry, An Essay in American Economic History,* (New York: Macmillan Co., 1897) part 1, p. 358; James L. Watkins, *King Cotton, A Historical and Statistical Review, 1790 to 1908* (New York: James L. Watkins & Sons, 1908) ch. 5; table 15, p. 305; *Cotton Movement and Fluctuation, 1900-1905* (New York: Latham, Alexander & Co., 1905) 127. *United States Department of Agriculture Yearbook, 1921* (Washington: Government Printing Office, 1922) 323-406.

[32]Statistics on draft animals based on unpublished Agriculture Census, 1880, Liberty County, Georgia.

Shave, who owned 750 head; Thomas B. Hylton, Sr., 572 head; James W. Parker, 400 head; and James Clark, with 275 head. The two black owners with the largest herd of sheep were John Stuart with 135, and Will Ryals with 90 head; both farmers were sharecroppers. According to a manual issued by the Georgia State Department of Agriculture in 1875, sheep husbandry could be highly profitable. It estimated the average annual profit on capital invested in sheep in Georgia at 63 percent. The predatory dog remained the bane of the sheep farmer.[33]

Adjustments made by Liberty County farmers to the new conditions created by the passing of the plantation-slave system in 1865 generated an agrarian revolution. Reconstruction ushered in a new era that fostered marginal and subsistence farming, a type of peasant agriculture that impoverished blacks and whites alike. Most farmers turned to the production of rice, corn, sweet potatoes, and a few cows and hogs for home consumption in lieu of the commericalized crops of antebellum days. Though the largest plantations did not break up, farmers shifted to lumbering, turpentining, sheep, and cattle-raising. New conditions affecting owners and laborers promoted not only an increase in the number of farm units, but also the rise of tenancy. Unlike the black belt of the Georgia Piedmont, the sharecropping system never flourished in Liberty County. Renting, however, was quite common. The vicious crop-lien system that made independent farmers subservient to commission-merchants exploited both former planters and freedmen. One of the noblest and indeed most successful achievements of the era was the struggle by blacks to become independent landowners. It is remarkable that so many recently freed from slavery acquired more than 45,000 acres in 35 years.

Rice and sea-island cotton, the major crops of the antebellum period, ceased to be important by the end of the century. By 1899, rice was planted on only 18,000 acres in the entire state, a decline of 40 percent in a single decade. For both crops, special problems caused by changed labor conditions, declining profitability, shortages of capital, and competition from other regions forced abandonment. Draft animals, depleted during the war, remained in short supply in Liberty County well into the twentieth century.

---

[33]Statistics on swine, cattle, and sheep based on the unpublished Agriculture Census, 1880: Liberty County, Georgia; Georgia State Department of Agriculture, *A Manual of Sheep Husbandry in Georgia* (Atlanta, 1875); Range, *Century of Georgia Agriculture*, 106-107.

Livestock were more plentiful, but continued to be unimproved and scarce for most Liberty County farmers. Hand labor and mule power, virtually unassisted by mechanical implements, would continue to be the principal means of production until the 1940s. As in other parts of the state, institutional forces and the coercive manifestations of racism hindered capital formation, technological innovation, and industrial development in Liberty County. These impediments to economic progress, readily diagnosed by latter-day historians, seemed insurmountable to those Liberty Countians who had few opportunities to change or escape the system. Liberty County farmers entered the new century poor, isolated, and lagging behind most Georgians, and the rest of the country, in every area indicative of agricultural progress.

TEN

Charging Head and Ring:
Martial Spirit
and Chivalry
in Coastal Georgia

*The word chivalry comes from "cheval," a horse, and so
if a man was not mounted there was no chance to be chivalrous.
A seat in a buggy wouldn't do at all. It won't churn up heroism
like the canter of a horse. That [Age of Chivalry] was called
"the fantastic age of famished Honor," for honor was said to be
always hungry for a fight with somebody, and the knights started
out periodically to provoke difficulties. Happy for us this age
has passed away and the knights are unhorsed, but unhappily for
us, like a comet, portions of the tail still linger in the land,
and ever and anon some valiant knight shows up and strikes his
breast and exclaims, "Mine honor, Sir, mine honor!"*

—Bill Arp

THE TERMS, "MILITANT SOUTH" and "romantic South," epithets
applied frequently to the region, have been repeated so often they are accepted as truisms. Pundits and "South-watchers" consider militancy and
romanticism as indigenous to Southern culture as Greek revival architecture and mint juleps. Although historians have not yet produced a satisfac-
tory explanation of their origins, they concede that these traditions are
embedded in the history and mythos of the region.

In spite of statistics on Southern volunteers in past wars, the number of
military academies in the region, and the popular usage of "colonel" as a
title, one can hardly prove that Southerners are more militaristic, or possess more courage or better fighting qualities, than other Americans. Few
would deny, however, that in past conflicts Southerners have freely, and
sometimes heedlessly, rallied to defend their section or country. Their ardent and tenacious devotion to the martial spirit has been ascribed to an
exaggerated preoccupation with honor that supposedly fosters an inclina-

tion toward violence, an overly enthusiastic reading of Sir Walter Scott's historical romances, and the persistence of a frontier environment that ebbed within a generation of the Civil War. Others cite the hierarchical and authoritarian character of Southern society, the legacy of slavery, poverty, and the idealization of the "lost cause" that made defeat not only admirable, but morally superior to victory.[1] Wilbur J. Cash, author of the classic study, *The Mind of the South*, commented that in the years following the Civil War the heroes of Southern boys were the dashing Stuart, the daring Pickett, and the swift and terrible Forrest, "forever charging the cannon's mouth with the Southern battle flag."[2] The Southern ring tournaments and cavalry tilts that began in the antebellum decades and reached the climax of their popularity in the 1880s are often considered the most anachronistic expression of this penchant toward militarism and chivalry. Little wonder that the "Old South" has been viewed as the last stand of obsolete romanticism.

---

[1]Studies of the militant nature of the South include John H. Franklin, *The Militant South, 1800-1861* (Cambridge: Harvard University Press, 1956); Samuel P. Huntington, *The Soldier and the State: The Theology and Politics of Civil-Military Relations* (Cambridge: Harvard University Press, 1959); Marcus Cunliffe, *Soldiers and Civilians, The Martial Spirit in America, 1775-1865* (Boston: Little, Brown and Co., 1968) 332-84; John T. Graves, *The Fighting South* (New York: G. Putnam's Sons, 1943); also see James C. Bonner, "The Historical Basis of Southern Military Tradition," *The Georgia Review* 9 (Spring 1955): 74-85; Robert E. May, "Dixie's Martial Image: A Continuing Historical Enigma," *Historian* 40 (February 1978): 213-34; Robert D. Meade, "The Martial Spirit of the South," *Current History* 30 (April 1929): 55-60; John H. Napier, III, "The Militant South Revisited: Myths and Realities," *The Alabama Review* 33 (October 1980): 243-65. Rollin G. Osterweis, *Romanticism and Nationalism* (New Haven: Yale University Press, 1949), and William R. Taylor, *Cavalier and Yankee: Old South and American National Character* (New York: G. Braziller, 1961) are still useful sources. John Fraser, *America and the Patterns of Chivalry* (London: Cambridge University Press, 1982), explores the political implications of a fondness for chivalric values embodied in works of romantic fiction. Also see G. Harrison Orians, "Walter Scott, Mark Twain and the Civil War," *The South Atlantic Quarterly* 40 (October 1941): 342-59; and Hamilton J. Eckinrode, "Sir Walter Scott and the South," *North American Review* 206 (October 1917): 595-603.

In his recent study, Bertram Wyatt-Brown offers the thesis that honor, instead of the right to own slaves, was the driving force in the Old South. He argues that honor, the keystone of Southern morality, both preceded and outlasted slavery. The Southern code of honor endured because it was based on family-blood purity, hierarchy of color and social rankings, white male dominance, and white community judgment of individuals. Bertram Wyatt-Brown, *Southern Honor, Ethics and Behavior in the Old South* (New York: Oxford University Press, 1982).

[2]Wilbur Joseph Cash, *The Mind of the South* (New York: Vintage Books, 1968) 124.

During the colonial and antebellum periods, Southerners were born to the saddle. Undoubtedly, geography and settlement patterns contributed to the development of this horse-oriented society. The Southern lad, rich or poor, was hardly rid of his bib and tucker before he was mounted on horseback and trained to fire a gun. Whether overseeing a farm or plantation, trading in the local market, or riding a professional circuit as doctor, lawyer, or preacher, or visiting the nearest neighbors who were likely several miles away, Georgians conducted their day-to-day life in the saddle. The pine barrens of the wiregrass lands in the southeastern coastal plain, unlike the deciduous forests of the Ohio and Central Atlantic regions, were easily traveled by men on horseback. The thick layers of pine needles, aided by periodic fires, stunted any dense undergrowth. Along the causeways of the rice coast and the forest trails of the interior, planters, farmers, and cattle herders relied upon the horse. The hunt, horse race, steeplechase, and tilt were popular amusements and social affairs that afforded coastal Georgians opportunities to display their finest horse flesh and equestrian skills. A man's status was commonly measured by the quality of his mount. The universal love of horses, their use as draft animals and mounts, along with their attraction in sport and pleasure, promoted a local cavalry tradition.[3]

From its inception, Georgia was intended to serve as a military buffer to protect the southern frontier against the Spanish in Florida. The trustees envisioned a colony of sober and industrious soldier-settlers who would double as farmers and militiamen. General James E. Oglethorpe, throughout his ten years in the colony, was preoccupied with building forts, negotiating Indian alliances, and waging war against the Spanish.[4] Two weeks after their landing in Savannah, the first settlers held a militia muster, and before

---

[3]Samuel Carter III, *The Last Cavaliers, Confederate and Union Cavalry in the Civil War* (New York: St. Martin's Press, 1979) 2-7; E. Merton Coulter, *The Confederate States of America, 1861-1865* (Baton Rouge: Louisiana State University Press, 1950) 338-39; Mills B. Lane, ed., *The Rambler in Georgia* (Savannah: The Beehive Press, 1973) 140.

[4]For military origins of Georgia, see Larry E. Ivers, *British Drums in the Southern Frontier: The Military Colonization of Georgia, 1733-1749* (Chapel Hill: University of North Carolina Press, 1974); Kenneth Coleman, *Colonial Georgia: A History* (New York: Scribner's, 1976); Paul S. Taylor, *Georgia Plan, 1732-1752* (Berkeley: University of California, 1972); Clarence Ver Steeg, *Origins of the Southern Mosaic: Studies of Early Carolina and Georgia* (Athens: University of Georgia Press, 1975) 69-102; Daniel J. Boorstin, *The Americans, The Colonial Experience* (New York: Vintage Books, 1958) 71-96; and Milton L. Ready, "The Georgia Concept: An Eighteenth Century Experiment in Colonization," *Georgia Historical Quarterly* 55 (Summer 1971): 157-72.

three years elapsed, Oglethorpe had already divided the colony into two military districts. Georgia gained control over its own militia in 1737 and it soon joined British regulars and Indian allies in an invasion of St. Augustine that culminated in the War of Jenkins' Ear.

In 1749 the residents of Savannah and neighboring plantations, threatened by an Indian raid, organized a troop of horse militia led by Noble Jones and John Milledge. A second troop of horse militia was formed south of the Ogeechee River under the command of Captain William Francis in 1757. Governor Henry Ellis commissioned Captain Noble Jones as colonel of the First Troop of Horse on 26 March 1758, marking the origin of the coastal cavalry as a unified command. The original Savannah troop that disbanded in 1771 was revived in 1778 to defend the city against Tory invaders. The Second Troop, recruited from Sunbury and the Midway district, was reactivated in January 1776 as the St. John's Rangers under the command of Captain James Screven. Both troops fought against British regulars, Tories, and Indians until coastal Georgia fell to the British in 1778-1779. They remained inactive after the Revolution until 1785 when they were again reorganized to protect the coastal frontier from Indian raids.[5]

The passage of the Federal Militia Act in 1792 required all able-bodied male citizens who were between the ages of 18 and 45 to enroll in the state militia. The persisting Indian menace led to the organization of four new cavalry troops in Chatham, Effingham, Glynn, and Camden Counties in 1793. An act of the state legislature in December 1808 formally organized the brigades of cavalry as Georgia militia. Brigadier General Daniel Stewart of Liberty County was commissioned to command the brigade that was a combination of four regiments. The First Cavalry Regiment, commanded by Lieutenant Colonel Jacob Robinson, included the Liberty Independent Troop, the Chatham Light Dragoons, the Effingham Troop of Horse, the Glynn County Troop of Horse, and the Camden County Troop of Horse. Two new troops, the Chatham Hussars and the McIntosh Troop, were organized during the era of the War of 1812. Lieutenant Colonel John M. Ber-

---

[5]Special appreciation is acknowledged to Major Gordon B. Smith and Sergeant Norman V. Turner for sharing their research on coastal cavalry companies. See Smith, "First Squadron Georgia Cavalry, 1758-1861," Vertical Files, Hodgson Hall, Georgia Historical Society, Savannah; also his Unit Work Sheets on Liberty Independent Troop, Richmond Hussars, Beaufort District Troop, and McIntosh Light Dragoons. Sergeant Turner has written "Official Statement of Lineage and Battle Honors of Battery 'C,' 2nd Battalion, 214th Field Artillery Georgia Army National Guard, Springfield, Georgia" (22 July 1976, unpublished).

rien led the First Regiment to the "Plains of Darien" early in 1815 to support the withdrawal of troops threatened by British Admiral George Cockburn's landing on Cumberland Island. Unaware that the Treaty of Ghent had already been signed in December 1814, Georgians feared an attack on Darien and Savannah.[6]

At the close of the War of 1812, all of the coastal cavalry units disbanded except the Liberty Independent Troop. General Stewart resigned in November 1815 and the regimental organization lapsed for the next 43 years. The legislature, alarmed by the lack of an organized cavalry and the vulnerability of the Georgia coast, passed an act in 1818 to reorganize the cavalry. Four years later, yet another law was enacted that created one or more squadrons within the First Division, Georgia Militia. The Liberty Independent Troop and the Georgia Hussars, joined periodically by other units that fluctuated in and out of the organization, were the principal companies of the First Squadron reorganized in October by Colonel Berrien. During the next four decades the Darien Hussars (1824), the Glynn County Hussars (1831), the Camden Chasseurs of Horse (1836), and the Liberty Guards (1845), joined the squadron. The old First Squadron was the training command of the regiments that established the legendary reputation of the coastal cavalry in the Civil War.[7]

When war came in 1861 the local cavalry companies rushed to join the Confederate cause. Throughout the South the cavalry was regarded as an elite branch, with troopers expected to provide their own mounts and often their own weapons. As the war wore on, however, few of the romantic visions of the dashing cavalry survived the realities of combat. Commanders complained of jaded horses, shortages, casualties, and battle fatigue; cavalrymen began to suffer disrepute as "deadbeats" and "incorrigible horse thieves."[8] Governor Zebulon B. Vance of North Carolina complained that if God had a greater plague for the Confederacy than He had sent against Egypt, then "it must have been a regiment or so of half-armed, half-disci-

---

[6]Smith, "First Squadron Georgia Cavalry, 1758-1861."

[7]Ibid.

[8]Carter, *The Last Cavaliers*, 1-24. There is no study of Confederate cavalry comparable to works by Stephen Z. Starr on Union cavalry. See Starr, *Union Cavalry in the Civil War* (Baton Rouge: Louisiana State University Press, 1979, 1981). A useful treatment of Confederate cavalry is found in John K. Herr and Edmund S. Wallace, *The Story of the U. S. Cavalry, 1775-1945* (Boston: Little, Brown and Co., 1953) chs. 5-6.

plined Confederate cavalry."[9] General William T. Sherman, the scourge of Georgia, however, had a more estimable opinion of the rebel cavalry. "War suits them," he observed, "and the rascals are brave and bold to rashness. . . . They are splendid riders, first rate shots, and utterly reckless—the most dangerous set of men which this war has turned loose upon the world."[10]

Coastal and wiregrass Georgia raised more than a dozen cavalry companies that served in the Fourth, Fifth, and Seventh Regiments, Georgia Cavalry. The Fourth Regiment under Colonel Duncan L. Clinch, Jr., was recruited south of the Altamaha River. It served on the Georgia coast, in the Atlanta campaign, against Sherman on his march to the sea, and into the Carolinas. The Fifth Regiment, commanded by General Robert H. Anderson and Colonel Edward Bird, patrolled the Georgia coast, served in South Carolina, Florida, the Atlanta campaign, Tennessee, and back through Georgia into the Carolinas. The Seventh Regiment, whose commanders were William P. White, Joseph L. McAllister, and Edward C. Anderson, Jr., fought with Young's Brigade, Fitzhugh Lee's Divison, Army of Northern Virginia.[11]

Although the coastal cavalry companies were prohibited from reorganizing immediately after the Civil War, former members of the Georgia Hussars celebrated the seventy-eighth birthday of the unit in 1866; the Liberty Independent Troop and the Effingham Hussars were reactivated in 1872, and the McIntosh Dragoons reorganized in the spring of 1875. That same year the First Squadron, Georgia Cavalry, commanded by Major Edward C. Anderson, Jr., composed of all these units, was reestablished.[12] In 1886 there were eight cavalry companies in the state with a total enrollment

[9]Edmund C. Burnett, "Letters of a Confederate Surgeon: Dr. Abner Embry McGarity, 1862-1865," Georgia Historical Quarterly 30 (March 1946): 39; Coulter, Confederate States of America, 338-40.

[10]Cited in Carter, The Last Cavaliers, 7.

[11]Smith, "First Squadron Georgia Cavalry, 1758-1861"; Clement A. Evans, ed., Confederate Military History (Atlanta: Confederate Publishing Co., 1899) vol. 6; campaigns of Fourth, Fifth, and Seventh Regiments can also be traced in The War of the Rebellion: A Compilation of the Official Records of the Union and Confederate Armies.

[12]"Minutes of the Liberty Independent Troop" (unpublished); Richard C. Cohan, The Liberty Independent Troop (1979), unpublished manuscript, no pagination; Smith, "Unit History Work Sheet—McIntosh Light Dragoons"; Turner, "Military History of Effingham County," and "Lineage and Battle Honors of Battery C" (unpublished). Smith, "First Squadron Georgia Cavalry, 1758-1861."

of 393 troopers. The Savannah Hussars was the only black cavalry unit in the state. The First Regiment was reorganized and incorporated at a cavalry convention in Savannah on 24 July 1889 under the command of Colonel William W. Gordon. The authorizing legislation specified that a regiment should not consist of more than 12 troops. The First Regiment included seven of the ten cavalry companies in the state. Units included in the regiment were the Brunswick Light Horse Troop, the Effingham Hussars, Georgia Hussars, Liberty Guards, Liberty Independent Troop, McIntosh Dragoons, and the Screven Troop. The First Regiment was designated Fifth Regiment, Georgia Cavalry, and renumbered with wartime designation by legislation in 1890; however, in 1899, it resumed its old name.[13]

Even though most state militias had already taken the title of National Guard by the time of the Spanish American War, the Dick Act which passed Congress in 1903 superseded the Militia Act of 1792 and created a new National Guard designed to serve as a component of the Regular Army. The Guard was financed by federal and state funds, trained under the supervision of army professionals, and supplied and equipped by the Regular Army. According to new specifications, the maximum strength of a company was a hundred men—three officers, 16 noncoms, and 76 privates; minimum strength was set at 51 enlisted men. The cavalry squadron was to be made up of four troops, a total of 405 men. Governor Hoke Smith reorganized the Georgia militia to comply with the new regulations, effective after 21 January 1908.[14] Unable to maintain minimum manpower quotas and to comply with these changes, several of the coastal cavalry companies disbanded. In 1909 the annual inspection of Company C, Effingham, reported that the officers were inexperienced and the men were unmilitary in their uniforms and bearing. In spite of the poor rating they received on records, drill, and equipment, the inspector observed that the troopers rode

[13]*The Savannah Morning News* (12 August 1886) 5; (25 July 1889) 8; (21 November 1889) 2, 8; *Darien Timber Gazette* (27 July 1889); Smith, "Unit Work Sheet—McIntosh Light Dragoons"; *Georgia Laws, 1890-1891*, 2:194-95; *Georgia Laws, 1899*, Act. no. 377, 60-65.

[14]Walter Millis, *Arms and Men* (New York: Capricorn Books, 1967) 179-80; "An Act to Promote the Efficiency of the Militia, and for Other Purposes," 21 January 1903; "Proposed U. S. Code," Circular, War Department, 8 October 1903, Section 22, Cavalry; Governor Hoke Smith to Hon. Robert Shaw Oliver, Acting Secretary of War, 13 December 1907. Reorganization in accord with General Order no. 222, U. S. War Department, State Military Records, Department of Archives and History, Atlanta. Unit Orders, 1907, General Orders No. 1 (2 January 1907), ibid.

well. The next year the inspector recommended that the unit be disbanded. An inspection of Troop E, the Liberty Guards, in 1910 produced a similar report, even though the men were considered fine riders.[15] Allowing for the numerous reorganizations, only the Liberty Independent Troop and the Georgia Hussars have lineages that span from the colonial period to the present.[16]

In a social order where horses and cavalry were so highly regarded, romanticism, flavored by the novels of Sir Walter Scott, found an appropriate clime. The singularly most popular and romantic account of a ring tournament was the "Gentle and Joyous Passage of Arms" at Ashby de la Zouche described in *Ivanhoe*. Published in 1820, the fictive image of Scott's tournament captured the public's imagination, even though he had taken a poet's license in depicting a tournament during the reign of Richard the Lion-Hearted.

The origin of the tournament is obscure although it was most likely invented in France during the eleventh century out of the mock battles fought by noble youth. Jousts—single combats where mounted knights charged with lances in the lists—were often included in tournaments to honor the ladies. The quintain and running at the ring were practice exercises for the joust and were designed to perfect aim while remaining steady in the saddle. Originally a mere post or suspended shield served as the target in the quintain; later, however, a human form usually made to resemble a Saracen was mounted on a pivot. A misdirected blow would cause the target to spin around, dealing the novice a buffet by an attached sandbag or a smart blow by the dummy Saracen. Tilting, the exercise of riding with a lance aimed at a mark, was a later adaptation of the quintain that required dexterity of arm, accuracy of eye, and equestrian skill.[17]

---

[15]The McIntosh Dragoons disbanded 17 March 1905 and both the Effingham Hussars and the Liberty Guard no longer existed by 1910. Inspection Reports, Unit Orders 2-7, Adjutant General's Office, Atlanta. Smith, "Savannah Militia," 17-20.

[16]Sergeant Turner concludes that the Effingham militia was mustered into the service of the colony in June 1751. The Effingham Hussars unit was organized 3 July 1846. Undeniably Effingham County has had a militia organization for more than 230 years.

[17]Fraser, *America and the Patterns of Chivalry*, 32-83; on origins of tournaments, see Robert C. Clephan, *The Tournament, Its Periods and Phases* (London: Methuen and Co., Ltd., 1919); Charles Mills, *The History of Chivalry: Of Knighthood and Its Times* 2 vols. (Philadelphia: Carey and Lea, 1826); Richard Barber, *The Knight and Chivalry* (London: Longman, 1970); Jean Froissart, *Chronicles of England, France, Spain, and the Adjoining Countries, from the Latter Part of the Reign of Edward II to the Coronation of Henry IV*, trans. Thomas Johnes

The rules for conducting martial games have been attributed to Geoffrey de Prueilli of Anjou; however, the German emperor, Henry I, issued rules for a tournament at Magdeburg 150 years earlier. These brutal contests drew condemnation from the medieval church, and consequently the tournaments were regulated by royal ordinances. The presence of ladies, who generally awarded the prizes, tended to refine the contests which in time were restricted only to men of noble birth. The tournament, according to one scholar, "was the crucible in which the ideas of feudal chivalry took form and remained throughout the Middle Ages."

By the fifteenth century tournaments were ritualized. Combatants were administered an oath of chivalry, and contests were conducted according to strict rules with severe penalties for offenders. The tournament was discredited in 1559 when King Henry II of France was fatally wounded by the stroke of Gabriel de Montgomeri in mock combat in Paris. Surviving longest in Germany, the tournament lasted nearly six centuries. Although its positive impact is debatable, some historians contend that the tournament helped tame and civilize restless and underemployed feudal knights, inculcated respect, and fostered courtesy and honor. The increased efficiency of firepower led to the decline of mounted knights in warfare and transformed the tournament into a colorful pageant and sport.

Although there were numerous attempts to revive the tournament in the nineteenth century, its day had passed. French aristocrats held a tournament at Namur in 1828, and their British counterparts staged another at Eglington in 1839 that featured 35 knights in combat and the coronation of Lady Seymour as Queen of Beauty. The "Triumph" at Earl's Court, London, likewise created a temporary sensation in 1912. Belgians were no more successful at the "Pas d' Armes," conducted at Rathausplatz in 1905.[18]

Sparked by the contest at Eglington in 1839, ring tournaments were staged in Virginia at Gilmore Estate and Fauquier Springs the next year. William Gilmore has been called the father of the Southern tournament. As a tourist in Scotland in 1839, he attended the highly publicized tournament at Eglington Castle. The next year he sponsored a meet at his es-

(New York: American Book Exchange, 1880); Sidney Painter, *French Chivalry: Chivalric Ideas and Practices in Medieval France* (Ithaca: Cornell University Press, 1964).

[18]Clephan, *The Tournament, Its Periods and Phases*, 1-16, 38, 47, 126, 138-39, 142-45. Louis Napoleon attended in the Eglington tournament that attracted more than 10,000 spectators.

tate, "The Vineyard," located in the environs of Baltimore. This event, modeled after the Eglington extravaganza, set the standard in rules and costumes for subsequent tournaments conducted in the United States. By the end of the decade, other resorts in Virginia were sponsoring ring tournaments, mainly as commercial attractions to draw large crowds to their watering places. Warren, Virginia, became the center for the sport in the South. Promotion and profit, rather than the insatiable hunger for the glories of a bygone age discovered in Scott's novels, offer an alternative explanation to the origin of Southern ring tournaments.[19] But who can say that antebellum Southerners did not also see themselves mirrored in the culture of the Saxons who refused to bow to the more sophisticated and dominant Normans?

The ring tournament was developed more elaborately in the South Carolina low country than anywhere else outside Virginia and Maryland. The spectacular tournament held in April 1851 at Pineville was replete with plumed knights who assumed romantic names like the "Knight of Eutaw" and the "Knight of the South," dashing and gaily caparisoned steeds, a Queen of Love and Beauty, and a moonlight ball. Herbert R. Sass idealized this romantic dreamworld of plantation pageantry in *Adventures in Green Places* (1935).[20] Realistically, the ring tournament was little more than delightful mimicry and cannot be construed as military except in the sense that any horsemanship competition was cavalry training, and any athletic contest a preparation for military discipline. A spirit of rivalry definitely pervaded the contests, but the ardor of combat never existed. Southerners were infatuated with these romantic games because they suited their tastes, supported their social system, and contributed decorative ideals and manners to their culture.[21]

---

[19]The major study of ring tournaments in this country is Esther J. and Ruth W. Crooks, *The Ring Tournament in the United States* (Richmond: Garrett and Mossie, 1936). Also, see Inez Parker-Cummings, "Vestige of Chivalry: Ring Tournaments in the South," *Georgia Review* 9 (Winter 1955): 407-21; and Robert L. Loeffelbein, *Knight Life: Jousting in the United States* (Lexington Park MD: Golden Owl Publishers, 1977). For origins of the ring tournament in Maryland and Virginia, see G. Harrison Orians, "The Origin of the Ring Tournament in the United States," *Maryland Historical Magazine* 36 (1941): 263-77.

[20] The Pineville Tournament is also romanticized in Sass's novel, *Look Back to Glory* (Indianapolis: Bobbs-Merrill Co., 1933).

[21]Orians, "Walter Scott, Mark Twain, and the Civil War," 346-50.

In coastal Georgia, cavalry tilts, rather than medieval pageants, were held by horse companies earlier in the nineteenth century. Cavalry companies like the Liberty Independent Troop and the Georgia Hussars conducted tilts as military drills. The Liberty Independent Troop held its first tilt in 1830, nine years before Eglington. Early cavalry manuals described the drill which was sometimes called "tilting at the head and ring," "running at the ring," or "charging at the ring and giving edge." According to Von Schmidt's *Instructions*, "handiness" was the first principle of cavalry. Dexterity of the mounted trooper in handling his arms depended on the training of man and horse, and a perfect understanding between them.[22] Hoyt's *Rules and Regulations* stated that the cavalry tilt, when properly and frequently performed, instructed the recruit in the use of his sword and confirmed him in the saddle. Captain George W. Behn, commander of the Georgia Hussars and later of the First Squadron, published a system of cavalry instruction in 1842 in which he also justified tilting as a useful drill for training cavalrymen in conducting their horses and in the use of arms. After the Civil War, when tilting received its most enthusiastic support in coastal Georgia, Upton's *Manual*, the authoritative source for all military drills, was the standard guide. "Running at the ring" was specifically adapted to train the mounted trooper to deliver his point with certainty at any given target against cavalry; "giving edge" was designed to train cavalrymen to execute cuts, guards, thrusts, and parries against infantry.[23]

A typical tilting track or course, like the home course of the Liberty Independent Troop at Goshen, was laid out in a straight line about 150 to 200 yards in length. The five stations on the course were at least 25 yards apart; runs of 25 yards also separated the start line and the first station, and the last target and the finish line. Wooden blocks or canvas bags stuffed with straw (heads), approximately seven inches high, were mounted atop standards of varying heights. The first station, the "low head," was only 18

---

[22]Carl von Schmidt, *Instruction for the Training, Employment, and Leading of Cavalry* (London, 1881) 3.

[23]E. Hoyt, *Rules and Regulations for Drill, Sabre Exercise, Equitation, Formation and Field Movements of Cavalry* (Greenfield MA: Denio and Phelps, 1813) 79-81; also see *A System or Rules for the Exercises and Manoeuvres of the Cavalry of the State of South Carolina* (Charleston: Wm. Riley, 1834) 71-72. George W. Behn, *A Concise System of Instruction Arranged and Adopted for the Volunteer Cavalry of the United States* (Savannah, 1842) 36-37, 54. Behn's *System* describes a rectangular course, a plan that enabled two troopers to compete simultaneously. Contenders used both sabers and pistols at heads.

inches high and represented an infantryman firing a rifle in either the prone or kneeling position. The "left hand" or third target was attached to a five-foot standard by a wooden peg and was comparable to the height of a standing soldier. The "right head," or last target was about six feet from the ground and was intended to represent a mounted cavalryman. Targets two and four were iron rings, three to five inches in diameter, which approximated an infantryman's throat. The ring was suspended by a wire from a wooden arm attached at right angles to standards of different heights. The "low ring" was about five feet from the ground, the height of a standing soldier; the "high ring," suspended from a six-foot standard, was supposed to represent the throat of a mounted trooper.[24]

At the sound of the trumpet and the command, "Charge, Sir Knight," the tilter, his saber drawn at "carry," brought his mount quickly from trot to canter, reaching full gallop as he approached the starting flag. Assuming the "guard" with his sword, he advanced to the "low head," which was executed at "right cut" against infantry, a target worth two points. After this cut, he returned to "guard" and dashed to the "low ring." Taking the position of "quarter point," the rider had to thrust the ring at "quartee." If successful, he discharged the ring to the ground according to the prescribed motion, feats worth three points. The trooper again resumed "guard" and charged to the next station, the "left hand." This target had to be executed at "left cut" and was worth four points. Back to the "guard," he raced toward the "high ring," thrust it at "tierce point," cast the ring to the ground and returned his saber to "guard." This ring counted two points. The final obstacle was the "right head," worth two points. The tilter made his blow at "right cuts"; afterwards he came to the "guard" and then returned to "carry saber." The clock stopped at the last head; in order to qualify the tilter had to complete the entire course in 13 seconds.

The sword drill involved 14 proper guards, points, and moulinets, each of which counted a half-point for a possible total of seven points. Horsemanship counted an additional four points. A perfect score for the drill, which was seldom achieved, was 24 points. Riders were not permitted to shout at or strike their mounts, and no horse could be ridden by more than one rider on the same team, nor could any tilter change his horse after his

---

[24]Richard C. Cohan, *Liberty Independent Troop*, gives a description of the Goshen course including a diagram. Also, see *Savannah Evening Press* (27 September 1901) 5, for rules composed by George W. Owens and Colonel Peter W. Meldrim of Savannah.

first run. If a trooper was thrown, except by his horse falling down, he received zero for horsemanship; if he dropped his saber, he received zero for saber exercises. If he failed to complete the course within the prescribed 13 seconds, he received zero for the round. Several officials were stationed around the course to score the contestants on time, horsemanship, and saber exercises. Both individual and team winners were declared in every competition and prizes were usually quite valuable articles such as spurs or medals, and were awarded to the first place team and tilter. Second and third place winners received lesser awards. If the contention was planned as part of a special celebration, a banquet or ball generally followed the competition. The trooper who made the highest score had the privileged honor of crowning the queen of the tournament.[25]

The minutes of the separate cavalry troops and the newspapers of the coastal region provide numerous accounts of tilts in both the antebellum and postbellum decades. The Liberty Independent Troop sponsored one of the earliest tilts in the region in 1830 and continued to hold contentions for more than a century. Captain Paul Caswell was the last to win the company medal in 1940.[26] Few records exist from the decade of the 1840s, but beginning in the 1850s tilts were common events at celebrations held on Washington's Birthday and the Fourth of July. In February 1851, a cavalry tournament was conducted in Savannah featuring trials of skill in horsemanship, sword exercises at head and ring, and target firing. The Liberty Independent Troop, the Liberty Guards, the Effingham Hussars, and the McIntosh Dragoons competed for the prizes. Cornet L. T. Elkins of the Effingham Hussars made the highest score and won a pair of silver spurs. In both 1858 and 1860 the troopers from Effingham captured the prizes at the squadron meets in Savannah.[27] Behind their champion tilter, Trooper Shearouse, Effingham teams dominated the squadron tilts throughout the 1850s. Shearouse was reputedly the finest sabreur of his day, and his horse was so well trained that he could carry a full glass of water at full speed without spilling the contents. According to a local wag, Shearouse had "tilting on the brain." He practiced daily in his private tiltyard, taking rings

---

[25]Ibid., and *Atlanta Constitution* (1 May 1888) 7.

[26]Cohan, *Liberty Independent Troop*; Letter, Judge Paul E. Caswell to R. F. Saunders, Jr., 9 September 1981.

[27]*Savannah Daily Morning News* (28 February 1851) 3; (4 March 1858) 2, 4.

and lopping heads as he went to and from his fields. Because they were so invincible and regularly won all the prizes, both he and his horse were eventually excluded from competitions.[28]

The Georgia Hussars, the leading Savannah company, frequently competed against the Charleston Dragoons. The Hussars were invited to Charleston 1 April 1856 to join the Dragoons in celebrating their twenty-first anniversary. Sergeant J. W. McAlpin of the Hussars took the first prize for head and ring, and leaping ditch and bar. The next year, Governor Hershell V. Johnson was invited as guest of the Georgia Hussars at their Washington's Birthday celebration. The Charleston Dragoons were challenged to test their skill at head and ring in a return match. The Hussars again defeated their rivals and Captain J. P. W. Read was the champion tilter for which he received a saddle cloth.[29] During the late 1850s the First Squadron under the command of Major George W. Behn, an ardent enthusiast of tilting, staged annual parades in Savannah that regularly featured tilts as the main attraction. Both the local citizens and the *Savannah Morning News* applauded the military display. Quoting the *Richmond Dispatch*, the *News* praised the increased attention being given to military education in the South. "There is a possibility," warned the papers, that "she [the South] may be called upon to defend her soil against an enemy whose numbers are superior; the South should encourage the military training and discipline of her sons."[30]

After the war, the Liberty Independent Troop, which was reactivated in 1872, repaired its track at Goshen and revived contention at head and ring. For the duration of the century there were several tilts annually.[31] The Georgia Hussars revived the drills at their Washington's Birthday celebration in 1874 when they conducted an impromptu tilt at two heads and a hat on the ground.[32] After the formation of the First Squadron in 1875, squadron parades and meets were resumed in Savannah that regularly culminated

[28]*Savannah Morning News* (27 August 1901) 10.

[29]Crooks, *The Ring Tournament in the United States*, 85-94.

[30]*Savannah Daily Morning News* (4 March 1858) 4; (21 February 1860) 2; (24 February 1860) 2; (8 August 1856) 2.

[31]"Minutes of the Liberty Independent Troop" (4 July 1872), (29 December 1873); Cohan, *Liberty Independent Troop*.

[32]*Savannah Morning News* (24 February 1874) 3.

in a competitive tilt at the Ten Broeck course.[33] In April 1884, the crack tilters of the Georgia Hussars participated in the interstate tilt in Charleston which they won by an overwhelming score. The Georgia Hussars hosted an interstate cavalry tournament on 30 April 1885 at Ten Broeck race course. More than 5,000 spectators witnessed the contests among five Georgia and three South Carolina teams, including the Beaufort District Troop, the Edgefield Rangers, and the Edgefield Hussars. After an impressive parade through the city to the race track, competition began at 11:00 A.M. and lasted late into the afternoon. The second team of the Georgia Hussars was victorious, followed by the Liberty Independent Troop and the Beaufort District Troop. Each member of the winning team was awarded a gold medal and badge. Private Fleming of the Hussars won $75 for the highest individual score; Private Norman of the Liberty Independent Troop received $50 for second prize; and Private Boyd of the Beaufort Troop as third-place winner received a gold pen and pencil. The closing event of the tournament was a grand ball at the Masonic Temple where the troopers and their ladies danced the lancers. At 11:00 P.M. the cavaliers "fell in" at the sound of the bugle for the awards ceremony. A midnight supper was served after which dancing continued until the early hours.[34]

The centennial celebration of the Liberty Independent Troop at McIntosh in July 1886 was one of the major contests that year. Following a morning of parading, oratory, and picnicking, the tournament began at 3:00 P.M. Among the eight competing teams were the Liberty Guards and the Georgia Hussars, each entering two teams, one team from the McIntosh Dragoons, and three teams from the Liberty Independent Troop. The distinguished panel of judges included heroes of the Civil War such as Colonel Edward Bird, Colonel Richard J. Davant, Jr., and Captain William Brailsford. By the time the McIntosh Dragoons took to the field, it was nearly dark, and consequently their performance was substantially handicapped. The first team of the Georgia Hussars made the highest score and won the $100 prize; the second team of the Liberty Independent Troop came in second, receiving $50. Private George R. Keller, Jr., first team, Georgia Hussars, won $25 for the highest individual score; his colleague, Private D. A.

---

[33]Ibid. (14 June 1875) 3; (12 October 1875) 3; (2 May 1876).

[34]Ibid. (18 April 1884); (1 May 1885) 8.

Fleming, compiled the second highest score. The visiting companies were treated to a sumptuous banquet which closed the long day.[35]

Washington's Birthday was celebrated in Savannah the next year with a parade of the local military companies which was reviewed by the governor. That afternoon the Georgia Hussars conducted an intra-company tilt at the Ten Broeck course. The second platoon was declared the winner and received $50; Private I. W. Keller received the company medal. A grand ball to honor Governor John B. Gordon followed the contest.[36] In July 1887, the Hussars attended a tilt in Effingham where they defeated the home team and captured the $50 prize. Private George R. Keller, Jr., of the Georgia Hussars won $25 for the highest score. After the tournament, the tilters enjoyed an elegant banquet at the courthouse in Springfield and returned to Savannah the next morning. In October 1887, the Piedmont Exposition in Atlanta designated a "Military Day" to attract military companies from around the state. The Central Railroad offered to the Georgia Hussars a special roundtrip fare of $3 per man and $2.65 per horse so the troop could participate.[37]

The first state cavalry convention held in Atlanta on 9-10 May 1888 was perhaps, next to the Piedmont Exposition, the grandest military display in Georgia during the late nineteenth century. Captain John Milledge organized the event and the Governor's House Guard served as host to ten tilting teams from Savannah, Augusta, Charleston, Philadelphia, Liberty and McIntosh Counties. The rules for the tilt to be held in Piedmont Park were announced in the Atlanta Constitution on 1 May. General P. M. B. Young was designated chief judge and was assisted by eight other experts from across the state. The first team prize was worth $600; second team prize, $200. The champion individual tilter was to receive $150 and the honor of crowning the queen of the convention.[38]

---

[35]Ibid. (21 July 1886) 8; (22 July 1886) 8; "Minutes of the Liberty Independent Troop" (21 July 1886), Centennial of Liberty Troop. For comments about a tilt in Darien, see Letter, Julia King to Bessie Lewis, 31 January 1943, copy in possession of authors.

[36]Savannah Morning News (20 February 1887) 8.

[37]Ibid. (8 July 1887) 2; (29 September 1887) 8.

[38]"Only a Week Off—The Big Cavalry Festival Told About in Detail," Atlanta Constitution (1 May 1888) 7.

After a spectacular opening parade led by a marching band and a review before the packed grandstands, the competition commenced around noon, 9 May. The First Troop of Philadelphia, dressed in flashy uniforms and mounted on thoroughbreds, created the greatest sensation prior to the competition and was favored to capture the prizes. Rumors circulated that every member of the Philadelphia Troop was worth no less than $100,000 each.[39] At best, the McIntosh Dragoons, represented by J. F. Wylly, S. F. Sinclair, James O'Brien, and R. D. Wylly were considered the underdogs. Riding their "marsh tackies," they drew the ninth round. When the contention ended late in the afternoon the spectators guessed that the first prize had been won by either the Charleston Dragoons, the Savannah Hussars, or the McIntosh Dragoons. After several hours of waiting, the judges, in a unanimous decision, awarded the first-team prize to the McIntosh Dragoons; second and third prizes went to the Savannah Hussars and the Liberty Independent Troop, respectively. Members of the Philadelphia Troop, claiming that they had never engaged in a contest of this sort, finished last. J. O'Brien of the McIntosh Dragoons won first prize for the highest individual score; S. F. Sinclair, also of the Dragoons, came in fourth. In the grand individual tilting contest held the next day, P. R. Martin of the Liberty Independent Troop captured the laurels by narrowly edging out R. D. Wylly and J. F. Wylly of the McIntosh Dragoons who came in second and third.[40] The teams from the coastal companies had swept all of the prizes.

On the last evening the troopers, their ladies, and friends gathered at Degives Opera House for the coronation of the "Queen of Love and Beauty" and her court. After an address by Colonel A. H. Cox, who lauded the virtues of Southern chivalry, and a review of the troops, J. A. O'Brien crowned Miss Eleanor Mansfield of Darien the reigning queen. Lieutenant Livingston, commander of the McIntosh Dragoons, then made a short speech and presented the queen with a gold star studded with brilliants and a saber covered with roses. Miss Mansfield responded with gratitude and paid tribute to the members of the home troop after which the assemblage adjourned to the grand ballroom of the Kimball House, and the royal cou-

---

[39]*Atlanta Constitution* (8 May 1888) 7; (9 May 1888) 7; (10 May 1888) 7.

[40]"It's a Success—Brilliant Opening of the Cavalry Festival at Piedmont Park"*Atlanta Constitution* (10 May 1888) 7. *Darien Timber Gazette* (12 May 1888) 3; (19 May 1888) 3. Upon their return, the champion Dragoons were given a grand reception by the mayor and citizens of Darien; *Savannah Morning News* (13 May 1888) 8.

ple opened the ball. The dancing lasted into the late hours. The *Constitu-tion* reported the next day that the first cavalry festival ended more brilliantly than it had begun, and praised Captain Milledge for its phenom-enal success.[41]

The celebration of the Fourth of July 1889 in Oliver, a small town on the Central Railroad in Screven County about 45 miles west of Savannah, was highlighted by a challenge tilt between the Screven Troop and the Ef-fingham Hussars. In addition to a large turnout of local citizens, an excur-sion train brought a large delegation from Millen. Outgoing trains from Savannah brought tilting enthusiasts and fun-seekers from the coast, along with a band and a detachment of the Georgia Hussars. An immense pavil-ion provided by the Central Railroad was erected to shelter musicians and dancers. The morning was spent in lively amusements and baseball. At 1 P.M. a long table was spread under a pavilion described as a "sight tempting to epicures." After the picnic the two teams competed at head and ring in which the Effingham Hussars vanquished the Screven Troop. Sergeant W. T. Green of the Hussars won a pair of spurs for highest individual score. Among the distinguished judges of the competition were Colonel Bird and ex-Captains E. J. Shepherd and J. D. Groover. Although the Georgia Hus-sars did not tilt, they conceded that they were "royally entertained."[42]

Cavalry tilts remained popular in coastal and wiregrass Georgia until after the turn of the century. Outside of the region, ring tournaments were also the rage. As early as 1870, the Grand Tournament Corps, a statewide organization of equestrian enthusiasts, was begun in Atlanta. The Gordon Knights of the capital city elected General John B. Gordon their president and practiced regularly in order to make a spectacular showing at the forth-coming state fair. On that occasion 20 knights competed before a crowd of 10,000 spectators. The contest was tragically interrupted when M. E. Kenny, "Knight of the Red Hood," was thrown from his horse and killed. Further competition was postponed, and the knights in procession followed the fellow knight home and to his final resting place. When the tournament resumed, winners contributed their prize money to erect a monument in honor of Kenny.[43] Ring tournaments were popular spectacles at fairs in

---

[41]"The Tourney Knights," *Atlanta Constitution* (11 May 1888) 5.

[42]*Savannah Morning News* (5 July 1889) 8.

[43]Episode described in Parker-Cummings, "Vestige of Chivalry," 416.

Thomasville, Albany, Macon, Athens, Rome, and other cities in the state. Gallant knights in true Scott fashion assumed romantic names like the "Black Knight," "Knight of the Lost Cause," and "Knight of the Red Rose," dressed in colorful costumes, and attempted to imitate the tournament at Ashby de la Zouche. The crowning of the queen and her court was always the climax of the grand pageant.[44]

Ridiculed as relics of an obsolete romanticism, anachronistic outgrowths of a feudal psychology, and nostalgic escapisms, these games were never confined to the South, yet they lingered there longer than in other sections. If so inclined, one may still attend a ring tournament at Middleton Place near Charleston in the spring. While the rest of the nation embraced industrialization and urbanization, the South remained predominantly rural, and Southerners, perhaps more than other Americans, developed a strong attachment to the land, revered traditions, and acknowledged social distinctions. Like the English gentry of the eighteenth century, they were devoted to horsemanship, manly pleasures associated with martial display, hunting, outdoor sports, and convivial gatherings. Tilts, like court days of yesteryear, protracted religious meetings, fairs, and school closings, brought the community together for entertainment and social intercourse. Southern women were among the most ardent champions of the tilt. They provided food and refinement to the events and obviously enjoyed the attention they received from the chivalry.

The demise of cavalry tilts in coastal Georgia can be attributed to a number of factors. The cavalry had known its finest hour during the Civil War and the young blades of the Spanish American War were never able to match the deeds or capture the public imagination like the old cavaliers who wore the grey. The passing of the old guard undoubtedly weakened the tradition. The reorganization of the militia under the Dick Act prescribed membership and training requirements that forced several of the old cavalry units into inactivity. Professional training exercises under the supervision of Regular Army personnel replaced the tilt. The building of better roads and expanded rail lines relegated the horse to draft animal or source of amusement. Within a few decades the automobile revolutionized transportation and dramatically altered social conventions and recreational patterns. After the turn of the century, coastal newspapers seldom reported

---

[44]Crooks, *The Ring Tournament in the United States*, 87-93, passim.

ring tournaments or cavalry tilts.[45] Instead they described rifle competitions, excursions, boat races, the scores of the men's and women's golf teams, and baseball games, the new national pastime. Coastal Georgians were among the last champions of the sport and were perhaps slower than their countrymen to realize that the wave of the future did not lie in the cultivation of romantic myths but in modernization. Just as chivalric ideals continued to enhance the virtues of honor and gallantry in an age little attuned to civility, tilts and ring tournaments afforded excitement for those who preferred an innocuous escape into medieval pageantry.

---

[45]Ring tournaments are still popular sports in Maryland, Virginia, and South Carolina. After designating jousting as the official state sport in 1968, the Maryland Tournament Association was founded the next year. In 1970 a National Jousting Association was formed; it now conducts an annual tournament in Washington, D. C. as part of the capital city's "Summer in the Park" program. The authors attended a lancing tournment at Middleton Place near Charleston, South Carolina, on 18 October 1981 that featured riders from the Cedar Swamp Lancing Association of Williamsburg County, South Carolina.

ELEVEN

The Liberty County
Christ Craze of 1889 ˑ

MILLENARIAN MOVEMENTS and religious fervor have occurred throughout history in both "advanced" and "primitive" societies. In periods of social upheaval, communities sometimes turn to bizarre ideals and mystical religious cults that offer escape from frustration and despair. If the adherents are already imbued with religious ardor, the leader may be regarded as a messiah, especially if he offers his followers a plan of redemption based on the Scriptures.[1] In the summer of 1889, Jacob Orth, alias DuPont Bell, a deranged wanderer and self-styled messiah, appeared in the coastal district of Liberty County and incited several hundred blacks to prepare for the "day of ascension" that was to come 16 August. Before the delusion subsided, its manifestations included disruption of family and community life, lunacy trials, a succession of leaders, violence, orgiastic rituals, and serio-comic episodes like the sale of a "cyar load of wings" to the credulous be-

---

[1] For discussion of millenarian movements and messianic cults, see Kenelon Burridge, *New Heaven, New Earth, A Study of Millenarian Activities* (New York: Shocken Books, 1969); Sylvia L. Thrupp, ed., *Millennial Dreams in Action* (The Hague: Mouton & Co., 1962); Norman Cohn, *The Pursuit of the Millennium* (New York: Oxford University Press, 1970); Vittorio Lanternari, *The Religions of the Oppressed, A Study of Modern Messianic Cults* (New York: Alfred A. Knopf, 1963); and W. D. Wallis, *Messiahs: Their Role in Civilization* (Washington: American Council on Public Affairs, 1943); Ken Levi, ed., *Violence and Religious Commitment* (University Park: Pennsylvania State University Press, 1982). For another treatment of the Christ craze that analyzes causes-effects, see Thomas F. Armstrong, "The Christ Craze of 1889: A Millennial Response to Economic and Social Change" in *Toward a New South? Studies in Post-Civil War Southern Communities*, ed. Orville V. Burton and Robert C. McMath, Jr., (Westport CT: Greenwood Press, 1982) 223-45.

lievers. The Reverend James Stacy, historian of the old Midway Church and Presbyterianism in Georgia, compared the Liberty County Christ craze to the Salem witch hysteria. Although his account of the craze was the first to appear, he was so offended by its excesses that he chose to "draw the vail."[2]

In the wake of the Civil War, emancipated blacks and their former masters were forced to restructure relationships. Liberty County blacks organized separate churches and schools—Macedonian Presbyterian Church, the Riceboro and Newport Baptist Churches, the McIntosh Methodist Church, and the new Midway Congregational Church and Dorchester Academy near McIntosh. The Freedmen's Bureau and Northern freedmen's aid societies, namely the American Missionary Association, furnished preachers, teachers, and assistance. A considerable number of blacks acquired small holdings of land and became marginal, subsistence farmers. Many left the county, especially in the decade before 1870, while others found employment as sawmill and turpentine hands. These industries attracted a new breed of rootless, migratory laborers who came mainly from the Carolinas. They lived in isolated quarters scattered through the swamps. Mostly male, rowdy, and unreliable, they were bound to their employer who extended them credit at the commissary and bailed them out of jail.[3]

For several decades following 1865, Liberty County blacks were active in county, state, and national Republican politics under the leadership of William A. Golding, the Reverend Floyd Snelson, the Reverend W. H. Styles, and S. A. McIver.[4] After they were abandoned by Republican lead-

[2]James Stacy, History and Records of Midway Church (Newnan GA: S. W. Murray Printer, 1951) 244-51.

[3]Richard B. Drake, "The American Missionary Association and the Southern Negro" (Ph.D. dissertation, Emory University, 1957); George A. Rogers and R. Frank Saunders, Jr., "The American Missionary Association in Liberty County, Georgia: A Mission of Light and Love," Georgia Historical Quarterly 62 (Winter 1978) 304-15; and Jacqueline Jones, Soldiers of Light and Love, Northern Teachers and Georgia Blacks, 1865-1873 (Chapel Hill: University of North Carolina Press, 1980). Also, see Ralph Schlomowitz, "The Transition from Slave to Freedman Labor—Arrangements in Southern Agriculture, 1865-1870" (Ph.D. dissertation, University of Chicago, 1979); Thomas F. Armstrong, "From Task Labor to Free Labor: The Transition Along Georgia's Rice Coast, 1820-1880," Georgia Historical Quarterly 64 (Winter 1980): 432-47.

[4]William A. Golding served in the Georgia General Assembly, 1868, 1870; Floyd Snelson served as chairman of the Liberty County Republican Party, Republican nominee for Congress (1888), delegate to national Republican convention (1888), and member of Lib-

ers in the post-Reconstruction era, a proscriptive backlash produced Jim Crowism, lynchings, the convict-lease system, and second-class citizenship. White racists justified supremacy by invoking anthropological and sociological doctrines that relegated blacks to a subordinate status—hewers of wood and drawers of water. The "Negro problem" was the popular label applied to the myriad of social ills that afflicted Southern blacks—poverty, ignorance, crime, disease; whatever the misfortune, the evil was commonly ascribed to the presence of the black race, to the biological inferiority of blacks, or to their supposed degenerate and bestial nature.[5]

In 1889, blacks outnumbered whites by more than two to one in Liberty County.[6] The 15th Georgia Militia District, the old rice belt, was almost exclusively black. Illiteracy in Georgia was deplorably high, averaging over 65 percent in 1889. Although a majority of Liberty County blacks were poor, culturally deprived, and landless, many were landowners and a goodly number were renters. Almost none were sharecroppers. Out of a total of 1,500 farmers in Liberty County in 1890, 725 were black. They owned 41,227 acres for an average of 57 acres per farm. Most of them engaged in subsistence farming on their small patches where they produced corn, rice, sweet potatoes, and some livestock and poultry.[7]

erty County Board of Commissioners. Styles, active in county politics, was a candidate for the General Assembly, 1888; S. A. McIver was a member of the General Assembly in the 1880s and 1890s and was considered "a colored gentleman of the old antebellum school."

[5]For studies of blacks in Georgia, 1865-1900, see James L. Owens, "The Negro in the Reconstruction of Georgia" (Ph.D. dissertation, University of Georgia, 1974); Horace C. Wingo, "Race Relations in Georgia, 1870-1908" (Ph.D. dissertation, University of Georgia, 1969); Clarence Bacote, "The Negro in Georgia Politics, 1880-1908" (Ph.D. dissertation, University of Chicago, 1955); Clarence Bacote, "Negro Proscriptions, Protests and Proposed Solutions in Georgia, 1880-1908," *Journal of Southern History* 25 (November 1959): 471-98.

[6]*Compendium of the Eleventh Census, 1890* (Washington: Government Printing Office, 1892) Part 1, 13, 101, 480; *Twelfth Census of the United States, 1900: Population* (Washington: United States Census Office, 1901) Part 1, 14.

[7]*Report on Population of the United States at the Eleventh Census: 1890* (Washington: Government Printing Office, 1897) Part 2, xxxiii-xxxvi; Armstrong, "Christ Craze," 233. *Report on the Statistics of Agriculture in the United States at the Eleventh Census: 1890* (Washington: Government Printing Office, 1895) 130, 203, 242, 281, 361, 393, 404, 427, 465; *Twelfth Census of the United States: 1900, Agriculture, Crops and Irrigation* (Washington: Government Printing Office, 1902) Part 2, 192; W. E. B. DuBois, "The Negro Farmer," *Bureau of the Census Special Reports, Supplementary Analysis and Derivative Tables, Twelfth Census of the United States: 1900* (Washington: Government Printing Office, 1906) 511-79; W.

The Christ craze of 1889 was preceded by a series of natural and imagined calamities that appeared as signs of some ominous event. In August 1886, the Charleston earthquake shook the Georgia coast. More immediately, Liberty Countians experienced a severe drought followed by flooding in the spring of 1889. These and other occurrences set the stage for the appearance of DuPont Bell, "the great original," who seem to fulfill their expectations.[8]

According to Bell, he arrived in Savannah on 2 April 1888; a few days later, the eccentric drifter agreed to an interview with a reporter of the *Morning News* in which he stated that he was 29 years old and had been born the son of a United Brethren minister in Circleville, Ohio. He claimed that he had worked as a dry-goods clerk in Chicago, Toledo and Wauseon, Ohio, and in Tampa, Key West, and Jacksonville, Florida. "The subject of mind-reading has been uppermost in my mind for the past three months," he told the reporter, and "I have been inspired to enlighten the world tomorrow night at Turner Hall. My lecture is inspired: 'Light, Way and Life.' I have not written it; never rehearsed it. It is original. It is not me that will speak, but the Great Original speaking through me." Taking a small, square block of wood from his pocket, he asserted that it was the basis of his lecture. Bell explained that when cast down the block would always find a firm footing. In the same manner, a "square" man will fall on a firm foundation and be righted. In a state of rapture, he professed perfection in all things—mythology, architecture, linguistics, drawing, painting, music, poetry, spiritualism, and marital relations. Bell announced that he planned to remain in Savannah until his mission was fulfilled.[9]

On Sunday evening, 15 April, nearly 600 curious people gathered in Turner Hall on Broughton Street to hear Bell's lecture. When, after 9:00 P.M., the speaker failed to begin, the audience became restless. Bell's only response was that the right man had not yet arrived. He was finally moved to sing a hymn that was interrupted by the booing and hissing of the crowd. When the lights suddenly went out in the hall, the audience departed in

E. B. DuBois, "The Negro Landholder of Georgia," Bulletin of the United States Department of Labor, no. 35 (July 1901).

[8]Charleston *Courier* (31 August 1886 and subsequent issues).

[9]*The Savannah Morning News* (15 April 1888) 8.

mass confusion.[10] On 18 April, Bell was arrested on a charge of lunacy and was given a hearing in the Court of Ordinary. When the court convened on 23 April, the charges against Bell were dropped on the grounds that the accused was more of a crank than a lunatic. Bell's presence was next noticed in June of 1889 when he began his mission among the blacks in coastal Liberty County.[11]

Bell, described as "an old white man" with long hair parted in the middle, dressed in a blouse suit and carrying a staff, was reputed to have scars on his hands and feet. He told the local blacks that the earthquake of August 1886 was the sign of his coming. Initially he wandered from house to house in the "swamp district," gathering a small band of followers who were awed by his knowledge of the Bible, his real or imagined miracles, and his prophecies. He proclaimed a mission to save the blacks, staying away from the McIntosh settlement where more whites resided.[12] As he gained several hundred followers from among the more backward and uneducated blacks, Bell moved his meeting place from a brush arbor located near the junction of the Riceboro and McIntosh roads to the old Walthour "Homestead Place," seven miles northeast of Walthourville. For about six weeks he preached to more than 400 followers—many of whom were members of the New Midway Congregational Church at Dorchester, the Baptist Churches at Newport and Riceboro, and the Methodist Church at McIntosh—beneath two sprawling live oak trees that shaded a pulpit surrounded by wooden benches. The inner circle which was about 40 feet in diameter was designated as the "Holy Ground" or "Jerusalem."[13] Bell's successors would hold meetings at the same site.

Bell's followers, a majority of whom were women, left their homes, families and employment to be near the "Christ." They camped in abandoned slave cabins or in the open around fires and held their worldly goods in common as they awaited the day of ascension. Bell denounced the local ministers for taking collections and instructed his followers to hand their

[10]Ibid. (18 April 1888) 8.

[11]Ibid. (24 April 1888) 8.

[12]Ibid. (14 June 1888) 6; *Atlanta Journal* (12 June 1889) 3; *The Savannah Tribune* (15 June 1889); (22 June 1889) 3; (29 June 1889).

[13]Stacy, *History and Records of Midway Church*, 244-51; *Atlanta Constitution* (31 July 1889).

money to him in envelopes. Floyd Snelson and W. H. Styles, pastors of the New Midway Congregational Church near McIntosh and the Baptist Church at Riceboro, respectively, were alarmed by Bell's growing influence and swore out a vagrancy warrant against the impostor. They retained ex-Congressman Thomas M. Norwood of Savannah, owner of a summer retreat near Walthourville, as their counsel. After interrogating Bell, Norwood reported he could not discover any "mal-intent in the man," and since the accused was supported by two congregations, the charge of vagrancy could not be sustained. Authorities feared a disturbance, and news circulated that the jury had decided to release Bell, a verdict that was interpreted by his followers as unquestionable evidence of their messiah's divinity and power.[14] Bell's last antic involved a request to the Father for a consignment of wings, 360 pairs, that were to be delivered to the faithful on the day of ascension. He offered them to his deluded followers for $5 per pair.[15]

Norwood advised his clients to change their charges from vagrancy to lunacy and on 21 June, the Reverend Styles, whose church had been nearly emptied by the craze, filed a petition against Bell for pretending to be Jesus Christ and for preaching to the local blacks in an incendiary manner. Judge Norwood later observed that Bell's "trump card" was his claim that on the day of judgment blacks would become white and whites would become black.[16]

Joseph Ashmore, county ordinary, named a commission of 18 citizens, including Dr. Alfred I. Hendry as examining physician, to conduct the hearing. Bell's case was heard on 28 June before Justice W. A. Fleming in an improvised courtroom set up in an abandoned store at McIntosh Station. Carey B. Townshend of Valdosta, an eyewitness to the proceedings, reported that fully 300 people, black and white, assembled for the hearing.

Bell, shabbily dressed, appeared meek, quiet, and nonviolent except when Judge Norwood interrogated him about his religious mission. He announced that this was his second appearance on earth, that he had appeared a thousand years earlier as King James of England. He claimed not

---

[14]New York Times (11 July 1889) 3.

[15]Atlanta Constitution (12 July 1889) 3; Macon Telegraph (13 July 1889) 6; The Savannah Tribune (20 July 1889) 3.

[16]The Valdosta Times (29 June 1889) 3; The Savannah Morning News (26 July 1889) 8; Atlanta Constitution (27 July 1889) 3.

only to be the resurrected Christ but also George Washington, Abraham Lincoln, and Jeff Davis. When asked to perform a miracle, Bell retorted that he would not "gratify idle curiosity." The audience was startled by Bell's ability to quote scriptures, but two hours of raving convinced the commission that the impostor was suffering from delusions of grandeur.[17] The verdict of the commission was that Bell was a dangerous lunatic and a pauper who should be held in the county jail prior to removal to the state asylum at Milledgeville. Due to crowded conditions at the asylum, Bell was not admitted to the asylum until 13 July.[18] He remained there for the next ten years when he was discharged as "restored" on 25 August 1899; thereafter he dropped into anonymity.

Five days after Bell was sent to the asylum, Edward James, a 31-year-old farmer and justice of the peace, emerged from a trance and proclaimed his divine mission as Bell's successor. His constable, seized by the same mania, announced that he was the "Holy Ghost." According to James, who claimed that Bell's spirit had entered him, "We are three in one." James, appearing stark naked, began to hold daily meetings at the same site under the oaks where Bell had preached. On the following Sunday, he urged the gathering to make sacrifices, to either throw their money away or give it to the Lord. He placed a dry-goods box, called the "ark of the covenant," in the circle and commanded his followers to put their money into it. James warned that anyone who touched the box would be struck dead. On Sunday, 18 July, $400 was offered as sacrifice. James reportedly tore up the paper money and scattered the silver coins through the woods.[19] One Tero, a nonbeliever, ignored the prophecy and showed up in Savannah with $22.75 that he had stolen from the ark.

Influenced by the idea of sacrifice from the biblical story of Abraham offering up Isaac, James demanded human blood. On Sunday, 21 July, while the parents attended James's meeting, the infant, Andrew Roberts, and his older sister were allegedly murdered by their aunt, Laura [Sarah] Roberts,

---

[17]Carey B. Townshend, *The Valdosta Times* (29 June 1889) 3; (6 July 1889) 2; *The Savannah Morning News* (23 June 1889) 8; (30 June 1889) 8; *Thomasville Daily Times Enterprise* (30 June 1889) 2.

[18]*The Savannah Tribune* (20 July 1880) 3; for proceedings against Bell, see *General Records, Book R, 1874-1891*, Ordinary, Liberty County, 792-94.

[19]*New York Times* (29 July 1889) 2; *Atlanta Constitution* (27 July 1889) 3; *The Valdosta Times* (27 July 1889) 1.

an avid follower of Bell and James. When a search failed to locate the children, suspicion began to point to the children's aunt who had a history of mental illness. When asked about the children, she answered "Ask the Lord: he has decided me," and "The buzzards will tell you where to find them." The body of the infant boy, mutilated with the sign of a cross on his forehead and breast, was discovered the next day in a railroad ditch with his throat cut and ears split. The records are silent about the fate of the other child. When the grand jury investigated the case of Laura Roberts it returned a "no bill" on grounds of insanity.[20]

At the afternoon meeting on 21 July, James claimed that he saw devils in the wife of Charlie Baker and he called upon his disciples to pound the devils out of her. A dozen men attacked her with clubs and broke the victim's jaw and inflicted other serious body injuries which subsequently caused her death. The next day James saw the devils moving in Eugene Richards, a sober, industrious farmer, who was likewise beaten insensible by the crazed mob. When David James and Sampson Carter tried to persuade the self-styled Christ to stop preaching, another brawl ensued and Carter was beaten unmercifully.[21]

According to Senator Samuel D. Bradwell, founder and publisher of the *Hinesville Gazette*, James presided over hideous orgies at the "Holy Ground." In a state of frenzy his followers formed two rings, one of men and another of women. They would dance around with torches making strange sounds, and as the excitement mounted, the participants began to strip off their clothing until they were stark naked. They would then fall on their hands and knees and grunt like hogs and bleat like sheep, leap to their feet, and run about screaming "fire." The noise was supposed to drive off the devil. James reputedly had a number of concubines and, according to Bradwell, he authorized his principal disciples to set up harems.[22]

By the last week in July, conditions in the county had reached a critical state. Hundreds of blacks had left their huts and many had turned their livestock into the patches that produced food crops. Turpentine stands, rice

---

[20]*Macon Telegraph* (24 July 1889) 3; *The Savannah Morning News* (25 July 1889) 8; State v. Sarah Roberts, *Record of Minutes of Liberty County Superior Court* (November 1884-April 1891) 360.

[21]*Atlanta Constitution* (25 July 1889) 3; *The Savannah Morning News* (26 July 1889) 8.

[22]*Atlanta Constitution* (13 August 1889) 11.

and cotton fields were neglected from want of labor. James, the "lion of the hour," held such absolute power over his followers that many whites feared that he would cause a massacre and the burning of every residence in the county.[23] Because the excesses of the craze appeared to threaten order and stability, the respectable blacks and whites demanded outside intervention. Ministers and officers of several black churches who "claimed to represent the interest and honor" of their people appealed to local civil authorities to disband the fanatical followers of DuPont Bell and Edward James. Their petition of seven resolutions condemned the band as a crazy mob. They had committed degrading acts, and their doctrines and ceremonies were vile and demoralizing. Fearing that many would become paupers or thieves from abandoning their crops and jobs, the petition denounced the crimes committed against opponents and followers. The leaders protested that the craze was injuring the honor and character of their people, 90 percent of whom were respectable, sane, and faithful to civil and ecclesiastical law.[24]

On Monday, 22 July, warrants were issued for the arrest of James and six of his followers; four others were arrested by the end of the week. W. J. James, brother of the deranged leader, filed a petition for a lunacy hearing on 23 July, and three days later Edward James was examined at McIntosh and found to be a dangerous lunatic. He was held in the county jail, a raving maniac, secured to his cell wall. Accompanied by his brother, James was admitted to the state asylum on 3 August 1889, where he died of consumption.[25]

Having lost two self-proclaimed messiahs, the deluded group accepted the leadership of Shadrack Walthour on Sunday, 28 July. An illiterate rice-field worker, Walthour claimed to be "King Solomon." Tony LeCount, a licensed teacher, became Walthour's assistant and called himself "Nebuchadnezzar." A visitor to the "Holy Ground," under the same spreading oaks where Bell and James had preached, described Walthour pacing across the circle as his followers chanted a strange dirge. He commanded them to cease their chant and to show honor "to the duty" by raising a wooden scepter

---

[23]*Thomasville Daily Times Enterprise* (30 July 1889) 1.

[24]*The Valdosta Times* (3 August 1889) 3.

[25]*Atlanta Constitution* (28 July 1889) 12, (1 August 1889) 4; *Macon Telegraph* (3 August 1889) 3; *The Savannah Morning News* (3 August 1889) 8. For lunacy proceedings against James, see *General Records, Book R, 1874-1891*, Ordinary, Liberty County, 797-800.

that he claimed was the source of his power. "King Solomon" then fired questions to the assembly that were answered in chorus. Apparently Bell and James had catechized the group, leading them to believe that they were animals who were placed in slavery because they did not honor God. They were short-haired and black because they had crucified the Son. After the catechism, "King Solomon" delivered a monologue that was accompanied by a strange melody. The meeting was disrupted by a party of black men who came to claim their wives and children. To avoid confrontation, "King Solomon" was bribed into dispersing the gathering until the following Tuesday. He announced that he was going to change the day of ascension from 16 August to 30 July, the next Tuesday. The crowd agreed to wait.[26]

"King Solomon's" reign ended the next day, 29 July, when he decided to go over to Hinesville to liberate the prisoners who were being held in jail on charges of lunacy. When Walthour and several of his followers arrived in Hinesville, the marshall arrested the entourage and placed them in jail. Charges were preferred against them for assaulting Sampson Carter.[27] When Tony LeCount, "Nebuchadnezzar," was arrested, Chris Lee became "Nebuchadnezzar" number two.

When news of "King Solomon's" arrest reached the believers who were still gathered at the "Holy Ground," Ellen (Ella) Roberts, announced that she was the "Queen of Sheba" and the "Virgin Mary," an assertion readily accepted by many of the deluded followers. She was a 28-year-old mother of eight who had deserted her family and was living as a "guest" of Alexander Walthour. Sheriff Smith visited the camp on Monday, 29 July, and ordered the assembly of about 250 persons to disband and to cease their preaching and religious exercises. Approximately a hundred, however, still congregated around the "Queen" who passed into trances every 10 to 15 minutes; upon waking she would reveal her visions to her disciples. A visitor to the camp found her lying on her back, surrounded by attendants fanning her majesty with palmetto fans. Her head and body were covered with a soiled sheet.[28]

---

[26]*Atlanta Journal* (29 July 1889) 1.

[27]*Atlanta Constitution* (31 July 1889). See State v. Simon Walthour, John Douglas, Q. Roberts, Jack Pray, Ned Stevens, Dicky Maxwell, William Quarterman, William Batey, *Records of Minutes of Liberty County Superior Court*, 8:371, 377-79, 392-93

[28]*Atlanta Constitution* (1 August 1889) 4.

After a visit home on 28-29 July, Representative S. A. McIver, the only local black in the state legislature, told an *Atlanta Journal* reporter that there was "no religion" in the excitement down in Liberty County. "There are about 500 Negroes gone crazy," he observed, "who had better be at work." He called both "King Solomon" and the "Virgin Mary" weak-minded. Quoting the Reverend Snelson, who was also a county commissioner, McIver confirmed that the accounts in the newspapers had not been exaggerated.[29]

By comparison to her predecessors, the "Queen" was mild and innocuous. She commanded her followers to bring their children to worship her. They were commanded to kiss her feet in exchange for blessings. After three days of waiting during which time the faithful subsisted only on green corn, most of the remaining followers drifted back to their cabins and patches.[30] On Sunday, 4 August, Sheriff Smith led a posse of 50 men, both white and black, to the camp. They destroyed the benches of the tabernacle and cleared out the goods of the squatters from the abandoned cabins. The "Queen" who was delirious from typhoid fever, was returned to her home. After the destruction of their camp, the leaderless believers, greatly reduced in numbers and fragmented, continued to meet for a short time in small gatherings at three separate places.[31]

When the local jail became crowded with both the insane and prisoners who were accused of either murder or assault, county officials filed a petition with Judge R. Falligant for a special session of state court. After most of the prisoners were sent to the asylum or released on bond, the petition was denied. In early August, Senator Bradwell returned to the county at the request of Governor John B. Gordon to assist in pacifying the disturbance among the blacks. Bradwell suggested that the county authorities establish a patrol of ten men to maintain surveillance over the "swamp district."[32]

Although the hysteria appeared to be passing, county authorities remained nervous about troubles that might occur on 16 August, the day of ascension when the wings Bell had promised were supposed to fall from the

[29]*The Darien Timber Gazette* (3 August 1889) 3.

[30]*Atlanta Constitution* (13 August 1889) 11.

[31]*Macon Telegraph* (7 August 1889); *The Valdosta Times* (10 August 1889) 1; *The Savannah Morning News* (17 August 1889) 8.

[32]*Atlanta Constitution* (13 August 1889) 11.

sky. Instead of the march to Canaan, big crowds of local blacks boarded the train at Walthourville and McIntosh on the morning of 16 August for an excursion to Thomasville. Mr. M. Pleasant, a prominent Savannahian, had organized the affair. En route a brass band from Jesup and the Valdosta Phoenix Riflemen joined the festive excursion. Upon arrival in Thomasville, the party enjoyed a parade down Broad Street that was followed by sightseeing and dancing. The local paper noted that curiosity-seekers were anxious to glimpse the Liberty Countians who had received so much notoriety because of the Christ craze. The Liberty County delegation was described as well-dressed and orderly. They remained good-humored in spite of the jostling they encountered from the Thomasville blacks. Back home, the worshipers did not assemble at the Walthour plantation and the day passed without excitement.[33]

The last noteworthy event associated with the Christ craze was the mysterious death of Shadrack Walthour, "King Solomon," who still remained in the Hinesville jail. On Sunday, 13 October, he was found dead in his cell with his head wrapped in a blanket. Initially, word circulated that he had smothered himself. A coroner's inquest the next day, however, revealed serious fractures on Walthour's skull which some believed were self-inflicted. While the inquest was being conducted in the jail yard, a black inmate interrupted the proceedings and accused A. R. Dean, jailer and deputy sheriff, of beating Walthour with brass knuckles. Another prisoner corroborated the testimony that the jailer beat Walthour for ignoring an order to stop reading his Bible so loudly. Dean admitted striking the victim but denied using brass knuckles, testimony that was substantiated by two of the jailor's relatives who were present. The coroner's jury reached the verdict that Walthour had died from bruises on his head and that the case should be thoroughly investigated by the grand jury. Solicitor W. W. Fraser, who was present at the inquest, stated that he was convinced that Walthour was murdered. On 22 November 1889, the Liberty County grand jury handed down a special presentment for murder in the case of State vs. Andrew R. Dean. When the case was tried before the Superior Court of Liberty County, the all-white jury found the defendant Andrew R. Dean "not guilty."[34]

---

[33]Ibid., (17 August 1889) 3; *Thomasville Daily Times Enterprise* (17 August 1889) 3; (20 August 1889) 1; *The Savannah Morning News* (17 August 1889) 8.

[34]*The Savannah Morning News* (19 October 1889) 8; (22 October 1889) 8; *The Savannah Tribune* (26 October 1889) 3; *The Valdosta Times* (26 October 1889) 1. For proceedings in

The Liberty County Christ craze of 1889 is not an incomprehensible aberration. The delusion occurred at a time of upheaval among people who were experiencing economic and social dislocation. Its adherents, poor and black, felt as powerless and alienated, as frustrated and marginal, as the unskilled peasants who followed the mystics of the middle ages or the tragic followers of Reverend James Jones who committed mass suicide at Georgetown, Guyana, in 1978. DuPont Bell, deranged as he was, offered his followers, who possessed neither wealth nor political power, an opportunity for redemption. By combining a hypnotic style and a message taken from their own cultural idiom, Bell attracted those who sought a personal religious experience, those who felt adrift and needy. Black women, among the most oppressed, flocked to Bell because he offered them a meaningful status, an alternative to motherhood and submission to their husbands. Bell, and to a lesser degree his successors, promised a new heaven and a new earth to those who viewed religion as a source of power. He offered them redemption, ordered intimacy, and escape—an end to doubt and despair.

The craze undoubtedly left lasting scars on the lives of many black Liberty Countians in personal suffering and tragedy. Leaders of the community like Judge Norwood and Senator Bradwell could explain the craze, at least to their satisfaction, as a lapse into barbarism.[35] They could point to the failure of black institutions and leaders, especially churches and preachers.

The Reverend Stacy, disturbed about the wisdom of organizing separate churches for blacks, observed that both the Midway Presbyterian congregation, led by a white minister, the Reverend J. T. H. Waite, and the black Presbyterian church near Riceboro, under the pastorship of the Reverend B. L. Glenn, were only slightly influenced by the craze. Likewise, he noted that the pupils of the Dorchester Academy were unaffected. The following spring Professor Payson E. Little of the academy reported in the *American Missionary* that a "work of grace" had transpired in Liberty County. "It is pleasant to know," he observed, "that nearly all of those who were brought under the influence of this crazy fanatic, have now returned to their

---

State v. Andrew R. Dean, see *Record of Minutes of Liberty County Superior Court*, 8:371, 9:11-12.

[35]See *Atlanta Constitution* (27 July 1889) 4; Senator Bradwell's views are found in *Atlanta Constitution* (13 August 1889); Judge Norwood reflected on the craze in "The Liberty County Case," *Address on the Negro*, 31 December 1907, Savannah GA (Georgia Historical Society, vertical files).

churches thoroughly ashamed of their experience."[36] The craze also solidified white racial attitudes based on the assumption that blacks were uncivilized and that they should be segregated and carefully controlled by the dominant white society. More objectively viewed, the craze was symptomatic of the deep-seated frustration and hopelessness of people in the black community whose yearning for escape outweighed their willingness to endure the present or to face the future.

---

[36]Stacy, History and Records of Midway Church, 250-51; American Missionary 44 (March 1890): 82.

TWELVE

Henry Ford at Richmond Hill: A Venture in Private Enterprise and Philanthropy*

WHILE MOST AMERICANS were intoxicated by the crass and transient prosperity of the 1920s, only a small minority actually shared the affluence that made their nation the economic wonder of the age. The marginal farmers and sharecroppers of Georgia might have fancied the symbols and ingredients of the "good life," but more realistically their lives were fraught with poverty, illiteracy, and hardship. Like most of coastal Georgia, Bryan County was a region of subsistence agriculture, low-paying sawmill and turpentine industries, and moonshining; it had not known flush times since the antebellum rice era.

In 1925, Henry Ford, already a multimillionaire and the world's most successful automobile manufacturer, came to Way's Station, a small village on the Atlantic Air Line Railroad. During the next quarter-century, he implemented dramatic reforms that altered the land and the lives of its people. The change in name from Way's Station to Richmond Hill in 1941, also accomplished by Ford's influence, marked its transition from a blighted area into a model community.

In the 1920s Henry Ford reached the zenith of his career; his name was a household word and the "flivver"—as Americans dubbed the Model T— was a symbol of the age. Ford had already perfected mass production of automobiles and proved to cynics the practicality of the five-dollar work day.

*This paper was presented to the Georgia Historical Society 20 April 1979, and has appeared previously in *Atlanta Historical Journal* 24 (Spring 1980): 42-52. It is reprinted here with permission.

Each year the Ford Motor Company set record sales, and in 1924 the ten-millionth Model T rolled off the assembly line. Working men around the country could now own a car that eventually cost as little as $290.[1]

Having reached the pinnacle of business success, Ford now directed his energies and resources elsewhere. Some of his activities like the peace ship, *Oscar II*, his anti-Semitic campaign, his ill-fated venture into politics, and his frequently absurd public statements exposed his bigotry, his naivete, and the one-sided nature of his genius. Ford, turned social engineer, viewed human problems as if they were susceptible to mechanical solutions. Good planning and careful design could create a society that would function as efficiently as the engine of a Model T. Enamored with the ideals of agrarian simplicity and William H. McGuffey morality, Ford wanted to "create the working design for all that [he thought] was right and good and desirable." Like Carnegie and Rockefeller, he subscribed to the "gospel of wealth." He felt obliged, therefore, that as a steward of great wealth he should improve society and ameliorate social injustice.

Unwittingly perhaps, Ford was an old-fashioned Jeffersonian. After becoming a billionaire, he once confided to a minister-friend that "money means nothing to me—neither the making of it nor the use of it as far as I am personally concerned. I just want to live a life to make the world a little better. . . ."[2] Apparently, Ford failed to recognize the contradictions of his actions—Ford the builder of modern, motorized, urbanized America versus Ford the sentimental champion of nostalgic, rural values.[3] A combination of motives—personal, philanthropic, and capitalisitc—would attract Ford to the remote and lethargic village of Way's Station.

---

[1]Helpful background studies include Irving Bernstein, *The Lean Years. A History of the American Worker, 1920-1933* (Boston: Houghton Mifflin, 1960); John B. Rae, *The Road and the Car in American Life* (Cambridge: MIT Press, 1971); Allan Nevins and Frank E. Hill, *Ford: the Times, the Man, the Company* 3 vols. (New York: Scribner's, 1954-1962).

[2]S. S. Marquis, Dean, Episcopal Cathedral of Detroit, in a newspaper series, "Henry Ford: Lights and Shadows of the Elusive Personality," *Savannah Morning News* (26 November; 3, 10, 17, 24, 31 December 1922).

[3]In addition to the Nevins-Hill biography, other interesting treatments of Ford's life are Anne Jardim, *The First Henry Ford: A Study in Personality and Business Leadership* (Cambridge: MIT Press, 1970); David L. Lewis, *The Public Image of Henry Ford* (Detroit: Wayne State University Press, 1976); John B. Rae, ed., *Henry Ford* (Englewood Cliffs NJ: Prentice Hall, 1969); and Keith Sward, *The Legend of Henry Ford* (New York: Rinehart, 1948).

John Burroughs, the famous author-naturalist, was the first to com-
mend the beauty and climate of coastal Georgia to Henry Ford. Burroughs
first came to the state in 1907 and returned frequently to visit R. J. H.
DeLoach, a native Bulloch Countian who was on the faculty of the University of Georgia. After meeting Burroughs in 1913, Ford became so captivated with nature studies that he brought home a collection of songbirds
from England with which he planned to stock America's forests. Burroughs
and Ford later joined the self-styled "vagabonds," Harvey Firestone and
Thomas Edison, on rollicking excursions around the country. On a jaunt in
1915, Ford, Edison, and Firestone visited Luther Burbank's plantation in
California to inspect his experimental work. Edison apparently raised the
issue of American dependence on foreign rubber trees and observed that if
the country should enter war, rubber would become the nation's first shortage. Ford and Firestone challenged the inventor to discover a domestic supply or a substitute for this vital resource. When rubber prices rose sharply
in the mid-twenties, Ford and Firestone offered to finance Edison's
research.[4]

A series of circumstances merged at this juncture that would ultimately
lead Ford to Bryan County: namely, the desire for a winter homesite in a
climate more moderate than that of southern Florida, the need for sizable
acreage on which to grow rubber-producing plants, and the timely receipt
of a letter from R. L. Cooper, a Savannah realtor, advertising Cherry Hill,
Richmond, and Strathy Hall Plantations for sale in coastal Bryan County.
In December 1924, Frank Campsall, Ford's private secretary, appeared in
Cooper's office to inquire about properties between Charleston and Brunswick. The next day Mr. and Mrs. Ford visited Bryan County and, before
leaving Savannah, instructed Cooper to purchase the plantations and all
other land along the Ogeechee River east of Highway 17.[5] Newspaper accounts reported that Ford paid approximately $20 per acre for these early
tracts.[6] During the next two years he bought over 16,000 acres in the area.[7]

---

[4]Clara Barrus, *The Life and Letters of John Burroughs* (New York: Houghton Mifflin Company, 1925) 2:185, 194; Matthew Josephson, *Edison: A Biography* (London: Eyre & Spottis-
woode, 1961) 458, 470.

[5]"The Reminiscences of Mr. R. L. Cooper," Oral History Section, 1951, Ford Archives.

[6]*Savannah Morning News* (17 April, 9 May 1935); Pamphlet Collection, "Henry Ford,"
Savannah Public Library.

[7]Compiled from Bryan County Deed Records, Pembroke, Georgia. Purchases in Bryan
County included Orange Grove, Silk Hope, Cherry Hill, Richmond (formerly Dublin),

In 1927, Ford, Firestone, and Edison organized the Edison Botanic Research Company. The Ford Motor Company and the Firestone Tire and
Rubber Company each advanced $93,500, and Edison, despite failing
health, agreed to contribute his labor. After extensive collecting and test-
ing of plants gathered from around the world, Edison and his technicians
focused research on the goldenrod. Selective breeding ultimately produced
a variety of the plant that grew 14 feet high and produced a yield of up to
12 percent latex. Rubber created from this source, however, cost about $2
per pound.[8] Nonetheless, Ford, encouraged by Edison's success, greatly expanded holdings in Bryan and Chatham Counties for raising the crop. During the years 1930-1932, he bought over 44,000 additional acres, and
ultimately his holdings rose to 69,122 acres.[9] He reportedly purchased Val-
lambrosia Plantation (4,700 acres) across the Ogeechee River just to protect his view.[10]

Edison was convinced that he could give the United States a competitive, domestic rubber crop within five years. Time, however, ran out for
the noted inventor in 1931. Actually, Edison's goldenrod experiment was
foredoomed by the development of a new German chemical process for converting coal or petroleum derivatives into synthetic rubber. Ford, ever loyal
to "Mr. Edison," continued to support his idol's research. According to one
Edison biographer, where the great inventor was concerned, the ruthless
Ford was all sentiment.[11]

Even though Edison's death seriously crippled the research on goldenrod, Ford was still optimistic about the future of the weed, at least for a few
more years. H. G. Ukkleberg, a young agronomist from Minnesota who
had worked with Edison at his Fort Myers laboratory, was employed to continue the experiments at Richmond Hill. Ukkleberg directed experimental

---

Sterling Bluff, Ricedale, Strathy Hall, Cape Genesis (Jenyss) Point, Cottenham, Belvedere,
Kilkenny, Lincoln, Retreat, Fancy Hall, Star, Milford, Palermo, Tivoli, Belfast, Republican
Hall, Waterford, Tiperary, Egypt, Mount Hope, Tranquilla, Pearcefield; in Chatham
County: Vallambrosa, Beech Tree, Pine Bluff.

[8]Josephson, Edison, 470-72; Alfred Lief, The Firestone Story, A History of the Firestone
Tire and Rubber Company (New York: Whittlesey House, 1951) 159, 166.

[9]Compiled from Bryan County Deed Records.

[10]Book 26-J, Chatham County Deed Records, 279.

[11]Josephson, Edison, 457, 473, 484.

work on agricultural products there until 1941, after which he was placed in charge of all farming on the plantation.[12] In 1936 Firestone withdrew from the goldenrod venture, largely due to the success of his Liberian rubber plantations and his interest in the new synthetic process. Thereafter, Ford planted only a little goldenrod for "sentimental reasons."[13]

Ford built a laboratory for Ukkleberg's research in 1937 and instructed him to find uses for farm-waste products. He wanted to produce fertilizer from sawdust and ashes, bricks out of clay, sawdust, and cement, and plastics from sawdust, corn cobs, and pine bark.[14] That first year Ford also became excited about the potential of ramie, an Asiatic plant used in textile manufacturing in China. The crop proved unprofitable, however, since the yield per acre was extremely low. In his enthusiasm for ramie, Ford suggested that overseer Jack F. Gregory's tung trees be cleared out for his latest novelty.[15]

Ford also became interested in sweet potatoes, especially when he discovered how easily they were produced by local blacks. Ukkleberg made flour from potatoes and also used the culls to distill alcohol that worked well in the farm trucks. Ukkleburg quipped that his 20 young assistants were "experts" since all were either on probation or had served time for moonshining.[16] This experiment pleased Ford because he predicted that someday there would be a shortage of gasoline. At one time or another, Ford showed fleeting interest in growing rice, chea, perilla, safflower, indigo, and crotolaria.[17] The laboratory produced a few plastic tiles from corn cobs at the laborious pace of three or four tiles per day. Ukkleberg developed a process for producing rayon from sawdust out of which he made a few pairs of socks that were sent to his employer.[18]

---

[12]"The Reminiscences of Mr. H. G. Ukkleberg," Oral History Section, 1951, Ford Archives; also interview with Mr. Ukkleberg, Richmond Hill, Georgia, 10 May 1979.

[13]Ibid.

[14]Ibid.

[15]Ibid. According to Ukkleberg, 20 acres of ramie were planted in 1937. Apparently J. F. Gregory, superintendent of Richmond Hill Farms, introduced tung trees and planted 100 acres.

[16]Ibid.

[17]Ibid.

[18]Ibid.

In spite of the publicity given to Ford's experimental farming, one searches in vain for records in the Ford Archives that document controlled, scientific experiments. While Ford talked of making Richmond Hill Plantation profitable and self-sustaining, his interests were mercurial and frequently focused on the exotic and novel. Ukkleberg recalled that his enigmatic patron "tried to push all of us to develop something really good." On one occasion he told Ukkleberg: "You should have something new everyday to show me."[19] Apparently Ford did not comprehend that scientific plant-breeding could not produce immediate results. By 1940, scientific operations were significantly curtailed, and when the laboratory burned in 1941, Ukkleberg was reassigned to supervise farming operations. During the war years, Ford directed Ukkleberg to concentrate on food production. Some 20 different truck crops such as potatoes, string beans, and lettuce were grown for commercial marketing.[20]

In contrast to these agricultural experiments, Ford's investments in health services for Bryan County achieved rapid and dramatic results. Besides endemic poverty and an illiteracy rate that exceeded 20 percent, local residents were seriously debilitated by disease and malnutrition.[21] In 1930, Mrs. Samuel P. Rotan of Philadelphia, owner of Folly Farms, established Way's Station Health Association. She sought the assistance of Dr. C. F. Holton, chief surgeon for the Central of Georgia Railway in Savannah, who volunteered to become medical director of the clinic without salary. Dr. Holton induced Dr. Eugene Baker, a local child specialist, to conduct clinics twice weekly. Mrs. Constance Clark was employed as the resident nurse for the clinic. Upon moving to the area, she was the most popular resident in Bryan's Neck.[22] Since most of the patients who came to the clinic were

---

[19]Ibid.

[20]Ibid.

[21]In the Fourteenth Census of the U.S. (1920), Bryan County's population was 6,343 (white: 3,409; black: 2,920). Illiteracy rate for 10-year-olds and over averaged 20.8 percent (native whites: 5 percent; black: 38.6 percent). In the Fifteenth Census of the U.S. (1930), total population for Bryan County was 5,952 (white: 3,286; black: 2,666). Total population of District 20, Way's Station, was 1,514. By 1930 the illiteracy rate had declined to 13.4 percent (native whites: 5.2 percent; black: 23.9 percent).

[22]"Dr. Holton's History of the Clinic," Fair Lane Papers, Box 41, Ford Archives; "The Reminiscences of Dr. C. F. Holton," Oral History Section, 1951, Ford Archives.

either Ford employees or occupants of his land, Ford supported the clinic from 1931 to 1951.[23]

The countryside around Richmond Hill was a low, poorly drained region, an ideal breeding environment for anopheles mosquitoes. Ford, always a relentless enemy of sand flies and mosquitoes, recognized the enervating effects of malaria on local residents and solicited assistance from the state Board of Health. Nurse Clark recalled that in spite of regular consumption of bromo-quinine and "666," practically everyone was infected.[24] The state sent Dr. M. E. Winchester from Brunswick to supervise 17 nurses who took blood samples and administered the new drug, atabrine, to the entire population. According to Dr. Holton's findings, atabrine accomplished a 79 percent cure in a five-day course; the curative rate increased to 99 percent after an additional three-day course of plasmochin was given to the resistant cases. This intensive eradication effort, along with Ford's land-draining programs, brought malaria under control in the region.[25]

Dr. Holton's records showed that syphilis was actually more prevalent than malaria, especially among black residents. The clinic administered the neoarsphenamine treatment to 2,700 patients during its first ten years.[26] Intestinal parasites, commonly hookworm, plagued both races in the district, especially the children. In conjunction with the state Board of Health, the Ford clinic treated 239 cases of hookworm during the period from 1930 to 1935, and in the following five years only five new cases were identified.[27]

Likewise, the clinic conducted a widespread immunization campaign against typhoid, smallpox, and diphtheria; treated pellagra; provided prenatal care; performed tonsil and adenoid corrections; arranged for dental work, glasses, and x-rays for tuberculosis; and dispensed first aid. After

---

[23]Ibid.

[24]"The Reminiscences of Mrs. Constance Clark," Oral History Section, 1951, Ford Archives.

[25]"Dr. Holton's History," and C. F. Holton, "The Use of Atabrine in the Treatment and Control of Malaria among a Group of Industrial and Agricultural Employees in Georgia," *The Journal of the Medical Association of Georgia* 27 (August 1938): 299-304; and C. F. Holton, "Syphilis, Malaria and Hookworm Disease and Industrial Hazards in the South," *Southern Medical Journal* 31 (September 1938): 1011-16.

[26]"Dr. Holton's History."

[27]Ibid.

1935, activities were directed mainly toward the youth of the county with an emphasis on education and preventive medicine. Weekly clinics were held in every grade from kindergarten through high school, and every child was given a yearly health examination. During its first ten years, the clinic treated nearly 15,000 patients. Dr. Holton concluded that Ford's rehabilitation efforts had "changed the population from a sickly, suspicious, illiterate, and undernourished group into one of the healthiest communities in Georgia."[28]

As Henry Ford became more deeply committed to rehabilitating the region, Mrs. Ford devoted her efforts to the construction of a winter home. She envisioned a dream house with columns, wide verandas, a magnificent staircase, and large spacious rooms. The Fords scouted Greek Revival houses in Athens and Washington, and seriously considered buying Orange Hall in St. Marys and moving it to Richmond Hill.[29] The new mansion would stand at the junction of three avenues of magnificent live oak trees a few hundred feet from the Ogeechee River, the site of an earlier plantation house. When Edward J. Cutler, chief draftsman at Dearborn who made the original drawings for the mansion, first viewed the site, he recalled that "it was just like stepping into a real cathedral the way those trees arched up and came together across the top."[30] Cletus W. Bergen, a Savannah architect, was retained to draw the blueprints. In 1935, Ford bought the "Hermitage," a Savannah River plantation house, from the City of Savannah for $10,000, and some of the bricks from the old structure were used in the building of "Richmond."[31] Actual construction began in 1936; the Fords lived in a private railroad car until their new residence was completed.

"Richmond" was a Northern version of a Greek Revival structure; it contained a ballroom, parlors, and a huge kitchen on the first floor; six upstairs bedrooms; and seven baths. Magnificent chandeliers, one of which cost $65,000, and elegant crystal, china, and silver complemented the ex-

---

[28]Ibid.

[29]Letter from R. L. Cooper to Frank Campsall, 11 June 1928, Fair Lane Papers, Box 41, Ford Archives.

[30]"The Reminiscences of Mr. Edward J. Cutler," Oral History Section, 1951, Ford Archives.

[31]*Savannah Morning News* (17 April 1935). Article gives a short history of the "Hermitage" and describes the dismantling of the old mansion.

quisitely appointed furnishings. Later, servants' quarters and a garage were added. Fifty-five acres of surrounding grounds were landscaped with camellias, azaleas, and exotic shrubs, all planned to create a fairyland of blossoms for the Fords' annual spring visits.[32] By 1939, disbursements for the mansion, furnishings, and grounds totaled about $360,000.[33]

Following the construction of the mansion, other facilities were erected at Richmond Hill from 1938 to 1946. These included an ice plant, a community house, a blacksmith shop, an office building, a chapel, a turpentine still, a carpenter shop, a white teacherage, a commissary, and 108 housing units that were located primarily in the residential villages known as "The Bottom" and "Blueberry." A new sawmill, a remodeled clinic, and Ford's various educational buildings were also built. Most of the lumber was cut and sawed on the plantation and labor was provided by Ford employees. The Martha-Mary Chapel, however, was prefabricated in Ford's plant at Wayside Inn, Massachusetts. Reports of capital investment revealed that annual expenditures rose to $420,000 in 1941. Total expenditures for developments and improvements in the period 1938-1946 were in excess of $1,645,000.[34]

Ford was most interested in the children of the region and took delight in watching them at work and play. Indeed, his concern for the health and education of children motivated his finest efforts at Richmond Hill. He was especially sympathetic to those with handicaps.[35] When he first arrived, Bryan County operated a consolidated white school in the 20th district and six one-room schools for black children that were scattered throughout Bryan's Neck. In 1937, Ford assumed responsibility for operating all of the schools in the district and soon provided a chemistry lab, dining room, and playgrounds for the whites. He emphasized the importance of vocational education for boys and home economics for girls, and supported such extracurricular activities as dramatics, music, sports, and student gardens. At the close of the school year in 1937, the senior class visited Dearborn as guests of the Fords. A new trade school, established in 1938, offered courses

[32]*Detroit Free Press* (23 March 1975).

[33]File 384.1, Fair Lane Papers, Box 41, Ford Archives.

[34]Acc. 97, Box 1, Fair Lane Papers, Ford Archives.

[35]See "Reminiscences of Mrs. Constance Clark" and "The Reminiscences of Mr. Aimar Martin," Oral History Section, 1951, Ford Archives.

in mechanical drawing, wood and metal working, blacksmithing, and welding.[36]

Ford built the George Washington Carver School for black youth in 1939 and employed H. G. Cooper, a professional educator, as its first principal. Dr. Carver personally came from Tuskegee to dedicate the new facility. This consolidated school operated nine months each year and was staffed by qualified black teachers who were paid the state scale plus a supplement. Carver School opened with 150 students in seven grades; an additional grade was added each year though the eleventh grade. At its peak, enrollment reached 300 students. The curriculum included academic and vocational classes. From 1939-1945, a night school was also conducted for six months each term to teach adults the fundamentals of reading, writing, and arithmetic. In 1939, Ford added a kindergarten for preschoolers. Professor Cooper praised the success of a cooperative gardening project that was started in 1943. Ford cleared 100 acres for this project, and before the first year was out, all boys in the fourth grade and up learned to operate a tractor. The boys sold their produce, kept records, and netted a profit of $250.[37] Ford provided school buses, textbooks, and libraries for both races, and operated school lunchrooms long before public funds were available for this program. Black patrons organized a P.T.A. at Carver that sponsored a financial program for graduates who wanted to attend college. Five students out of the first graduating class in 1945 attended Savannah State College and three of these earned their degrees.[38]

According to Cooper, Ford felt that both races should be given equal opportunity and equal compensation for the same work. In an attempt to evaluate the impact of Ford's various projects on race relations, Cooper concluded that Ford's work did not last long enough for the "good to become a

---

[36]For Ford's educational projects, see "The Reminiscences of Mrs. Harry Gill," Oral History Section, 1951, Ford Archives; "The Reminiscences of Mr. Edward J. Cutler"; folder, 384.1, Fair Lane Papers; Acc. 517, Auditing Reports, 1928-1946, Box 1, Richmond Hill Plantation Operation Reports, Fair Lane Papers, Box 41, Ford Archives; "Education at Richmond Hill Plantation and Fort McAllister," Box 41, Ford Archives; and J. F. Gregory to Frank Campsall, 5 February 1940, Box 41, Fair Lane Papers, Ford Archives.

[37]Ibid. Also especially useful, "Reminiscences of Mr. H. G. Cooper," Oral History Section, 1951, Ford Archives.

[38]Ibid.

reality." "Just as soon as Mr. Ford dropped out of the picture," Cooper observed, "all that he had done and built up was torn down again."[39]

Jack F. Gregory, a local Scotch-Irishman who was superintendent at Richmond Hill for 12 years, was the pivotal figure both in fostering amicable race relations and in overseeing all phases of plantation development. While Gregory was described by a Detroit visitor as a "regular chain-gang man," Professor Cooper considered him the best man for whom he had ever worked. Cooper observed that while Gregory had little formal education, he was a man of good common sense who would sometimes side with the blacks against his own race. H. G. Ukkleberg praised Gregory as "the right man for the job" because he knew the local people and how to work them.[40] Undoubtedly influenced by his wife, Ford lost confidence in Gregory in later years. Mrs. Ford's enmity reportedly stemmed from a dispute about a fence to protect her rosebushes at "Richmond." Too, Gregory was accused of employing his relatives and some of his practices were allegedly slipshod. But in his defense it should be noted that he supervised the reclamation of several thousand acres and the work of approximately 800 employees during the era when the plantation was at maximum operation.

Ray Newman, a subforeman from the Ford Farms in Michigan, replaced Gregory in 1946. Newman was summoned to Richmond Hill by Mrs. Ford who offered him the position under two conditions that he "cut down the overhead and show a profit, or else."[41] Plantation tax records showed mounting losses that peaked at over $400,000 in 1941.[42] Newman immediately began to reorganize and trim operations. The kindergarten and training school were discontinued, the white high school was restored to county control, and the Carver School budget was slashed. With cutbacks in labor and savings from the introduction of machinery, farming operations were placed on a profitable basis. Sawmilling was expanded and became the most profitable enterprise on the plantation. Ford, already suffering from declining health, was merely a spectator in these decisions.

Although Newman's reorganization was operative for only a part of 1946, he cut the losses of the previous year by half. In 1947, the plantation

---

[39]Ibid.

[40]Ibid. Cutler, "Reminiscences"; Interview with H. G. Ukkleberg, 10 May 1979.

[41]"The Reminiscences of Mr. Ray Newman," Oral History Section, 1951, Ford Archives.

[42]Federal Income Tax Returns of Henry Ford, 1925-1947, Ford Archives.

showed a net operating profit of nearly $50,000.[43] Henry Ford died that year, and the Richmond Hill properties passed to the Ford Foundation with Clara Ford as executor. After her death in 1950, the plantation was sold in 1951 to the Southern Kraft Timberland Corporation which in turn sold it to the International Paper Company the next year.[44] Essentially, this ended the Ford era.

What then was the Ford legacy at Richmond Hill? If one seeks only tangible reminders of the Ford era, then only the name of the community and a few buildings still survive. Yet, Richmond Hill was more than just a winter home for Henry and Clara Ford. While he undoubtedly enjoyed the privacy of his Georgia retreat where he acted the part of a paternalistic country squire, his rehabilitation projects were a "godsend" to the people of Richmond Hill. Compared to a "private T.V.A.," his remarkable improvements changed health and education, provided jobs and vocational training, created decent housing, and restored several thousand acres to production. Perhaps more significantly, Ford altered the lives of at least two generations of coastal Bryan Countians. He showed them a better way to live and launched them upon it. By instilling hope and providing opportunity, he

---

[43]Memorandum from Ray Newman to R. T. Ross, 17 January 1947, and subsequent operation reports, Box 41, Fair Lane Papers, Ford Archives; also Annual Report, 1947, Box 41, Fair Lane Papers, Ford Archives.

[44]Wills of Henry and Clara Ford, Bryan County Deed Record 3B, 409-410, and 3E, 161; Indenture, Bryan County Deed Record, 3E, 73-145; Indenture, Bryan County Deed Record, 3E, 251. Hereafter the chain of title becomes much more complicated. The property has attracted many ambitious investors and developers like Gilbert Verney, James W. McCook, Jr., Maurice Coley, and George P. Tobler. All lacked either the resources or management skills to realize their dreams. The Ford estate was added to the National Register of Historic Places on 30 January 1978. In December 1978, an entangled litigation—George P. Tobler and Henry Ford Plantations, Inc. vs. Yoder and Frey Auctioneers, Inc. (U.S. District Court, Southern District of Georgia)—ruled against the defendant. Subsequently, part of the original Ford holdings including the decaying and vandalized mansion, were sold to A. G. Proctor, a Brunswick developer. The new owner began to develop a resort community in the area and the partially refurbished mansion was converted into a fashionable restaurant to serve both a local clientele and tourists from I-95. Currently Bryco Corporation owns the property, and the individual backer, Ghaith Pharaon, has begun to develop an exclusive resort community called "Cherry Hill" on the 1800-acre tract. Th Ford mansion and its environs have become Pharaon's private estate. Development plans for "Cherry Hill" include 250 single-family lots, a golf course, a country club, a canal system with lagoons, tennis courts, nature trails, and an equestrian center. See WAPORA, Inc., *Cherry Hill Development Environmental Report*, Project 381 (15 April 1983) 1; *Cherry Hill Plantation Development Report, Appendices*, Project 381 (15 April 1983) 34-37.

broke the vicious cycle of poverty, ignorance, and disease. While his agri-cultural experiments were often hampered by his impatience, he pioneered future uses of the soybean and gasohol, and demonstrated that scientific for-estry was both practical and profitable. Even his shortlived projects with rice, tung trees, and goldenrod left posterity a tradition of bold experimen-tation that might prove useful to future generations. As Mrs. Harry Gill, a Richmond Hill housewife, reminisced after Ford's death: "We knew that we had lost a good neighbor and a true friend."[45]

---

[45]Gill, "Reminiscences."

THIRTEEN

The Mighty Altamaha River*

ALTAMAHA, THE LILTING name of Georgia's largest river, is one of the oldest place-names in Georgia. Apparently of Indian origin, it was mentioned by De Soto's chroniclers in 1540. Older spellings were "Alatamahaw" or "Alatamaha"; the second "a" was dropped in the mid-nineteenth century. The older spelling persists, however, in the scientific name of the botanical specimen, *Franklinia alatamaha*, that was first discovered by John Bartram near Fort Barrington in 1765. All along the river one encounters other colorful place-names like Hell's Shoal, Stooping Gum, Marrowbone Round, Hog Pen Slough, and Doctortown. At a site where the river sharply reverses its direction, it forms Knee Buckle Island with a cutoff channel known as Dick Swift. Soon one comes upon Cole Eddy and Bugs Suck, hazardous currents where log rafters were sometimes swept into the banks or grounded in shallow water. Another tight curve difficult for the rafters was Old Bell Bight. Upriver was Rag Point where raftsmen making their first trip downriver customarily left a piece of a shirt tied to a tree. Other features that enhance the river's lore include Oglethorpe and Sansavilla Bluffs, Buffalo Swamp, Old Woman's Pocket, and Buttermilk Sound.

The Altamaha River is formed by the junction of the Oconee and Ocmulgee Rivers, its major tributaries. The headwaters of the Oconee rise

*This essay was written for publication in Richard A. Bartlett, ed. *Rolling Rivers: An Encyclopedia of America's Rivers* to be published by McGraw-Hill. It is published here with permission of McGraw-Hill Book Company.

along the base of the Chattahoochee River not far from Gainesville and form the North Oconee and the Middle Oconee. These form the greater Oconee a few miles south of Athens. The Apalachee River and other tributaries flow into the Oconee farther downstream. Above the fall line near Milledgeville, the river valley of the Oconee is narrow and bounded by hilly terrain; its stream bed commonly contains rocks and shoals.

The headwaters of the Ocmulgee rise near Atlanta where they divide to form the South and Yellow Rivers. Their confluence, along with the Alcovy River, is impounded by Lloyd Shoals Dam, creating Jackson Lake. Below the dam the combined waters flow as the Ocmulgee to the fall line at Macon. The Oconee and the Ocmulgee meet head-on at the "Forks" where Jeff Davis, Wheeler, and Montgomery Counties border. The mighty Altamaha River then flows about 140 miles southeastwardly to the Atlantic Ocean. It meanders most of that distance through "wiregrass" Georgia, being joined by the Ohoopee River and numerous creeks. Approximately 23 miles from the Atlantic, the river forms a delta and divides into several branches, namely, the Altamaha, the South Altamaha, and the Darien Rivers. Ocean tides affect these streams as far as 39 miles inland. Sapelo and St. Simons Islands, which lie on either side of the river's estuary, like the other major offshore islands of the Georgia coast, are closely connected with the history of the Altamaha.

This coastal area was the home of the Guale Indians, a tribal confederacy numbering perhaps as many as 4,000 persons prior to depletion by white contact and Indian invasion from the north. The Guale belonged to the Muskogean linguistic family and were relatives of the Yamasees and the Creeks with whom they ultimately merged. The "mico" or chief of these tribes originally resided on St. Catherines Island. As a sedentary people, the Guale engaged in hunting, fishing, and agriculture. Their burial mounds and shell middens have been discovered on all the islands along the Georgia coast.

Almost from the beginning of European colonization, Georgia was a "debatable land." For more than two centuries after the voyages of Columbus, the Spanish plotted with the Indians and fought against the French and English to control the coastal islands of Georgia and the narrow strip of adjacent mainland. Earlier, Spanish explorers had claimed the area; Pedro Menendez de Aviles had visited Guale in 1565, set up a cross, planted the Spanish flag, and left behind a garrison of 30 men.

Spanish presidios and missions, antedating those established in California by two centuries, were established and periodically destroyed during the next century. Jesuit priests first introduced Christianity to the natives in 1568 and organized missions on St. Catherines and Cumberland Islands. Even though these lasted only two years, Franciscans resumed missionary work in 1573 and subsequently erected five major missions: San Pedro (Cumberland Island), San Buenaventure (St. Simons Island), Santo Domingo (on the mainland near the Altamaha River), San Jose (Sapelo Island), and Santa Catalina (St. Catherines Island). The missions were destroyed in 1597 and rebuilt during the next decade. In 1606 the Bishop of Cuba made the first pastoral visit to the mainland and confirmed more than a thousand Guale Indians into the Catholic faith. South Carolinians, in violation of the Treaty of Madrid of 1670, pushed all Spanish outposts in Guale southward to the Altamaha River in 1680. In 1686, the northernmost Spanish settlement was on the St. Marys River; by 1702 the Spaniards and their Indian allies were restricted to Florida.

For nearly 50 years Guale remained uninhabited by white men and undisturbed except for occasional pirate raids. In 1721 South Carolinians built Fort King George on the high ground where Snow Creek entered an old meander of the Darien River. Constructed as a barrier against the Spanish in Florida and the French from the interior, it was the first English fort on Georgia soil. Fort King George was abandoned in 1727 because of mutinous garrisons, a destructive fire, and high maintenance costs.

The original grant given to the "Trustees for Establishing the Colony of Georgia in America" by George II was that territory between the Savannah and Altamaha Rivers, from the coast northward to their headwaters, and thence westward to the Pacific Ocean. General James E. Oglethorpe, a trustee and member of Parliament, founded Savannah at Yamacraw Bluff on 12 February 1733 to serve as a military buffer for South Carolina, to promote English mercantilism, and to begin a philanthropic experiment to relieve England's crowded debtors' prisons. Relying upon the friendship of Tomo-Chi-Chi, mico of the Yamacraws, and the services of Mary Musgrove as interpreter, Oglethorpe hosted a meeting of more than 50 Indian chiefs in May 1733. He successfully won the friendship of the chiefs and convinced them to cede the lands designated in the charter of 1732.

In January 1734 Oglethorpe visited St. Simons and Jekyll Islands and selected sites for two major defensive outposts, New Inverness and Frederica. A band of Scotch Highlanders, recruited for their fighting qualities, was settled at the mouth of the Altamaha in 1736. That settlement became known as Darien in honor of an ill-fated Scotch settlement on the Isthmus of Panama that was destroyed by the Spaniards about 40 years earlier. By late March 1736, a fort and town were also nearing completion on St. Simons, facing a southerly branch of the estuary of the Altamaha. It was called Frederica in honor of the son of George II. Fort Frederica was the largest and perhaps the most costly fortification erected by the English in North America. In 1740 Frederica had a population of 1,000 including the regiment of English regulars. Among its inhabitants was Oglethorpe, who resided there until he left Georgia in 1743. Fort St. Simons was constructed at the south end of the island and was connected with Fort Frederica by the Military Road. Fort Frederica and the fort at Darien on the other side of the Altamaha's delta were connected by waterways. To facilitate this communication, a canal was cut through General's Island. It is known as General's Cut and is still in use. To complete his communication network, Oglethorpe ordered that a road from Darien to Savannah be surveyed and built; it is now the Atlantic Coastal Highway.

The effectiveness of Oglethorpe's defensive strategy was soon tested in the War of Jenkins' Ear, a phase of the imperial rivalry between England and Spain that developed into King George's War. The land operations of the conflict in this area were fought largely on St. Simons Island. In July 1742 the Spaniards invaded the island with 50 vessels, 1,000 seamen, and 1,800 soldiers. Oglethorpe's entire force numbered only 600 men. The Spaniards took possession of Fort St. Simons and pursued the retreating Georgians toward Frederica. Following several skirmishes, Lieutenants Sutherland and Mackay surprised a Spanish detachment and killed or captured 200 Spaniards. This clash came to be called the "Battle of Bloody Marsh", and, while it was far from a decisive victory, it sufficiently demoralized the Spaniards to cause them to return to Florida.

Although this encounter substantially established Georgia's possession of lands north of the Altamaha, Georgians encountered difficulties from the Spanish, South Carolinians, and Creek Indians before gaining undisputed control over the region south of the Altamaha. Oglethorpe claimed the territory but King George's War ended without a settlement of the boundary between Georgia and Spanish Florida. While in limbo, the region became a refuge for outlaws and a target for schemers. South Carolina laid claim to the trans-Altamaha country in 1760 and started a major land speculation when South Carolina's Governor Boone granted 343,000 acres to influential South Carolina planters such as Henry Middleton and Henry Laurens. After the Treaty of Paris in 1763, the territory was ceded to Georgia by royal proclamation. Georgia's Governor Wright disputed South Carolina's legal right to preempt Georgia lands before the Board of Trade and, while the land scheme was declared unwarranted, the colonies were left to resolve their differences. Georgia later agreed to confirm the grants if the South Carolinians would conform with Georgia laws and register their patents. Some 20 claims were finally established. In the Treaty of Augusta in 1763, the Creeks ceded the lands along the Atlantic coast from the Altamaha to the St. Marys River, the area that would later become Glynn and Camden Counties. With the removal of these obstacles, the region could now be opened for settlement. The rising spirit of revolution would, however, postpone this development for 20 years.

Prosperous and contented under the leadership of their governor, Sir James Wright, Georgians lagged in support for the revolutionary cause. Beginning with the stamp-act crisis, however, the Midway settlement in St. John Parish was the center of anti-British agitation. As the struggle became more widespread and heated, Georgians began to hold meetings at Tondee's Tavern in Savannah that led to the organization of a provincial congress. Within a month after Lexington and Concord, revolutionaries seized control of the colony from British-appointed Governor Wright and joined the other 12 colonies in rebellion.

Although few major battles were fought on Georgia soil, widespread devastation was caused by invading British regulars and bitter conflicts between Whigs and Tories. Florida and the region south of the Altamaha became the haven for Tories, runaway slaves, and hostile Indians. For three years Georgia troops marched up and down the coast in what Dr. Coulter described as "a border war game, half-comic though tragic enough." The infamous Florida Rangers, operating from St. Augustine, remained an ominous threat to Fort Howe (Fort Barrington) on the Altamaha. In 1778 Georgia's Governor John Houston planned a campaign to destroy the British base in Florida. A force of 2,000 soldiers, composed of Colonel Samuel Elbert's Georgia Continentals, General Robert Howe's Continental regulars, and Houston's militia, was to rendezvous at Fort Howe for a march into Florida. The ambitious strategy failed, however, because of jealousy among the commanders, lack of preparation, weather, and the swampy route of the march.

Late in 1778, Florida forces composed of British regulars, Indians, and Schopolites under the command of Colonel Mark Prevost launched a campaign directed at the Midway district, and ultimately at Savannah. Lieutenant Colonel L. V. Fuser was to provide naval support for the mission and their combined forces were to join Lieutenant Colonel Archibald Campbell who was sailing from New York with 2,000 British regulars. Prevost reached the Altamaha in mid-November and went on to Midway but could contact neither Fuser nor Campbell. When he realized the strategy had gone awry, Prevost retreated to Florida leaving destruction in his wake.

Campbell's expedition from New York landed near the mouth of the Savannah River and captured the city of Savannah 29 December 1778. Colonel Augustine Prevost's forces advanced again from Florida, captured Fort Morris at Sunbury, and swept on to the junction at Savannah. By the end of January 1779, Ebenezer and Augusta were in British hands as Georgia fell under British occupation. Guerrilla resistance on land and sea, however, kept the patriot cause alive. A bold move to evict the British from Savannah failed miserably in 1779 in spite of French aid. Finally, through the heroic efforts of Elijah Clarke, John Dooly, and other fearless leaders, the British were defeated in the Georgia backcountry. By July 1782, Governor Wright had again fled the colony. British troops had evacuated Savannah, and the rebel government of Georgia was restored to power.

From the very first English settlement, agriculture, cattle raising, and lumbering were the main economic interests along the Georgia coast. One of the earliest resources harvested was live oak timber. The USS *Constitution*, famous as *Old Ironsides*, was built of oak grown on St. Simons. Similarly, an unexpected windfall of funds from a cattle roundup on St. Simons helped pay for the construction of Fort Barrington on the Altamaha in 1760. In the early nineteenth century sea-island cotton was the leading crop on the coastal islands. First grown by the Scots on St. Simons as early as 1778, sea-island cotton quickly spread to other islands along the coast and replaced indigo as the staple crop. By 1829 coastal planters produced 13,729 bales. Production peaked in 1894 when Georgia produced 39,367 bales. Thomas Spalding's plantation on Sapelo Island produced the first sugar cane in Georgia. By 1830 the culture of sugar cane had spread upriver into the hinterland as far as Milledgeville and Macon. Other crops common to the sea islands included corn and sweet potatoes.

The limited zone marked by the "ebb and flow" of the tides was the preeminent domain of the great rice plantations—an extension of the

South Carolina rice plantation culture. Local planters developed an ingenious and extensive hydraulic engineering system of dikes, canals, sluice gates, and dams that controlled the flow of river water into the fields at high tide and drained them at low tide. James Hamilton Couper's plantation, Hopeton, was one of the most productive in coastal Georgia. At Hopeton, located on the south side of the Altamaha in Glynn County about five miles above Darien, Couper rotated rice, sugar cane, and sea-island cotton on his swamplands.

A short distance upriver from Hopeton, the tidewater region, then as now, gives way to "wiregrass" country. Here in the vast forests of longleaf pine early settlers made small clearings where they built crude houses and planted small fields of corn, tobacco, sugar cane, and patches of subsistence crops. Their main livelihood came from cattle and hogs that ranged freely through the "piney woods" and grazed on wiregrass, shrubs, acorns, and pine mast. William Bartram, the naturalist-explorer who visited the region in the 1770s, referred to these settlements as "cowpens." Regional writer, Caroline Miller, won the Pulitzer prize in 1934 for her novel, *Lamb in His Bosom*, a story of pioneer life in wiregrass Georgia during pre-Civil War days. This sparsely settled region still retains its unique cultural identity; its residents still farm and harvest lumber, pulp wood, and naval stores.

For most of the nineteenth century, the Altamaha River system was the main artery of commerce between middle Georgia and the coast; Darien was its seaport. Flatboats were largely used to float cotton down river to Darien. Incapable of returning upstream, these boats would be dismantled and sold for lumber. One of the earliest to drift a flatboat down the Oconee and Altamaha was Freeman Lewis who brought down 5,000 bushels of corn in July 1806. Poleboats, operated by thrusting long poles into the river bed, carried passengers and freight in both directions. By 1806, A. Mills, a poleboat operator, reported that he had made seven round-trips between Milledgeville and Darien. Traveling upstream from Darien to the "Forks" by poleboat sometimes required 15 to 20 days.

Darien prospered and, although its population was never very large, it was designated the county seat of McIntosh County in 1818. That same year its first newspaper was published and the Bank of Darien was chartered with a capitalization of one million dollars. This bank, with branches in seven Georgia cities, was the major financial institution in Georgia for several decades. A new aspect of Darien's port city function was ushered in when the first steamboat to travel the Altamaha left Darien late in 1818 and arrived in Milledgeville early in 1819. Actually steamboats never completely replaced poleboats because the latter could navigate at low water. The Macon-Atlantic Navigation Company, the last line to operate on the river, continued until the 1930s. On a typical haul, cargo included groceries, hardware, sugar, and fertilizer that was put off at Doctortown and other landings on the Altamaha—at Lumber City, Jacksonville, Hawkinsville, and Macon on the Ocmulgee, and Mount Vernon and Dublin on the Oconee. Cargo downstream was cotton, naval stores, and lumber. During the prohibition era, numerous whiskey stills along the river supported a lively sugar traffic. When the Central of Georgia Railroad reached Macon in 1843, steamboat lines were forced to reduce freight rates to meet this competition. Other rail lines and a network of highways, completed in the early twentieth century, doomed the surviving steamboats. Today the river is used largely by pleasure craft and fishermen.

Darien suffered a number of serious fires in the nineteenth century, not the least of which occurred in 1863 when it was burned by Northern troops stationed on St. Simons Island. It was rebuilt in the 1870s and again became a major port, deriving a great part of its commerce from the timber floated down the Altamaha. For about 40 years prior to World War I, log rafting thrived on the Altamaha and its tributaries. The virgin "yellow pine" forests of the interior were harvested by squatters, landowners, and large land companies. These trees, 60 to more than 100 feet long, were felled, crudely squared, dragged to the edge of a stream, and floated to either the Oconee, Ocmulgee, Ohoopee, or Altamaha. They were then formed into rafts, sometimes 200 feet long. Raftsmen partially controlled their unwieldy craft with a long sweep at bow and stern. At Darien the logs were sold to lumber companies that sawed them into timber for shipment to markets around the world. In the early days many raftsmen walked back home. These rivermen were a tough and colorful breed who disappeared when the vast forests were cut. The depletion of the forests in the vast hinterland also ended Darien's booming prosperity and the old town has never recovered.

Just south of Darien lies Butler Island, formerly owned by Major Pierce Butler of South Carolina. His grandson and namesake married Fanny Kemble, the beautiful English actress, and brought her to live at Hampton in 1838. It was here that she began to write her *Journal of a Residence on a Georgia Plantation*, a passionate denunciation of slavery. After a brief and stormy marriage, the Butlers were divorced and Fanny Kemble returned to the stage, never again to visit the Georgia coast. Her daughter, Frances Butler Leigh, inherited and managed the Butler plantations for four years during the Reconstruction years. Her experiences are recorded in *Ten Years on a Georgia Plantation Since the War*, a major study of the problems of coastal planters without slaves.

Along the south branch of the Altamaha near the Couper plantation of Hopeton were Elizafield, Grantly, and Evelyn, the plantations of Dr. Robert Grant. Adjacent to these were Broadfield and New Hope which belonged to William Brailsford of Charleston. These baronial estates were tended by hundreds of Gullah slaves whose descendants still speak quite differently from their white neighbors. For decades linguists, anthropologists, and historians have been fascinated by Gullah culture, a unique blend of European and African traits. Modern influences still have not obliterated the beliefs and customs of a people who were isolated for generations. One can still discover believers in "conjuring," "haints," and "root doctors." Some religious groups still sing the old spirituals and dance frenetically to the beat of drums and tambourines.

During the Civil War Darien was burned in 1863 and the Savannah, Albany and Gulf Railroad was destroyed by Sherman's troops in December 1864 as far south as the Altamaha. Otherwise the impact of the war was felt in the heavy casualties sustained by the numerous companies raised in the various counties on both sides of the river. For example, out of three full companies raised in McIntosh County, barely 50 men, including the wounded, returned.

Reconstruction brought a new social order to the entire South. Along the lower Altamaha, one of the most controversial personalities was Tunis G. Campbell, a black carpetbagger from New Jersey. After an unsuccessful attempt to establish a black separatist regime on St. Catherines Island, Campbell became the labor and political boss of the former Gullah slaves in McIntosh County. He served in Georgia's Constitutional Convention, 1867-1868, and was later elected to the state senate. While serving as a magistrate in Darien he falsely arrested a British ship's captain. In 1875 Campbell was prosecuted, found guilty, and sentenced to a year in prison after which he fled the state.

By 1900 shortages of labor and capital, a series of destructive hurricanes, and competition from Louisiana growers ended plantation rice culture in the Altamaha delta. Naval stores, lumbering, and later shrimping replaced agriculture as sources of livelihood. Like the rest of the South, the

Altamaha region languished into economic and cultural deprivation and for several decades experienced a population drain. Meanwhile, small towns along the railroads and paved highways a few miles north and south of the river developed a measure of local prosperity and cultural achievement based largely upon local resources. Some like Claxton, Glennville, Ludowici, and Jesup drew upon a growing tourist traffic. All over the region slash and loblolly pine forests were planted and harvested for lumber and paper products. New jobs were created by the Rayonier Company, which operates a large pulp manufacturing plant along the Altamaha near Jesup in Wayne County. Other paper corporations like Georgia Pacific and Brunswick Pulp and Paper Company also own or lease large tracts of forested land in the region. Another aspect of modern economic development is the Edwin I. Hatch Nuclear Plant near Baxley in Appling County located about 20 miles below the "Forks." The plant, utilizing the river water in a closed circulatory system, has a generating capacity of 1,600,000 kilowatts. When completed it will represent an investment of nearly one billion dollars and the promise of energy abundance for the upper Altamaha area.

Major changes have occurred also in the lower reaches of the Altamaha as its marshlands, coastal mainland, and especially the offshore islands have felt developmental pressures. Beginning with Thomas Carnegie's purchase of the greater part of Cumberland Island in 1881, the coastal islands of Georgia soon became the playground of Northern millionaires. In 1886 Jekyll Island became one of the most exclusive winter resorts in the world; the Jekyll Island Club was composed of 100 of the nation's wealthiest men. In 1911 Howard E. Coffin, Detroit automobile magnate, purchased Sapelo. After Coffin's death, R. J. Reynolds bought the property. Today Sapelo is the site of the Marine Institute of the University of Georgia and is preserved in a nearly natural state. St. Simons has become an extensive residential community that retains many of its giant live oaks and miles of beaches. Georgia's coastal lands are coveted by conservationists, real estate developers, and industrialists, each attracted by the natural resources, beaches, the wild beauty of the Altamaha River, and a history reaching back over four centuries. These same attributes constitute a rich legacy for all Georgians.

Suggested Readings on the Altamaha Basin

Bagwell, James E. "James Hamilton Couper, Georgia Rice Planter." Ph.D. dissertation, University of Southern Mississippi, 1978.

Cate, Margaret Davis. *Our Todays and Yesterdays.* Brunswick GA: Glover Bros., 1926.

Chalker, Fussell M. *Pioneer Days Along the Ocmulgee.* Carrollton GA: 1970.

Coleman, Kenneth. ed., *A History of Georgia.* Athens: University of Georgia Press, 1977.

Coulter, E. Merton. *Georgia, A Short History.* Chapel Hill: University of North Carolina Press, 1960.

_____. *Thomas Spalding of Sapelo.* Baton Rouge: Louisiana State University Press, 1940.

Edwards, Norman. "The Old Southeast and Fort King George: Borderland of Three Empires." M.A. thesis, Georgia Southern College, 1980.

Grant, Hugh F. *Planter Management and Capitalism in Antebellum Georgia,* ed. by Albert V. House. New York: Columbia University Press, 1954.

Fancher, Betsey. *The Lost Legacy of Georgia's Golden Isles.* Garden City NJ: Doubleday and Co., 1971.

Huxford, Folks. comp., *Pioneers of Wiregrass Georgia.* Homerville GA, 1951, 4 volumes.

Kemble, Frances A. *Journal of A Residence on A Georgia Plantation.* New York: Harper and Bros., 1863.

King, Spencer B., Jr. *Darien: The Death and Rebirth of a Southern Town.* Macon GA: Mercer University Press, 1981.

Leigh, Frances B. *Ten Years on A Georgia Plantation Since the War.* London: Richard Bentley and Son, 1883.

Lewis, Bessie. *McIntosh County.* Darien GA: Ashantilly Press, 1966.

_____. *Patriarchial Plantations of St. Simons Island.* Darien GA: Darien News, 1974.

Lovell, Caroline C. *The Golden Isles of Georgia.* Boston: Little, Brown, and Co., 1932.

Morrison, Carlton. "Raftsmen of the Altamaha." M.A. thesis, University of Georgia, 1970.

Van Doren, Mark. *The Travels of William Bartram.* New York: Dover Publications, 1928.

Vanstory, Burnette. *Georgia's Land of the Golden Isles.* Athens: University of Georgia Press, 1970.

Novels

Cheney, Brainard. *River Rogue*. Boston: Houghton Mifflin Co., 1942.
Miller, Caroline. *Lamb in His Bosom*. New York: Harper and Bros., 1933.

Select Bibliography

Part of the excitement in writing local history comes from the detective work necessarily involved in locating sources—plundering courthouses, newspaper files, family and institutional records. Although Savannah and the golden isles of Georgia have attracted numerous historians and writers, the mainland between the Ogeechee and St. Marys Rivers and the pine barrens of the hinterlands have not received the same attention. Consequently, any historian of this neglected region will soon discover the dearth of collected and published materials. The official archives of the state, the Georgia Department of Archives and History, and the libraries of the University of Georgia, Emory University, the Georgia Historical Society, the University of North Carolina, Duke University, the Library of Congress, and the National Archives are major depositories for materials relating to Georgia. How lamentable that so many of the invaluable manuscript collections are outside of the state.

The most useful bibliographies proved to be the *Catalogue of the Wymberley Jones DeRenne Georgia Library at Wormsloe, Isle of Hope near Savannah, Georgia* 3 vols. (Savannah, 1931) for materials published prior to 1900; Arthur R. Rowland and James E. Dorsey, *A Bibliography of the Writings of Georgia History, 1900-1970* (Spartanburg: Reprint Company, 1978); and John E. Simpson, *Georgia History: A Bibliography* (Metuchen NJ:The Scarecrow Press, Inc., 1976). A convenient, one-volume guide to the extensive literature of local history and genealogy relating to Georgia is James E. Dorsey, *Georgia Genealogy and Local History: A Bibliography* (Spartanburg: Reprint Company, 1983).

Special acknowledgment is due to the ladies who seem to have been the first to recognize the need and have subsequently dominated the study of the region. Both amateurs and professionals, they include Mary Ross, Margaret Davis Cate, Caroline Couper Lovell, Julia Harn, Bessie Lewis, Josephine B. Martin, Caroline P. Wilson, Pearl Gnann, Margaret Jordan, Lucille Hodges, Mary Effie Smith, Burnette Vanstory, Betsey Fancher, Rhea C. Otto, and Alpharetta K. Register. The forthcoming study of slavery at tidewater by Julia F. Smith promises to be a major

32 / *Swamp Water and Wiregrass*

contribution to the scholarship on coastal Georgia in the antebellum decades. As writers of fiction, Caroline Miller and Eugenia Price have used local history, culture, and folklore in their works which have received national recognition.

Manuscripts

American Missionary Association Archives. Georgia Southern College, Statesboro, and University of Georgia, Athens. Microfilm.

Andrews, R. Q. "Recollections of War Times" (unpublished).

Baldwin, William—Stephen Elliott Correspondence. New York Botanical Garden Library.

Baldwin, William Letters. Forman-Bryan-Screven Papers, Georgia Historical Society, Savannah.

Cate, Margaret Davis Collection. Georgia Historical Society, Savannah.

Cay, Raymond. "Captain Remount Detachment of the Liberty Troop" (unpublished).

Couper, James Hamilton Plantation Records. Southern Historical Collection, University of North Carolina, Chapel Hill.

Darsey, Squire Ben Diary, of Liberty County. (Unpublished, in possession of Mrs. Mary Sue Ginter, Midway, Georgia).

DeRenne Collection, fascicle No. 1 of Stephen Elliott's *Sketch*. Special Collections, University of Georgia, Athens.

Elliott and Gonzales Family Papers. Southern Historical Collection, University of North Carolina, Chapel Hill.

Elliott, Stephen—James Macbride Correspondence. Charleston Museum Library, Charleston, South Carolina.

Elliott, Bishop Stephen Papers. University of the South, Sewanee, Tennessee.

Elliott, Stephen Letterbook 1862-1864. Southern Historical Collection, University of North Carolina, Chapel Hill.

Ford, Henry Papers. Greenfield Village, Dearborn, Michigan.

Hofwyl Plantation Papers. Georgia Department of Archives and History, Atlanta.

Jones, C. C. Papers. Special Collections, Tulane University, New Orleans, Louisiana.

Jones, C. C. Papers. Special Collections, University of Georgia, Athens.

LeConte, Sr. James A. Collection. Special Collections, University of Georgia, Athens.

Macbride, James Papers. Library of Congress, Washington, D.C.

Mackay and Stiles Family Papers. Southern Historical Collection, University of North Carolina, Chapel Hill.

Midway Records. Copies in Georgia Department of Archives and History, Atlanta.

Minutes of the Liberty Independent Troop (unpublished).

Muhlenberg, Henry—Stephen Elliott Correspondence. Arnold Arboretum Library, Harvard University, Boston, Massachusetts.

Muhlenberg, Henry—Stephen Elliott Correspondence. Historical Society of Pennsylvania, Philadelphia.

Read, Keith M. Collection. "John H. Ash, Confederate Diaries (1860-1865)." Special Collections Department, Woodruff Library, Emory University, Atlanta, Georgia.

Records of the Quartermaster-General, Files on Fort Lawton and Millen, Georgia. RG245 (Washington, National Archives).

Records of the United States Bureau of Refugees, Freedmen, and Abandoned Lands. Reports of the Georgia Superintendent of Education, 1865-1870, Records of the Field Offices of the Bureau, 1865-1870. National Archives, Washington, D.C. Available on microfilm.

Stevens, John. "Personal Narrative of Sherman's Raid in Liberty County, Georgia" (unpublished). Stevens Papers, Georgia Historical Society, Savannah.

Warnell, James Smart. "The Diary of James Smart Warnell, 1862-63." (unpublished). Georgia Department of Archives and History, Atlanta. Microfilm.

Courthouse Records.

Bryan County, Georgia.

Bulloch County, Georgia.

Burke County, Georgia.

Camden County, Georgia.

Candler County, Georgia.

Charleston County, South Carolina.

Chatham County, Georgia.

Effingham County, Georgia.

Emanuel County, Georgia.

Evans County, Georgia.

Glynn County, Georgia.

Jenkins County, Georgia.

Laurens County, Georgia.

Liberty County, Georgia.

McIntosh County, Georgia.

Montgomery County, Georgia.
Screven County, Georgia.
Tattnall County, Georgia.

Newspapers

The Atlanta Constitution.
The Atlanta Journal.
The Augusta Chronicle.
The Bulloch Times.
Brunswick Daily Advertiser.
The Charleston Courier.
The Darien Timber Gazette.
The Hinesville Gazette.
The Macon Telegraph.
The New York Times.
The Savannah Morning News.
The Savannah Tribune.
The Sylvania Telephone.
The Thomasville Daily Times Enterprise.
The Valdosta Times.

Unpublished Materials

Cohan, Richard C. "The Liberty Independent Troop" (1979).

Fraser, H. B., comp. "The War Record of the Five Military Organizations from Liberty County, Georgia in the Confederate Army" (Mrs. Eliza Matin, Hinesville, Georgia).

Smith, Gordon B. "First Squadron Georgia Calvary, 1758-1861," Vertical Files, Georgia Historical Society, Savannah.

Turner, Norman V. "Lineage and Battle Honors of Battery C, Effingham County."
_____. "Military History of Effingham County."

Government Publications

Cemetery Service Historical Records. *Roll of Honor*. National Archives, Washington, D.C.

Compendium of the Eleventh Census, 1890. Washington, D.C.: Government Printing Office, 1892.

Compiled Service Records of Confederate General and Staff Officers. Washington, D.C., National Archives.

Compiled Service Records of Confederate Soldiers from Georgia. Georgia Department of Archives and History, Atlanta.

DuBois, W. E. B. "The Negro Farmer." *Bureau of the Census Special Reports, Supplementary Analysis and Derivative Tables, Twelfth Census of the United States: 1900.* Washington, D.C.: Government Printing Office, 1906.

_____. "The Negro Landholder of Georgia." *Bulletin of the United States Department of Labor.* No. 35, July 1901.

Report on Population of the United States at the Eleventh Census: 1890. Washington, D.C.: Government Printing Office, 1897.

Report on the Statistics of Agriculture in the United States at the Eleventh Census: 1890. Washington, D.C.: Government Printing Office, 1895.

Report on the Treatment of Prisoners of War by Rebel Authorities During the War of the Rebellion (Shanks' *Report*), 3rd Session, 40th Congress. Washington, D.C.: Government Printing Office, 1869.

Statement of the Disposition of Some of the Bodies of Deceased Union Soldiers. Washington, D.C.: Government Printing Office, 1868.

Twelfth Census of the United States, 1900: Population. Washington, D.C.: U.S. Census Office, 1901.

Twelfth Census of the United States: 1900, Agriculture, Crops and Irrigation. Washington, D.C.: Government Printing Office, 1902.

The War of the Rebellion: A Compilation of the Official Records of the Union and Confederate Armies. Washington, D.C.: Government Printing Office, 1882-1900, 130 vols. with atlas.

Books

American Missionary Association, Annual Reports. Emory University, Atlanta, Georgia.

Anderson, Richard L. *LeConte History and Genealogy.* 2 vols. Macon: R. L. Anderson, 1981.

Association for Religious Instruction of the Negroes in Liberty County, Georgia, Annual Reports. Savannah: Various Publishers, 1836-1848.

Armes, William D., ed. *The Autobiography of Joseph LeConte.* New York: D. Appleton and Company, 1903.

Banks, Enoch M. *The Economics of Land Tenure in Georgia.* New York: Columbia University Press, 1905.

Barnwell, Stephen B. *The Story of an American Family.* Marquette, Michigan, 1969.

Bartram, William. "Travels in Georgia and Florida, 1773-74: A Report to Dr. John Fothergill," annotated by Francis Harper, in *Transactions of the American Philosophical Society.* n.s., vol. 33, part 2. Philadelphia: American Philosophical Society, 1943.

_____. *Travels Through North and South Carolina, Georgia, East and West Florida.* Philadelphia: James and Johnson, 1791.

Beard, Augustus F. *A Crusade of Brotherhood: A History of the American Missionary Association.* Boston: Pilgrim Press, 1909.

Behn, George W. *A Concise System of Instruction Arranged and Adopted for the Volunteer Cavalry of the United States.* Savannah, 1842.

Blake, James. *Annals of the Town of Dorchester.* Boston: David Clapp, Jr., 1846.

Bonner, James C. *A History of Georgia Agriculture, 1732-1860.* Athens: University of Georgia Press, 1964.

Brooks, Robert P. *The Agrarian Revolution in Georgia, 1865-1912.* Bulletin 639. Madison: University of Wisconsin, 1914.

Bryant, Pat. *English Crown Grants for Island in Georgia, 1755-1775.* Atlanta: Georgia Department of Archives and History, 1972.

_____. *English Crown Grants in St. Andrew Parish in Georgia, 1755-1775.* Atlanta: Georgia Department of Archives and History, 1972.

_____. *English Crown Grants in St. George Parish in Georgia, 1755-1775.* Atlanta: Georgia Department of Archives and History, 1974.

Georgia State Department of Agriculture. *Reports of the Georgia State Commissioner of Agriculture,* 1874-1940.

Candler, Allen D., comp. *The Colonial Records of the State of Georgia.* 39 vols. Atlanta: Various printers, 1904-1937.

Cash, Wilbur J. *The Mind of the South.* New York: Vintage Books, 1968.

Cate, Margaret Davis. *Our Todays and Yesterdays.* Brunswick: Glover Bros., 1926.

Catesby, Mark. *The Natural History of Carolina, Florida and the Bahama Islands Containing two hundred and twenty figures of Birds, Beasts, Fishes, Serpents, Insects and Plants.* Introduction by George Frick, notes by Joseph Ewan. Savannah: Beehive Press, 1974.

Chalker, Fussell M. *Pioneer Days Along the Ocmulgee.* Carrollton, Georgia, 1970.

Clapp, Ebenezer. *History of the Town of Dorchester, Massachusetts.* Boston: Ebenezer Clapp, Jr., 1859.

Clarke, Erskine. *Wrestlin' Jacob.* Atlanta: John Knox Press, 1979.

Clifton, James M. *Life and Labor on Argyle Island*. Savannah: Beehive Press, 1978.

Coleman, Kenneth. *Colonial Georgia: A History*. New York: Scribner, 1976.

Coleman, Kenneth, et. al. *A History of Georgia*. Athens: University of Georgia Press, 1977.

Coleman, Kenneth, and Charles Stephen Gurr, eds. *Dictionary of Georgia Biography*. 2 vols. Athens: University of Georgia Press, 1983.

Coleman, Leodel. *Statesboro . . . 1866-1966 . . . A Century of Progress*. Statesboro: Bulloch Herald Publishing Company, Inc., 1969.

Colquitt, Neyle. *An Historette of Midway*. 1915.

Coulter, E. Merton. *Georgia, A Short History*. Chapel Hill: University of North Carolina Press, 1960.

_____. *The Confederate States of America, 1861-1865*. Baton Rouge: Louisiana State University Press, 1950.

_____. *Thomas Spalding of Sapelo*. Baton Rouge: Louisiana State University Press, 1940.

Crooks, Esther J., and Ruth Crooks. *The Ring Tournament in the United States*. Richmond: Garrett and Mossie, 1936.

Darlington, William, comp. *Reliquiae Baldwinianae*. Philadelphia: Kimber and Sharpless, 1843.

Darsey, B. W. *A War Story, or My Experiences in a Yankee Prison*. Statesboro: News Print Co., 1901.

Davidson, H. M. *Fourteen Months in Southern Prisons*. Milwaukee: Daily Wisconsin Printing House, 1865.

DeVorsey, Louis, Jr., ed. De Brahm's *Report of the General Survey in the Southern District of North America*. Columbia: University of South Carolina Press, 1971.

Dorsey, James E. *Footprints along the Hoopee: A History of Emanuel County, 1812-1900*. Spartanburg: Reprint Company, 1978.

Dorsey, James E., and John K. Derden. *Montgomery County, 1812-1900*. Spartanburg: Reprint Company, 1978.

_____. *Montgomery County Georgia, A Source Book of Genealogy*. Spartanburg: Reprint Company, 1983.

Douglass, Paul H. *Christian Reconstruction of the South*. Boston: Pilgrim Press, 1909.

DuBois, W.E.B. *The Souls of Black Folk, Essays and Sketches*. Chicago: A. C. McClurg and Co., 1903.

Elliott, Stephen. *A Sketch of the Botany of South Carolina and Georgia*. 2 vols. Charleston: J. R. Schenck, 1824.

Evans, Virginia F., comp. *Liberty County, Georgia: A Pictorial History*. Statesville: Brady Printing Co., 1979.

Ewan, Joseph, ed. William Bartram: Botanical and Zoological Drawings, 1756-1788. Philadelphia: American Philosophical Society, 1968.

Fagin, N. B. William Bartram, Interpreter of the American Landscape. Baltimore: Johns Hopkins Press, 1933.

Fancher, Betsey. The Lost Legacy of Georgia's Golden Isles. Garden City: Doubleday and Co., 1971.

Flanders, Ralph B. Plantation Slavery in Georgia. Chapel Hill: University of North Carolina Press, 1933.

Flynn, Charles L., Jr. White Land, Black Labor, Caste and Class in Late Nineteenth Century Georgia. Baton Rouge: Louisiana State University Press, 1983.

Frick, George Frederick, and Raymond Phineas Stearns. Mark Catesby the Colonial Audubon. Urbana: University of Illinois Press, 1961.

Georgia State Department of Agriculture. A Manual of Sheep Husbandry in Georgia. Atlanta, 1875.

Glazier, William W. The Capture, the Prison Pen, and the Escape. Hartford: H. E. Goodwin, 1868.

Grant, Hugh F. Planter Management and Capitalism in Antebellum Georgia. New York: Columbia University Press, 1954.

Gray, Lewis C. History of Agriculture in the Southern United States to 1860. 2 vols. Washington: Carnegie Institute of Washington, 1933.

Gunn, Virginia Reeves. Hofwyl Plantation. Atlanta: Georgia Department of Natural Resources, 1976.

Hanckel, Thomas M. Sermons of the Right Reverend Stephen Elliott, D.D., Late Bishop of Georgia With a Memoir. New York: Pott and Amery, 1867.

Heath, Milton S. Constructive Liberalism: The Role of the State in Economic Development in Georgia, 1733-1860. Cambridge: Harvard University Press, 1954.

Hemperley, Marion R. English Crown Grants for Parishes of St. David, St. Patrick, St. Thomas, St. Mary in Georgia 1755-1775. Atlanta: Georgia Department of Archives and History, 1973.

_____. English Crown Grants for St. Philip Parish in Georgia, 1755-1775. Atlanta: Georgia Department of Archives and History, 1972.

_____. English Crown Grants in St. John Parish in Georgia, 1755-1775. Atlanta: Georgia Department of Archives and History, 1972.

_____. English Crown Grants in St. Matthew Parish in Georgia, 1755-1775. Atlanta: Georgia Department of Archives and History, 1974.

Hesseltine, William. Civil War Prisons, a Study in War Psychology. Columbus: Ohio State University Press, 1930.

History of the American Missionary Association. New York, 1891.

Hodges, Lucille. History of Our Locale, Mainly Evans County, Georgia. Macon: Southern Printer, Inc., 1965.

Hollingsworth, Clyde. *Pioneer Days: A History of the Early Years in Screven County.* Sylvania: *Sylvania Telephone*, 1947.

Hoskins, Charles L. *Black Episcopalians in Georgia: Strife, Struggle and Salvation.* Savannah: Hoskins, 1980.

Huxford, Folkes. *Pioneers of Wiregrass Georgia.* Homerville: Pattern Publishing Co., 1951-1975.

Hvidt, Kristian, ed. *Von Reck's Voyage: Drawings and Journal of Philip Georg Friedrich von Reck.* Savannah: Beehive Press, 1980.

Isham, Asa B., et. al. *Prisoners of War and Military Prisons, Personal Narratives of Experience in the Prisons at Richmond, Danville, Macon, Anderson, Savannah, Millen, Charleston and Columbia.* Cincinnati: Lyman and Cushing, 1890.

Ivers, Larry E. *British Drums on the Southern Frontier: The Military Colonization of Georgia, 1733-1749.* Chapel Hill: University of North Carolina Press, 1974.

Jones, Charles C. *A Catechism for Colored Persons.* Charleston: Charleston Observer Office Press, 1834.

_____. *A Catechism of Scripture, Doctrine and Practice: For Families and Sabbath Schools. Designed also, for the Oral Instruction of Colored Persons.* Savannah: T. Purse and Co., 1837.

_____. *The Religious Instruction of the Negroes in the United States.* Savannah: Thomas Purse, 1842.

Jones, Charles C., Jr. *Dead Towns of Georgia.* Savannah: Georgia Historical Society, 1878.

_____. *The History of Georgia.* 2 vols. Boston: Houghton, Mifflin Co., 1883.

Jones, Jacqueline. *Soldiers of Light and Love, Northern Teachers and Georgia Blacks, 1865-1873.* Chapel Hill: University of North Carolina Press, 1980.

Jordan, Margaret C. *Wayne Miscellany.* Jesup: *Jesup Sentinel*, 1976.

Kellogg, Robert H. *Life and Death in Rebel Prisons.* Hartford: L. Stebbins, 1866.

Kemble, Frances A. *Journal of a Residence on a Georgia Plantation in 1838-1839.* New York: Harper and Brothers, 1863.

King, Spencer B., Jr. *Georgia Voices, A Documentary History to 1872.* Athens: University of Georgia Press, 1966.

_____. *Darien.* Macon: Mercer University Press, 1981.

Kirbye, J. Edward. *Puritanism in the South.* Boston: Pilgrim Press, 1908.

Knauss, William H. *The Story of Camp Chase.* Nashville: Publishing House of the Methodist Episcopal Church, South, 1906.

Kuhns, Maude P. *The "Mary and John:" A Story of the Founding of Dorchester, Massachusetts, 1630.* Rutland: The Tuttle Publishing Co., Inc., 1943.

Lane, Mills B., ed. *The Rambler in Georgia.* Savannah: Beehive Press, 1973.

_____, ed. *War is Hell.* Savannah: Beehive Press, 1974.

LeConte, Joseph. 'Ware Sherman. Berkeley: University of California Press, 1938.

Lewis, Bessie. McIntosh County, Georgia. Darien: Ashantilly Press, 1966.

————. Patriarchial Plantations of St. Simons Island. Darien: Darien News, 1974.

————. They Called Their Town Darien: Being a Short History of Darien and McIntosh County, Georgia. Darien: Darien News, 1975.

Leigh, Frances Butler. Ten Years on A Georgia Plantation Since the War. London: Richard Bentley and Son, 1883.

Lightcap, W. H. The Horrors of Southern Prisons During the War of Rebellion. Lancaster, Wisconsin, 1902.

Lovell, Caroline C. The Golden Isles of Georgia. Boston: Little, Brown, and Co., 1932.

Lyell, Sir Charles. A Second Visit to the United States of North America. New York: Harper and Brothers, 1849.

Mallard, R. Q. Plantation Life Before Emancipation. Richmond: Whittet and Shipperson, 1892.

————. Montevideo-Maybank, or The Family Life of the Rev. Charles Colcock Jones, D.D. Richmond: Presbyterian Committee of Publication, 1898.

Malone, Henry T. The Episcopal Church in Georgia, 1733-1957. Atlanta: The Protestant Episcopal Church in the Diocese of Atlanta, 1960.

Martin, Arthur M. The Flemington Martins. Columbia: The State Printing Co., 1970.

Martin, Josephine B. Midway, Georgia in History and Legend. Savannah: Southern Publishers, 1936.

Matthews, Donald G. Religion in the Old South. Chicago: University of Chicago Press, 1977.

McIlvaine, Paul. The Dead Towns of Sunbury, Ga. and Dorchester, S.C. Ashville: Groves Printing Co., 1975.

Monroe, Haskell, ed. Yankees A 'Coming. Tuscaloosa: Confederate Publishing Co., 1959.

Myers, Robert M., ed. The Children of Pride. New Haven: Yale University Press, 1972.

Olmstead, Frederick L. A Journey in the Seaboard Slave States, with Remarks on their Economy. New York: G. P. Putnam Sons, 1904.

Orr, Dorothy. A History of Education in Georgia. Chapel Hill: University of North Carolina Press, 1950.

Park, Orville A. The Puritan in Georgia. Savannah: Georgia Historical Society, 1929.

Pond, Cornelia Jones. Life on a Liberty County Plantation. Edited by Josephine Martin. Darien: Darien News, 1974.

Pratt, William. "Journal of the Elder William Pratt." *Narratives of Early Carolina*. Edited by Alexander S. Salley. New York: Charles Scribner's Sons, 1911.

Range, Willard. *A Century of Georgia Agriculture, 1850-1950*. Athens: University of Georgia Press, 1954.

_____. *The Rise and Progress of Negro Colleges in Georgia, 1865-1949*. Athens: University of Georgia Press, 1951.

Ransom, John L. *John Ransom's Diary*. New York: Paul S. Erikson, Inc., 1963.

Ransom, Roger L., and Richard Sutch. *One Kind of Freedom, the Economic Consequences of Emancipation*. London: Cambridge University Press, 1977.

Records of the First Church at Dorchester in New England, 1636-1734. Boston: David Clapp, Jr., 1846.

Reddick, Marguerite, comp. *Camden's Challenge: A History of Camden County, Georgia*. Woodbine: Camden County Historical Commission, 1976.

Rose-Troup, Frances. *John White the Patriarch of Dorchester and the Founder of Massachusetts, 1575-1648*. New York: G. P. Putnam's Sons, 1930.

Rowell, John W. *Yankee Cavalrymen Through the Civil War with the Ninth Pennsylvania Cavalry*. Knoxville: University of Tennessee Press, 1971.

Sheftall, John M. *Sunbury on the Medway*. Atlanta: Georgia Department of Natural Resources, 1977.

Sherman, William T. *Memoirs of General W. T. Sherman*. 2 vols. New York: Charles L. Webster and Co., 1891.

Shriver, Philip R., and Donald J. Breen. *Ohio's Military Prisons in the Civil War*. Columbus: Ohio State University Press, 1964.

Smith, Mary Effie D., ed. *The Willie Community*. Reidsville: *Tattnall Journal*, 1973.

Stacy, James. *History of the Midway Congregational Church, Liberty County, Georgia*. Newnan: S. W. Murray, Printer, 1951.

Stephens, Lester D. *Joseph LeConte, Gentle Prophet of Evolution*. Baton Rouge: Louisiana State University Press, 1982.

Swint, Henry L. *The Northern Teacher in the South*. Nashville: Vanderbilt University Press, 1941.

Thompson, C. Mildred. *Reconstruction in Georgia*. Savannah: Beehive Press, 1972.

Townsend, Billy. "Camp Lawton, Magnolia Springs State Park." Atlanta: Parks and Historic Sites Division, Georgia Department of Natural Resources, 1975.

Urban, John W. *Battle Field and Prison Pen*. Philadelphia: Hubbard Bros. Publishers, 1882.

U. S. Christian Commission. *Record of the Federal Dead Buried from Libby, Belle Isle, Danville, and Camp Lawton Prisons*. Philadelphia: James B. Rodgers Printer, 1865.

Vanstory, Burnette. *Georgia's Land of the Golden Isles*. Athens: University of Georgia Press, 1970.

White, George. *Historical Collections of Georgia*. Baltimore: Genealogical Publishing Co., 1969.

Works Project Administration, Georgia Writers Project, Savannah Unit. *Drums and Shadows: Survival Studies Among the Georgia Coastal Negroes*. New York: Doubleday and Co., 1972.

Wrightman, Orrin S., and Margaret Davis Cate. *Early Days of Coastal Georgia*. St. Simons Island: Fort Frederica Association, 1955.

Wyatt-Brown, Bertram. *Southern Honor, Ethics and Behavior in the Old South*. New York: Oxford University Press, 1982.

Yarbrough, Paul, and Bird Yarbrough, eds. *Taylor's Creek*. Pearson: Press of the Atkinson County Citizen, 1963.

Articles in Periodicals

The American Missionary, 1846-1934. Published by The American Missionary Association.

Armstrong, Thomas F. "From Task Labor to Free Labor: The Transition Along Georgia's Rice Coast, 1820-1880." *Georgia Historical Quarterly* 64 (Winter 1980): 432-47.

————. "The Christ Craze of 1889: A Millennial Response to Economic and Social Change." *Toward A New South? Studies in Post Civil War Southern Communities*. Edited by Orville V. Burton and Robert C. McMath, Jr. Westport: Greenwood Press, 1982.

Barnhart, John Hendley. "John Eatton LeConte." *The American Midland Naturalist* 5 (1917-1918): 135-38.

————. "Dates of Elliott's Sketch." *Bulletin of the Torrey Bontanical Club* 27 (1901): 680-88.

Barnwell, Stephen. "The Confederate Episcopacy, Slavery and Stephen Elliott." *The Michigan Academican* 1 (Spring 1969).

Bartram, John. "Diary of a Journey through the Carolinas, Georgia, and Florida from July 1, 1765 to April 10, 1766." Annotated by Francis Harper. *Transactions of The American Philosophical Society*. n.s., vol. 33, part 1. Philadelphia: American Philosophical Society, 1942.

Bonner, James C. "The Historical Basis of the Southern Military Tradition." *The Georgia Review* 9 (Spring 1955): 74-85.

Bacote, Clarence. "Negro Proscriptions, Protests and Proposed Solutions in Georgia, 1880-1908." *Journal of Southern History* 25 (November 1959): 471-98.

Clifton, James M. "The Rice Driver: His Role in Slave Management." *South Carolina Historical Magazine* 82 (October 1981): 331-53.

Flanders, Ralph B. "Planter Problems in Ante-Bellum Georgia." *Georgia Historical Quarterly* 14 (March 1930): 17-40.

Gordon, Alexander. "An Account of an Agricultural Excursion Made into the South of Georgia in the Winter of 1832." *The Southern Agriculturist and Register of Rural Affairs* 6 (1833): 298-304, 413, 416.

Harden, William. "William McWhir, An Irish Friend of Washington." *Georgia Historical Quarterly* 1 (September 1917): 197-219.

Harper, Roland M. "Development of Agriculture in Lower Georgia from 1850 to 1880." *Georgia Historical Quarterly* 6 (June 1922): 97-121.

House, Albert V. Jr. "The Management of a Rice Plantation in Georgia, 1834-1861." *Agricultural History* 13 (October 1939): 208-17.

Jones, C. C. Jr. "Sherman's March from Atlanta to the Coast." *Southern Historical Society Papers* 12 (July-August-September 1884): 294-309.

Journals of the Protestant Episcopal Diocese of Georgia. Georgia Historical Society, Savannah.

Lambright, James T. "The Liberty Independent Troop." Address to members of Clement A. Evans Chapter, United Daughters of the Confederacy, Brunswick, Georgia, 1910. Pamphlet.

Levy, Babette M. "Early Puritanism in the Southern and Island Colonies." *American Antiquarians Society Proceedings* 70 (1960): 69-348.

Martin, Josephine. "The Society of Midway." *Georgia Historical Quarterly* 11 (December 1927): 321-29.

Mathews, Donald G. "Charles Colcock Jones and the Southern Evangelical Crusade to Form a Biracial Community." *The Journal of Southern History* 4 (August 1975): 299-320.

Monroe, Haskell. "Men Without Law: Federal Raiding in Liberty County, Georgia." *Georgia Historical Quarterly* 44 (June 1960): 154-71.

Norwood, Thomas M. "The Liberty County Case." Georgia Historical Society. 31 December 1907. Vertical files.

Orians, G. Harrison. "The Origin of the Ring Tournament in the United States." *Maryland Historical Magazine* 36 (1941): 263-77.

Parker-Cummings, Inez. "Vestige of Chivalry: Ring Tournaments in the South." *Georgia Review* 9 (Winter 1955): 407-21.

Pennington, Edgar L. "Stephen Elliott, First Bishop of Georgia." *Historical Magazine of the Protestant Episcopal Church* 7 (September 1938): 203-63.

Rogers, George A., and R. Frank Saunders, Jr. "The Impact of Rice Culture upon Antebellum Georgia." *An Introduction to LeConte-Woodmanston.* Institute of Community and Area Development, University of Georgia (1978) 19-23.

Rogers, George A. "Stephen Elliott, A Southern Humanist." *The Humanist in His World.* Edited by Barbara W. Bitter and Frederick K. Sanders. Greenwood: The Attic Press, 1976.

Sargent, C. S. "Portions of the Journal of Andre Michaux, botanist, written during his Travels in the United States and Canada, 1785 to 1796, with an Introduction and Explanatory Notes." *Proceedings of the American Philosophical Society* 26 (January to July 1889).

———. "A Sketch of the Ogeechee Mission." *Southern Episcopalian* 1 (February 1835): 494-97.

Smith, Henry A. M. "The Upper Ashley; and the Mutations of Families." *South Carolina Historical and Genealogical Magazine* 20 (July 1919): 151-98.

———. "The Town of Dorchester in South Carolina—A Sketch of Its History." *South Carolina Historical and Genealogical Magazine* 6 (April 1905): 62-75.

Spalding, Thomas. "On the Introduction of Sea Island Cotton into Georgia." *Southern Agriculturist* 4 (March 1831): 131-33.

———. "Cotton—Its Introduction and Progress of Its Culture in the United States." *Southern Agriculturist* 8 (January 1835): 35-46.

Tankersley, Allen P. "Midway District: A Study of Puritanism in Colonial Georgia." *Georgia Historical Quarterly* 32 (September 1948): 149-57.

Tyner, Wayne C. "Charles Colcock Jones: Mission to Slaves." *Journal of Presbyterian History* 55 (Winter 1977): 363-80.

Wilson, Carrie P. "Candle Lights in Old Liberty County." *Georgia Historical Quarterly* 11 (March 1927): 44-53.

Wims, Douglas C. "The Development of Rice Culture in Eighteenth Century Georgia." *Southeastern Geographer* 12 (May 1972): 45-57.

Theses and Dissertations

Bacote, Clarence. "The Negro in Georgia Politics, 1880-1908." Ph.D. Dissertation, University of Chicago, 1955.

Bagwell, James E. "James Hamilton Couper, Georgia Rice Planter." Ph.D. Dissertation, University of Southern Mississippi, 1978.

Berry, James W. "Growing Up in the Old South: The Childhood of Charles Colcock Jones, Jr." Ph.D. Dissertation, Princeton University, 1981.

Chesnutt, David R. "South Carolina's Expansion into Colonial Georgia, 1720-1765." Ph.D. Dissertation, University of Georgia, 1973.

Collins, Doris K. "The Episcopal Church in Georgia From the Revolutionary War to 1860." M.A. Thesis, Emory University, 1957.

Davis, Ronald L. "Good and Faithful Labor: A Study in the Origins, Development and Economics of Southern Sharecropping, 1860-1880." Ph.D. Dissertation, University of Missouri, 1974.

Davis, Virgil S. "Stephen Elliott: A Southern Bishop in Peace and War." Ph.D. Dissertation, University of Georgia, 1964.

Drake, Richard B. "The American Missionary Association and the Southern Negro." Ph.D. Dissertation, Emory University, 1957.

Edwards, Norman. "The Old Southeast and Fort King George: Borderland of Three Empires." M.A. Thesis, Georgia Southern College, 1980.

Johnson, Clifton H. "The American Missionary Association, 1841-1861: A Study of Christian Abolitionism." Ph.D. Dissertation, Emory University, 1957.

Lines, Stiles B. "Slaves and Churchmen: The Work of the Episcopal Church Among Southern Negroes, 1830-1860." Ph.D. Dissertation, Columbia University, 1960.

Loring, Edward N. "Charles C. Jones: Missionary to Plantation Slaves." Ph.D. Dissertation, Vanderbilt University, 1976.

Menn, Joseph K. "The Large Slaveholders of the Deep South, 1860." Ph.D. Dissertation, University of Texas, 1964.

Morrison, Carlton. "Raftsmen of the Altamaha." M.A. Thesis, University of Georgia, 1970.

Owens, James L. "The Negro in the Reconstruction of Georgia." Ph.D. Dissertation, University of Georgia, 1974.

Swan, Dale E. "The Structure and Profitability of the Antebellum Rice Industry." Ph.D. Dissertation, University of North Carolina, 1972.

Wingo, Horace C. "Race Relations in Georgia, 1870-1908." Ph.D. Dissertation, University of Georgia, 1969.

Index

The authors gratefully acknowledge the assistance of Julius Ariail, Associate Director, Georgia Southern Library, in preparation of the index.

MUP Swamp Water and Wiregrass

Designed by Margaret Jordan Brown
Composition by MUP Composition Department

Production Specifications:
    text paper—60 pound Warren's Olde Style
    endpapers—Multicolor Antique Celadon printed PMS 343
    cover—(on .088 boards) Holliston Roxite B51538, Vellum finish
    dust jacket—100 pound enamel, printed four colors (PMS 134, cream,
    PMS 468 light brown, PMS 343 dark green, and black) and varnished.

Printing (offset lithography) by Omnipress of Macon, Inc., Macon, Georgia
Binding by John H. Dekker and Sons, Inc., Grand Rapids, Michigan

DATE DUE
